Dubbing, Film and
Performance

NEW TRENDS IN TRANSLATION STUDIES
Volume 16

Series Editor:
Professor Jorge Díaz Cintas

Advisory Board:
Professor Susan Bassnett
Dr Lynne Bowker
Professor Frederic Chaume
Professor Aline Remael

PETER LANG

Oxford • Bern • Berlin • Bruxelles • Frankfurt am Main • New York • Wien

Dubbing, Film and Performance

Uncanny Encounters

Charlotte Bosseaux

PETER LANG

Oxford • Bern • Berlin • Bruxelles • Frankfurt am Main • New York • Wien

Bibliographic information published by Die Deutsche Nationalbibliothek.
Die Deutsche Nationalbibliothek lists this publication in the Deutsche National-
bibliografie; detailed bibliographic data is available on the Internet at
http://dnb.d-nb.de.

A catalogue record for this book is available from the British Library.

Library of Congress Control Number: 2015939713

ISSN 1664-249X
ISBN 978-3-0343-0235-7 (print)
ISBN 978-3-0353-0737-5 (eBook)

© Peter Lang AG, International Academic Publishers, Bern 2015
Hochfeldstrasse 32, CH-3012 Bern, Switzerland
info@peterlang.com, www.peterlang.com, www.peterlang.net

This publication has been peer reviewed.

Printed in Germany

Contents

Acknowledgements

This book is the fruit of many years of research and I would not have been able to write it without the input of a great many people.

I would like to thank my Translation Studies colleagues and friends, particularly my 'AVT chums', Jorge Díaz-Cintas, Frederic Chaume and Pablo Romero-Fresco, who have provided feedback, guidance, ideas and support along the way. I would also like to thank my Edinburgh colleagues Sebnem Susam-Saraeva and Hephzibah Israel for their continuing support.

I am also thankful to my Film Studies and Music Studies colleagues and friends, especially Martine Beugnet, Mark Cousins, Helen Julia Minors and Sarah Artt, for giving me advice when I did not know where to start when embarking on this journey and for providing feedback at various points of my research.

I also would like to thank everyone who had something to say about my topic when it was developing in mysterious ways: friends, students, Translation Studies and Film Studies conference-goers, editors, reviewers and random people I met on the train, bus, boat or plane who did not know what they were letting themselves in for when they asked me what my job was!

Thanks also to the staff at Peter Lang and the anonymous reader for her or his positive response and constructive feedback.

Many thanks also to Conor O'Loughlin for his careful proofreading and indexing of the book.

Thanks also to the Carnegie for funding part of the publication cost of this book and to the University of Edinburgh for a grant towards the proofreading and editing cost.

Many thanks to Daniel Chandler for granting me permission to reproduce images published on his website (reproduced here as Figures 1, 2 and 3).

My special thanks also go to my sangha and amazing friends, particularly Steve Earl, Sharon Deane-Cox, Zhu Zhu and Geoffrey Baines; your friendship, time, positive energy and enthusiasm really made a difference at times when I was wondering why I was doing all of this, so thank you once again. I also would like to thank Coll Hutchinson for his valuable reading recommendations and Véronique Desnain and Sarah Artt for watching *Buffy* with me and discussing her awesomeness for many hours.

And finally, I would like to thank my family for their ongoing support and love, particularly my grandmother and my parents; without you, I would never have been able to write any of this. This book is dedicated to you.

Introduction

Popular culture TV series and films reach millions of people and are usually remembered through their main characters. However, as they travel the world in translation, audiences may perceive these very same characters differently even though the images remain the same. The premise of this monograph is my deep conviction that translation is a complex multi-layered process that has an impact on the way fictional characters are presented to their new audiences. Specifically, my point of entry is characterization: the way characters are created and presented in original and translated texts in an audiovisual context. I am particularly fascinated by audiovisual texts, which prove complex to deal with in translation owing to the fact that elements from various channels need to be taken into consideration; translators have to navigate both images and sounds, including words.

Characterization in the framework of Film Studies refers to the way characters are created on-screen through features such as actors' performance, voice quality, facial expressions, gestures, camera angles and soundtrack (Dyer 1979/1998). This book will investigate how characterization and performance (including voice quality, facial expressions and gestures) are intrinsically linked and show how dubbing affects performance. My main interest is in voice, since in dubbing the original actors' voices are replaced by new ones from the target culture. Film Studies and Audiovisual Translation Studies have seen little discussion of actors' voices as an integral part of their identity and of the way actors use language, i.e. their idiolect. Therefore, the primary goal of this monograph is to raise further awareness of the multimodality of the translation process and demonstrate how important it is to consider the above-mentioned aspects in original texts and in translation.

Audiovisual Translation is arguably the most widespread mode of translation: foreign movies and television series or programmes reach us through translation every day. However, less research has been done in this field in comparison to other genres (such as literary translation). Research started in the late 1980s with an emphasis on the media constraints inherent in dubbing and subtitling and the relative merits of these two modes of translation; it also focused on the search for norms or conventions that operate when translating into the target culture. Various studies have addressed issues such as the translation of ideological and cultural elements and the translation of humour. However, only a limited number of studies have looked into the presentation of characters, i.e. characterization and the potential impact of translation on characterization. This monograph therefore intends to fill this gap by investigating performance in the context of Audiovisual Translation and suggesting a new line of development in Audiovisual Translation research that has the potential to galvanize further studies and inspire other scholars and academics.

In this monograph specifically, I elaborate a methodological tool for studying characterization through performance in audiovisual texts by means of acoustic (or oral) and visual analysis. My two principal objectives are to delve into an area that, so far, has been overlooked in Translation Studies – characterization and performance shifts in Audiovisual Translation – and to foster a new line of research that will be instrumental in the analysis of audiovisual material, using a multimodal approach focusing on elements from both acoustic and visual channels.

The material chosen for investigation is the popular culture series *Buffy the Vampire Slayer* (1997–2003) and its dubbed French version. Through close analysis of shifts in performance between the original and dubbed versions, I will seek to establish which visual and oral (including linguistic) elements of a narrative audiovisual product need to be taken into account when investigating possible translation-induced characterization shifts. This meticulous analysis shall show the extent to which dubbing affects the portrayal of characters by identifying shifts in the presentation of these characters and any possible patterns in the translation strategies applied.

When looking at characterization and performance, I am ultimately interested in the 'feel' of the text, i.e. the fictional universe presented in the text and how this is conveyed in translation. In Bosseaux (2007), I developed a model that uses linguistic elements derived from Systemic Functional Grammar (markers of deixis, transitivity and modality) to identify how point of view is manifested in the original and shifted in translation. This

work has been crucial to my understanding of the complexity of the translation process. However, as I had been dealing with novels, my main consideration was the linguistic aspect of translation. In this present monograph
on audiovisual material, I will be focusing primarily on elements from the
acoustic and visual channels. This is not to say that the linguistic component is not important; given that we are also dealing with words, there will
have to be a linguistic consideration. However, many AVT studies have
overplayed the role of linguistics in AV translation, and my work shall be
seen as an attempt to counterbalance the current situation. Linguistic elements will therefore be incorporated, where appropriate, with the acoustic/
oral and visual analysis. My emphasis is on non-linguistic codes of film,
or what Chaume calls the 'signifying codes of cinematographic language'
(2004b: 16), i.e. elements of non-verbal communication and how these elements interact to create characterization. Although these features have been
explored in studies of characterization in the area of Film and Television
Studies (e.g. Branigan 1984, Dyer 1979/1998, and Klevan 2005), it is fair
to say that this is a topic which remains under-researched.

This monograph thus presents a comparative study which aims to
pinpoint significant differences between the original and translated texts
by comparing the original with its dubbed version(s). I will conduct two
case studies focusing on the way the protagonists come across in the original
and dubbed versions, first by looking at scenes from the original deemed
representative of the characters' personas and then comparing these to the
dubbed French version. My ultimate goal is to add to the existing research
in Audiovisual Translation by highlighting further the complexity of the
translation process for AV texts, with a specific focus on dubbing.

Outline

In the first three chapters, I shall present and define what is meant by
performance and characterization in audiovisual material. I will review
works from various fields, including Film Studies, Performance Studies

and Audiovisual Translation Studies, in order to contextualize my model for analysing audiovisual material in translation. In Chapter 1, the notion of *mise-en-scène* and its various elements will be examined. In Chapter 2, characterization will be defined further and linked to performance. In Chapter 3, my emphasis will be on voice and identity specifically, since in dubbing the actors' original voices are replaced by new ones. This chapter ends with a discussion of the effect dubbing can be said to have on viewers. It is in this section that I introduce Sigmund Freud's concept of the uncanny (1919) and apply it to dubbing, thereby contextualising further my method for analysing original and dubbed products.

In Chapter 4, I will introduce my multimodal model. When looking at characterization and performance, I primarily consider the universe presented in the audiovisual text and how this is conveyed in translation. The model is composed of non-linguistic codes of film and focuses on how these elements interact to create characterization and performance. These elements manifest themselves in aspects of performance such as speech delivery, voice characteristics, kinesics (facial expressions and gestures), proxemics and paralinguistics, as well as camera angles, lighting and soundtrack, all of which have a direct effect on how characters are portrayed. As words have been over-emphasized in previous AVT studies, it is the audio and visual elements that will be given prominence; however, linguistic elements will still be integrated into the acoustic presentation. Since visual elements such as facial expressions and gestures remain intact in translation, it is all the more important to consider how these dimensions interact with verbal dialogues given that we are dealing with an audio *and* visual product; a polysemiotic whole in which the image cannot be dissociated from the dialogue. Specific constraints attached to dubbing will be incorporated into the analysis, along with institutional constraints, cultural traditions and policies regarding audiovisual translation.

Chapter 5 introduces the material chosen for the case studies. My innovative multimodal approach will be used to analyse a corpus composed of selected scenes from the popular culture series *Buffy the Vampire Slayer* (Joss Whedon 1997–2003) and its dubbed French version. As we shall see, *Buffy* has been praised for, among other things, its construction of believable characters and its creative language, 'Buffyspeak', characterized by neologisms, humour and slang. Another aspect of 'Buffyspeak' worthy of investigation in translation is the recurrent use of British English as opposed to American English, as the show features two British characters whose characterization is primarily based on accent, vocabulary and cultural differences. The dubbing of *Buffy* into French provides interesting material for researching characterization, given that accents, voice and vocabulary tend to undergo changes in translation. Three characters from the series have been chosen for investigation: Buffy, Spike and Giles. The corpus will be analysed to highlight 'the factors contributing to the many-faceted meaning-making whole, as the various semiotic modalities are seen to operate in unison' (Taylor 2003: 195). Specific features of performance will be identified, including voice characteristics and vocabulary choices related to (for instance) Britishness, as well as non-verbal behaviour such as facial expressions. My qualitative analytical method will aim to uncover how these elements have been treated in translation, e.g. whether they are removed, reflected or reinforced, thereby leading to a change in characterization.

The final chapter, Chapter 6, presents the model in practice. The comparative study sets out to discover differences in characterization through performance between the original and dubbed versions. When analysing the corpus, the focus will be on the way the protagonists come across in the original and dubbed versions by comparing scenes from the original with those from the French version. These examples will be analysed with an emphasis on the interaction between the visual and oral channels. In my analysis of the scenes, I will comment on the visual image, kinesic action and soundtrack, emphasizing the interplay of paralinguistic features, kinesics, voice and linguistic elements used to create and portray characters. Voice quality, paralinguistic features, facial expressions, gestures and vocabulary will be analysed to show how these dimensions interact and create meaning. The first case study considers an excerpt from *Buffy*'s musical episode, with the emphasis on the function of songs as an important part of the series' narrative. The second case study shall investigate performance in normal or 'pure' film dialogues, with a particular focus on Britishness and accents as well as paralinguistic features (e.g. tone of voice) and visual elements (e.g. gestures and facial expressions).

Before exploring the theoretical material on which my understanding of translation, characterization and performance is based, I would like to emphasize the transdisciplinary aspect of my work. In order to conceptualise dubbing and performance and create a method to analyse characterization in originals and dubbed AV texts, I have relied on works from various fields, including Film Studies, Theatre Studies, Television Studies, Audiovisual Translation Studies, and Sound Studies. This has made the research process a rich and complex one, and I hope that researchers and readers in all of these areas will find my work intellectually stimulating.

CHAPTER 1

Understanding audiovisual material: A multi-layered meaning process

1.1 Introduction

Gavin Lambert explains that: '[U]ntil we know how a film is speaking to us, we cannot be sure what it is saying' (Lambert 1952: 7 in Gibbs 2002: 100). What Lambert highlights in this short quote is the fact that audiovisual materials, such as films and television series,[1] have a language of their own and that in order to understand them, we must learn to read and decode the various layers of meaning presented to us. Broadly speaking there are two levels of communications in films, known as the horizontal and vertical levels (Vanoye 1985). The vertical level corresponds to the interaction between directors and the audience, whereas the horizontal level corresponds to the interaction between characters. These two levels are interrelated since meaning comes from the interaction between audience and film (Phillips 2000: 88) and both the audience and directors interpret meaning based on the interaction between the characters.

Interpretation is therefore an important process when it comes to understanding films – so much so that Stafford notes that 'a film would not exist without an audience' (2007: 73). Consequently, this process of making meaning is not a straightforward one, as the audience responds to films on various levels. Patrick Phillips explains that there are two main

---

[1]   For the sake of simplicity, the word 'film' will hereafter be used to talk about both films and television series.

levels, the intellectual level and the emotional level (2000: 4–7), including previous experiences (Stafford 2007: 87), all of which will inform our appreciation of what is happening on-screen. Furthermore, this viewing experience is both shared and personal (Phillips 2000: 5); for instance, we can laugh at the same time as other people while also having our own personal interpretation.

Therefore, films can be discussed both in terms of their own language and of our viewing experience, and the first step towards conveying this experience to readers is to describe films; to put into words how they convey meaning. However, decoding a film's meaning is a complex task given that a film is generally understood as a 'polysemiotic medium'; a whole that audiences have to reconstruct (Gottlieb 2005, Desilla 2009: 120). Indeed, various elements or aspects combine to create meaning in a film, such as the *mise-en-scène*, editing, sound, and cinematography. For instance, when discussing the choice of music in the opening credits of *Desperately Seeking Susan* (Susan Seidelman 1985), Douglas Pye (2007: 33) explains that when we watch a film, 'we experience simultaneously the interaction of elements – colour, framing, action, sound and so on – that analysis inevitably separates'. Consequently, we can only analyse films by breaking them down into these smaller units; a process of description or dissection necessary in order to understand how films elicit particular reactions from audiences. Even though this process may run the risk of 'deconstructing' the whole and the magic of the carefully created atmosphere that goes with it, it is only by the act of describing that we can take the first step towards trying to understand the mechanics at work in audiovisual materials, be they originals or translations. Films are therefore complex repositories of meaning conveyed through various elements which must be read both individually and as part of a whole. In this first chapter, I examine the concept of *mise-en-scène* in order to show how audiovisual materials 'speak' to us or how they can be 'read'; that is, how films convey meaning and how this can be linked to characterization and performance, which will be examined in more detail in Chapter 2.

1.2 Elements of films: The visual elements of *mise-en-scène*

Mise-en-scène is a complex concept 'concerned with visual style in the cinema' (Gibbs 2002: 1), which translates literally as 'to put to stage' (ibid.: 5) or 'putting into scene' (Dix 2008: 11). Gibbs offers a very simple yet useful definition of *mise-en-scène* as 'the contents of the frame and the way they are organised' (2002: 5). Therefore, following Gibbs' definition, my work considers audiovisual materials in terms of the contents of their frame and, more specifically, 'lighting, costume, décor, properties and the actors themselves [...], framing, camera movement, the particular lens employed and other photographic decisions' (ibid.). From this definition, one can see that *mise-en-scène* is concerned with cinematographic features and 'encompasses both what the audience can see, and the way in which we are invited to see it' (ibid.). In the present book, the description of scenes in originals and dubbed versions will therefore take into consideration a selection of communicative elements in film following Gibbs' classification (2002: 6–26): lighting, colour, costume, props, décor, action and performance, space, the position of the camera and framing. The following paragraphs will examine each of these elements in turn.

Lighting specifically concerns how light is used or organized to present characters, i.e. to emphasize or minimize their presence on-screen. Lighting creates mood and can be used to highlight elements or characters in a scene through 'high key lighting' and 'low key lighting', each of which has a different connotation (Dix 2008: 18–19). What we are interested in is, for instance, whether characters are in the foreground or in the background (e.g. in the light or in the dark), or whether one character in a scene is better lit than the other protagonists, as this could mean that he or she is also in a clearer position in their emotional life. Audience perception will therefore be dependent on the way characters are lit, what they are saying and their facial expressions and gestures, all of which are elements of performance, as we shall see in Chapter 2. In the context of translation, the connotative messages attached to lighting may lead to different perceptions given that cultures are not monolithic spaces of meaning. This is why it is important to be sensitive to the specific elements of *mise-en-scène*. *Colours* are also crucial to creating meaning, particularly the way they are used and their associations. Colours carry connotations; in the West, for instance, 'red' is usually culturally associated with passion and 'white' with purity. These associations may vary across cultures, although there are some colours which have cross-cultural associations. For instance, when analysing the opening credits of *Desperately Seeking Susan* (Susan Seidelman 1985), Pye (2007: 32–3) comments on the use of pink and how this colour is widely used as a symbol of femininity. As noted previously, dissecting elements of *mise-en-scène* is necessary to our understanding of what these elements are and how they interact to make meaning. Colours and lighting are in fact linked, as colours may be considered as 'feature[s] of the lighting, the set decoration, or props' (Gibbs 2002: 8). Moreover, Baldry and Thibault (2006: 199) also note that a colour can act as a cohesive device: a 'colour is not an isolate – it is not a question of pure chromatic quality – but has its significance in relation to other features of the visual field with which it is integrated'. Hence, colours are related to various coding orientations (Kress and Van Leeuwen 1996, Baldry and Thibault 2006: 200). There are three different codings: naturalistic, sensory/sensual and the hyperreal, all of which will convey different meanings and have an impact on the audience's perception. Additionally, colours can also be used as *linkages*: 'details which will make the audience, consciously or more often unconsciously, connect one scene or character or action with another' (Ian Cameron 1963: 8). Throughout films, these linkages will act as motifs and through them the audience will associate particular images or scenes with one another. For instance, the use of the colour red in Lynne Ramsey's *We Need to Talk About Kevin* (2011), present in food, clothes, paint and nature, permeates the whole film and can be seen as a constant reminder of or clues about Kevin's looming atrocious act. Mentioning clothes leads us to *costume*, another important parameter that is concerned with the way clothes, hairstyles and make-up are used to convey meaning. All elements of costume prove highly significant in terms of characterization. Take Marilyn Monroe, for instance: her peroxide blonde hair and tight dress in *Gentlemen Prefer Blondes* (Howard Hawks 1953) contribute to expressing her oozing sexuality.

Another significant element of *mise-en-scène* is the category of *props*, which comprises the objects used by actors on set. Andrew Klevan notes that actors' 'interaction with domestic objects delineates their emotional progression' (2000:146, quoted in Gibbs 2002: 9). For instance, holding a bunch of flowers can be interpreted as a gesture conveying either affection or sympathy, depending on the context, or a character may be associated with their favourite hat – like Charlie Chaplin – or favourite shoes, such as Dorothy's red shoes in *The Wizard of Oz* (Victor Fleming 1939). Props can therefore be used to convey a character's emotional or psychological status (Dix 2008: 13–15) and their use is context-sensitive, not only in the context of the film itself but also in that of the original's source culture and the target culture of the translation. Props are an integral part of a film's *décor*, another element related to *mise-en-scène*. Indeed, what is present on set (e.g. doors, columns, tables etc.) can be used to 'express a character's emotions or predicament' (Gibbs 2002: 69). It is important to take note of the furniture in a scene, for instance; a chair could be seen to share the characteristics of a certain character in a scene: 'straight, simple, slim and firm' (Klevan 2005: 65). Furthermore, décor refers not only to that which a character possesses; location proves important too, as the way actors occupy space contributes to our understanding of their character. Klevan explains that 'the discovery of location is inseparable from the investigation of psychology: the performers look to their environment to realize their characters. Discreet and considerate disclosure of personality replaces definite announcement and revelation' (2005: 71). Hence, like props, décor can also reflect a character's personality and 'the way in which the background or composition of a shot' is presented 'can express what a character may not be able to put into words' (ibid.). For instance, when discussing *Imitation of Life* (Douglas Sirk 1959), Gibbs (2002: 94) explains that 'the set helps the film solve its structural problem': the design of the house in which the characters live and the architecture of the house reflect 'the way in which these characters' lives are interlinked' (ibid.).

Hence, all the elements of *mise-en-scène* we have seen so far serve to establish characters and are used to reveal information about these characters, such as their age, gender, socio-economic background etc. It will have also become obvious that some of these elements may be easier to 'read' than others, while it can likewise be argued that not everybody will be able to get the connotations or associations related to colours, lighting, costumes, décor or props. However, it is worth knowing how audiovisual materials generate meaning if we are interested in how these meanings are transferred and received in translation. The next two elements of *mise-en-scène*, action and performance, will be presented separately in Chapter 2, as these prove crucial where characterization in concerned. Indeed, Gibbs puts them in the foreground when he explains that:

> at an important base level, *mise-en-scène* is concerned with the action and the significance it might have. Whilst thinking about décor, lighting and the use of colour, we should not forget how much can be expressed through the direction of action and through skilful performance. (2002: 12)

Thus, a single gesture, a swift look at another actor whether on or off-screen, can be charged with meaning and convey valuable information about the characters' backgrounds, their relationships and their desires or emotional states. As we shall see, performance is a fascinating yet complex topic that proves very difficult to put into words. In the present book, performance is given priority and will be developed at length in Chapter 2, as it is 'central to our understanding of narrative film' (ibid.).

According to Gibbs (2002), there are three additional aspects that are important to take into consideration when analysing the elements that generate meaning in a film: space, the position of the camera and framing (or composition).[2] *Space* refers to the '*organisation* of the contents of the

---

2   Some critics establish a difference between *mise-en-scène* and cinematography (see, for instance, Dix 2008: 22–3 and Bordwell and Thompson 2007). Cinematography refers to 'how' we see the elements of *mise-en-scène* and is concerned with the functioning of the camera (distance, angle, movement). However, Gibbs (2002) treats all of this as being under the remit of *mise-en-scène*, claiming that *mise-en-scène* 'must include framing [and] composition' (2002: 54), which is why these aspects are covered in this section. For Bordwell and Thomson (2007), *mise-en-scène* includes setting, props, costumes, and lighting; they make 'no reference to framing, camera movement or the position of the camera' (Gibbs 2002: 54), which are dealt with under 'cinematography'.

frame' (2002: 18). In other words, it is the 'personal space between performers and our sense of when it is impinged upon', as well as 'the relationships
expressed and patterns created in the positioning of actors' (2002: 17).
Space thus refers to the way actors are organized on-screen and can give
an indication of their characters' relationships. To illustrate this, Gibbs
analyses a scene from *North by Northwest* (Alfred Hitchcock 1959) in which
two male characters and one female character are physically positioned in
a triangle, which on an emotional level can also be said to convey important information about their personal struggles. The *position of the camera*
is also paramount as it 'governs our access to the action and 'determine[s]
our understanding of the scene' (Gibbs 2002: 19). The subjective tracking
shot is a perfect example to illustrate this. With this shot, the audience sees
things through a character's eyes, giving the impression that we are moving
with them. Certain directors are well known for using this particular technique; for instance, it is one of the 'identifiable characteristics of Hitchcock's
mise-en-scène [...] [A] logical extension of the Hitchcockian principle of
audience-identification, an expression of his desire to "put the audience
through it"' (Wood 1976: 125–6 in Gibbs 2002: 20). The last element,
framing, also relates to camera position, albeit in a different way. When we
watch a film, 'what is in the frame is only a selective view of a wider fictional
world [...] [T]he act of framing an action presents the film-maker with a
whole range of choices, including those concerning what is revealed and
withheld from the audience' (Gibbs 2002: 26). A variety of camera movements and positions can be used to frame shots. Directors have at their
disposal various shooting techniques to tell a story from a specific point
of view, from 'long takes', which are used to keep us at a distance, to 'short
shots' and 'close-ups', used to isolate a character's face and their emotions.
Pye comments that 'the emotional dynamics of [a] scene are mirrored [...]
in the editing, framing and camera movement' (2007: 70). These shots are
therefore very significant when analysing audiovisual materials and trying
to understand the dynamics at work in a film. Shots, camera movements
and camera angles create meaning and establish a relationship between or
an engagement with audience and characters. For instance, Kress and Van
Leeuwen (1996: 131) talk about the 'proxemics of interpersonal communication' by which distance, intimacy, personal, social, and public views are all

created through the camera work (see, for instance, Dix 2008: 23–7, Baldry and Thibault 2006: 193–8, Wharton and Grant 2005: 51 and Kress and Van Leeuwen 1996: 140–8). To put it another way, proxemic signs are concerned with the distance between the characters themselves as well as between the characters and the camera – the horizontal level mentioned previously – and therefore includes types of shots.

All of these shooting techniques generate meaning; images act as clues to help the audience understand what is happening on-screen and more particularly to our understanding of characters. For instance, when discussing Orson Welles' *The Magnificent Ambersons* (1942), Victor F. Perkins explains that:

> [a] vital aspect of Welles' long-take practice is its refusal of the easy rhetoric of emotional and psychological exposure that analytical editing makes available. In conventional practice the timing of cuts and especially the deployment of close-up provide a means to assert the special significance of a gesture, a glance, a reaction [...] It is routine to bang in close-ups where the drama has no valid climax and where the actor has nothing of substance on display. Welles seems to wish to dissociate himself from the notion that the camera can supply insight not achieved in performance; and his practice can be taken to reflect a recoil from an excessively easy confidence in the camera's assertion of motive and undeclared feeling. (Perkins 1999: 58–9)

One can see from this quote how camera movements and positions impact on the way audiences perceive situations and characters, meaning camera work is intrinsically linked to performance and characterization. The different types of shots, camera angles and movements available to directors will be scrutinized at more length in Chapter 4 when I introduce my multimodal model designed to analyse originals and dubbed versions.

Hence, it is through the combination of the elements of *mise-en-scène* that a film produces meaning. Gibbs (2002: 26) emphasizes that it is the interaction of the elements of *mise-en-scène*, the 'interplay of elements that is significant' (ibid.) to generate meaning. Moreover, all of these separate elements take on even more 'significance' by 'virtue of *context*: the narrative situation, the "world" of the film, the accumulating strategies that the film-maker adopts' (ibid.). In other words, a film has a tone or register (Pye 2007) created through the interplay of the elements of *mise-en-scène*.

It is important to emphasize that this interplay is an integral part of the filmic material whether considering films in their original languages or their translated versions.

Hence, *mise-en-scène* can be defined simply as 'the organization of space' (Wharton and Grant 2007: 55), as opposed to editing, the organization of time. Editing and sound are often not included in the definition of *mise-en-scène*, save for figures like Gibbs (2002) and Robin Wood (1960/61). Gibbs, for instance, claims that it is not possible to describe a long take without mentioning the editing, while Pauline Reay (2004) argues that music can also be treated as part of *mise-en-scène*. Drawing from the work of the above-mentioned scholars, I have chosen to include sound and, by extension, music and dialogue in my analysis of characterization and performance through *mise-en-scène*. A further reason for doing so is because integrating sound into *mise-en-scène* does not relegate the script to a secondary position, which is an important consideration in the context of translation given that words also need to be translated in audiovisual translation.

1.3   The oral elements of *mise-en-scène*: Sound and dialogue

As mentioned previously, the various elements of a film's soundtrack generate meaning in different ways and the oral dimension must also be examined alongside the visual elements. This dimension is called the soundtrack and is composed of speech (dialogue, voiceover), music, sound effects and silence, which Dix claims should also be taken into consideration (2008: 81). There are two main types of sounds in a film soundtrack: diegetic and non-diegetic. Diegetic sounds belong within the world of the story, whereas non-diegetic sounds come from outside the world of the story (e.g. a sound or piece of music which does not have its source in the world of the story).[3]

---

3   There is also a difference between non-diegetic/diegetic and off/on-screen (or voice-off) sound. Voice-off is diegetic since it is a voice from within the story of

Both types of sound can have different levels of importance; they can be central, middle-ground or in the background (Van Leeuwen 1999: 23) and play an important part in setting the mood. For instance, non-diegetic music carries '"editorial" authority, not as comment necessarily (though it can have this function [...]) but as setter of a mood and dramatic register' (Pye 2007: 13). Let me begin by looking at the role of sound.

As demonstrated by Adam Melvin (2011) in an article on the use of sound in Steve McQueen's *Hunger* (2008), sound can be used to structure a film. Melvin argues that the 'sparse use of dialogue in much of the film affords space for a rich and prominent use of sonic material – including musical cues – and an attention to aural detail that mirrors that of the film's visual imagery' (2011: 23). In *Hunger*, sound acts as a 'structural tool, framing its [the film's] narrative content' (ibid.). Melvin further explains that 'sound and image enter into a dialogue of sorts that serves to emphasize the aural content of [these] actions' (ibid.: 27). Elements of the visual and the aural therefore combine to make meaning as a whole, even if the aural dimension takes precedence in *Hunger*. The sonic aspect of the opening scene is described in detail; according to Melvin, this scene 'resonates with us the most' because of a mixture of 'close-ups' and 'heightened sounds level in the mix' (ibid.). In *Hunger*, sound is a 'framing device' (ibid.: 28) and its most striking sonic motif is a 'uniform rhythmic pulse' that permeates throughout the film. Melvin describes how the 'painfully slow, monotonous pulse of the sweeping [of a prison officer cleaning up urine] captures the air of futility and resignation of the somewhat mammoth dialogue scene that it immediately follows, enabling us to digest and reflect upon it' (ibid.: 28). Hence, sound (including dialogue) and visual elements work together to create a universe that is an integral part of the film narrative structure. In such a configuration, 'diegetic sound' may become a 'musical statement' (ibid.: 29), and when the

---

the film. The source of the music need not be seen for it to be diegetic. It can come from, for example, a car driving past a building behind the action. Off-screen is always diegetic as off-screen means unseen by the camera but still within the world of the story; to the camera's left or right, above it or below it, or else behind it. Non-diegetic means something like 'non-screen', i.e. music or sounds that the characters could never be aware of because they were added in the editing process.

prisoners demolish their cells to oppose a decision, the resulting 'fusion of dialogue, sound, motif and musical gesture provides an orchestrated, yet expressive moment of sonic freedom in an otherwise oppressive world of uniform ritual' (ibid.: 29). Music and sound give 'structural cohesion' to the film by 'punctuating' and 'framing' the film's narrative: 'the absorption of the film's musical content into the fabric of its soundscape, coupled with the almost musical sensibility with which sound itself is at times handled, further enhances and unifies its dynamic' (ibid.: 29–30). I find Melvin's approach particularly helpful in its claim that films are semantically complex. In order to describe films, we must dissect or deconstruct them while not forgetting that we are dealing with a whole which only makes sense when all of the elements are considered alongside one another.

Many scholars agree that music creates atmosphere and heightens emotions (see, for instance, Kozloff 2000: 118, Wharton and Grant 2005: 61, Philips 2000: 38). Gorbman (1987) is one of the major works in the area of film music, being the first work in Film Studies and music in film to draw on narrative theory and apply the term diegetic and non-diegetic to music. Other works include Lak (1997), who discusses the emotional impact of music on the audience; Kalinak (1992), who looks at the conventions and strategies of film scoring in Hollywood; and Brown (1994), who offers a history of film music in American and European cinema. There are also a number of studies on music and emotions[4] as well as works in cognitive Film Studies relating to music (e.g. Jeff Smith 1996, 1999). More recently, David Machin (2010: 7) investigates the way visuals, sounds and lyrics are all able to communicate discourses multimodally. He comments that '[i]n Film Studies there has been work explaining *what* music does in film but none that has dedicated itself to showing specifically *how* it does this' (2010: 12). Machin sets out to explain 'how music creates setting, character and action' (2010: 12) by investigating the use of music and sound in *ER* and *Sex and the City*. In a similar way, my multimodal model will attempt to demonstrate how songs contribute to the creation of characters.

---

4   <http://csml.som.ohio-state.edu/Music829D/music829D.bibliography.html> (last accessed on 15 January 2013).

When it comes to music and songs, a number of studies have been conducted on music in films and its impact on the audience. One notable example
is Pauline Reay in *Music in Film: Soundtrack and Synergy*, who examines –
among other things – the 'textual functions of film music' (2004: 3). Music
supports and is seen as an integral part of *mise-en-scène*; it has a narrative function as well as cultural connotations. Reay looks specifically at how diegetic
and non-diegetic music is used to establish mood and setting in films. With
particular reference to Martin Scorsese's *Goodfellas* (1990), she comments that
'the songs [...] work on the first level of musical allusionism being appropriate
for setting, characterization and mood, as well as operating an integral part
of the narrative' (2005: 52). The other level of allusionism is when song lyrics
point to features of a character they would rather not acknowledge (2005:
52), thus contributing to character construction. Although Reay does not
consider musicals, parallels can be drawn with this genre and particularly
with my own corpus, given that the protagonists of *Buffy the Vampire Slayer*
articulate or release their doubts and anxieties against their will through the
songs in the musical episode 'Once More With Feeling'.

Susan Smith's research on musicals (2005 and 2007) is also worth mentioning, as she argues that musicals are perfect material to study the release
of emotions. Songs in musicals have an expressive potential; they are used
for dramatic effect and contribute to characterization. Smith (2007: 181)
discusses the use of songs in *Gigi* (Vincente Minnelli 1958) to express male
anxiety linked to a 'girl's growing up', which she contrasts with *Father of
the Bride* (Vincente Minnelli 1950), another film that deals with the same
theme but through spoken dialogue. She argues that:

> musical elements provide the opportunity for a much more extensive exploration
> of the male protagonist's feelings as Gaston is shown walking through the streets
> of Paris and engaging in singing form a soliloquy that marks a further development
> in the film's overall strategy of using Jourdan's voice to bring out a deeper state of
> interior reflection in his character. (2007: 181)

Hence, music is important when it comes to creating mood and giving
us information about what is happening on-screen. There is an obvious
relationship between a film's soundtrack and the images we see. Pye, for
instance, describes how the use of a pop number in the opening credits of

Desperately Seeking Susan (Susan Seidelman 1985) has an 'informing effect in orientating us to the action' (Pye 2007: 32). According to Pye, songs can be a musical commentary on the events that are taking place (2007: 28–9). This highlights the importance of music and songs as part of *mise-en-scène*, since they can be used for character and plot construction. Moreover, in the context of translation, we have to wonder what happens to songs that provide information about the narrative. For instance, when discussing the French dubbed and subtitled versions of Oliver Stone's *Natural Born Killers* (1994), Régine Hollander (2001: 82) laments that a Leonard Cohen song that plays at the beginning of the film is not translated and its meaning is therefore lost on the French audience. Thus, it seems relevant to consider the translation of the lyrics of film songs, given that lyrics can be considered an integral part of film dialogue. It is to this which I now turn.

Film dialogue encompasses all spoken lines, namely conversations both between and among characters as well as voiceover (Katz 1991/8: 366). Interestingly, the study of film dialogue has been a secondary pursuit in Film Studies:

> Although what the characters say, exactly how they say it, and how the dialogue is integrated with the rest of the cinematic techniques are crucial to our experience and understanding of every film since the coming of sound, [...] canonical textbooks on film aesthetics devote pages and pages to editing and cinematography but barely mention dialogue [...]. Dialogue has been perceived too transparent, too simple to need study. (Kozloff 2000: 6)

The fact that dialogue has been neglected in Film Studies may be related to the status sound has held in this field; sound has traditionally been seen as secondary to *mise-en-scène*, cinematography and editing. Shaviro explains that, in 'traditional analogue cinema':

> the soundtrack serves as a support to the images, giving them emotional resonance and a guarantee of (seeming) naturalism. That is to say, sound provides what Chion calls 'added value'; it enriches a 'given image' in such a way as to give the false impression that 'this information or expression "naturally" comes from what is seen, and is already contained in the image itself' (Chion 1994: 5). Film sound is therefore a supplement (in Derrida's sense of the term): it subliminally supports the primacy of an image that nonetheless would not mean or feel the same without it. (Shaviro 2010: 81)

Nevertheless, Shaviro acknowledges that the situation is changing with 'post-cinematic media like television and video' (ibid.), and I hope that my work will also contribute to showing the importance of considering dialogue in original films and their translated versions.

According to Kozloff (2000: 33), dialogue has two functions: the first one is at the level of the narrative, while the second relates to aesthetic effects. When it functions as a narrative device, dialogue is used to anchor diegesis to time and space, communicate and create narrative causality, sustain the plot, reveal character and for dramatic irony (Mernit 2001: 191–3, Kozloff 2000: 34–51, Phillips 2000: 32–4). Through spatial and temporal references, dialogue provides information related to where and when a story unfolds, as well as providing information on narrative cause and effect (e.g. past events, Mernit 2001: 192, Kozloff 2000: 37–9). Finally, and most importantly for my purposes here, dialogue also provides information related to characterization (Kozloff 2000: 43–7), revealing information about emotional states, personality and social background, as well as about the relationship between characters (Kozloff 2000: 46–7, 70–1, Phillips 2000). In terms of aesthetic effects, the main attribute of dialogue is its power 'to define the tone and set the mood of a film' (Desilla 2009: 118, Mernit 2001: 192, Kozloff 2000: 51–6). Indeed, it is through dialogue that audiences are stimulated emotionally and intellectually.

However, dialogue can only take its full meaning when considered within the semantic whole, as alluded to in Melvin's above-mentioned work. John Sayles, making particular reference to screenplays, comments that:

> [r]eading these [screenplays] without having reference to the movies made from them may be a little stark. The music is not here, the acting, the visceral power of the locations, no camera movement or lighting – all the things that make a movie a movie. So try to take them as the blueprints they are, outlines that helped people come together and make a story. (1998: x)

Considering the integrality of the communicative situation is a very important aspect of my approach to understanding original audiovisual materials and their translations. Dialogue is only one aspect of *mise-en-scène* and, by extension, only one element of audiovisual translation. This is something

AVT scholars have acknowledged in recent years as the study of audiovisual material in translation began to go beyond the simple linguistic level (as we shall see in Chapter 3), but it is interesting to note that dialogue is still considered to be of marginal importance in Film Studies. Indeed, nowhere in his book does Gibbs (2002) mention that he is dealing with translated words and dialogue, even though he is referring to foreign films, e.g. *La Règle du Jeu* (Jean Renoir 1939). However, Pye (2007), Klevan (2002) and Smith (2007) all argue that dialogue is an important aspect of the *mise-en-scène*, performance and voice within film. These works demonstrate that, even though dialogue has not been at the forefront of analysis, it is nevertheless a vital factor to consider when analysing the aforementioned aspects, given that the elements of *mise-en-scène* can only generate meaning when they are combined with one another. For instance, Douglas Pye (2007: 62), when discussing Frank Sinatra's performance in *Some Came Running* (Vicente Minnelli 1958), comments that the 'gaucheness of' Dave's (Sinatra's)'s reply: 'It's about love and I think I've learned a great deal more about it now' is 'heightened by the clumsiness of his attempt, as he negotiates the inelegant final clause, to perch on the narrow arm of Gwen's desk chair and pull her face towards him.'⁵ Thus, words are important not only from a linguistic angle but also in terms of paralinguistics, i.e. tone and voice, and I believe that studies in Audiovisual Translation can contribute to showing that the study of dialogue should be given more emphasis in film analysis. Indeed, is it not significant to know what has happened to the 'inelegant final clause' when it is dubbed into French, Japanese or Arabic, or subtitled in Portuguese and Swedish? Could the text reduction involved in subtitling have an impact on the sentence where it combines with the actor's physical expression? Or if the film has been dubbed, should we not be concerned whether the voice indeed conveys the 'gaucheness' of the original? Could the choice of vocabulary when matched to the movement of the mouth affect the 'inelegant final clause of the original'? And in the case that the tone or the words are not conveyed, is the gesture by itself enough to convey

---

5   See also Smith's discussion of Spencer Tracy's voiceover in *Father of the Bride* (1950): (2007: 165–74), as well as Pye (2007) on tone.

the meaning of the original? It is therefore my hope that the conclusions I present in this book will contribute to demonstrating the importance of dialogue, i.e. any changes may impact on narrative developments and characterization. When considering dialogue and enunciation, we must also remember to mention the real life actors who embody the characters and pronounce these words, an aspect which will be treated in more depth in the next chapter. The notion of context is also crucial to analysing and interpreting the elements of *mise-en-scène*, as shall be seen in the next section.

1.4   On analysing films: The importance of context

When examining the various elements of *mise-en-scène*, it was noted that analysing films is a complex task with many aspects to be taken into consideration, all of which will only assume their full meaning when interpreted within their respective contexts. Indeed, before making any claims about the meaning of a sequence in a film, it is imperative to consider the film as a whole and not just isolated scenes:

> [I]n order to make sense of the one moment, we have had to balance a detailed examination of the sequence itself with perspectives derived from an understanding of the rest of the film, knowledge of the traditions and conventions within and with which the film is working (those of the western, for example) and information from the world outside of the film (Gibbs 2002: 39).

Gibbs' reference to the 'outside world of the film' proves very relevant in a translating environment. The audience of a film in its original language, e.g. English in an American context, might be expected to have particular knowledge that the target cultures composed of French, Japanese or Swedish audiences may not possess. Brands like Pepsi may be easy to place for audiences throughout the world, but when references are more culturally specific, such as a reference to San Pellegrino or the Brazilian beer Antarctica, this could create a potential problem in terms of the overall coherence of the material – coherence both 'across the work' and 'between the different elements of a single moment' (ibid.: 40). What this highlights is not so much the importance of elements of *mise-en-scène* individually, but 'rather the relationship between elements, their interaction within a shot and across the narrative' (ibid.: 41).

Finally, it must be noted that, as with other material (e.g. novels), one also has to be aware of the danger of 'assigning particular effects to specific techniques' (Gibbs 2002: 43) when trying to understand the meaning of audiovisual materials. Once again, context – whether internal or external – is a very important parameter, and it is crucial to remember that:

> the nuances, and the range of effects, that can be provided by the position of the camera are considerable and we cannot simply identify one meaning with one technique [...] the context in which a technique appears, including the content to which it gives form, will contribute to determining its effect. (ibid.: 44)

Gibbs' words draw attention to the importance of context in translation: one cannot translate words in isolation but only within their particular context, both in the text and also outside of the text. Whether it is a film, a novel or another text type, the relationship between style and meaning can only be made in context, since the focus is on how various elements combine or work together to make meaning and 'one stylistic means can contribute to a range of different semantic ends' (ibid.: 51). In other words, '[i]n the integrated film, the individual stylistic element will have consequences for a complex network of meanings' (ibid.: 52) and 'style determines meaning, how an event is portrayed on the screen defines its significance [and] single moments or images of films cannot be adequately considered when extracted from their context' (ibid.: 100).

1.5 Conclusion

This first chapter has looked into the different aspects that create meaning in film with an emphasis on *mise-en-scène*. We have seen that the *mise-en-scène* offers 'a wordless commentary on the action' and 'creat[es] a central

point of orientation for the spectator' (Mulvey 1977/8: 55). Moreover, the
concept itself has 'enabled critics to understand film as a visual and sensory
experience rather than just a literary one, to engage with film as a medium
in its own right, and to consider the determining influence of style upon
meaning' (Gibbs 2002: 66). *Mise-en-scène* criticism has helped us to look
at various films in an artistic manner, and although it is associated with
Hollywood cinema, it is not 'only relevant to popular cinema' (ibid.: 66);
it can be used to discuss other types of audiovisual material, e.g. television
series, as will be seen in my case studies. Finally, what we have discussed
in this chapter can be related to the notion of point of view. The concept
of point of view in the framework of Film Studies is used to 'designate
the total network of a film's relationships to its material and its attempts
to position the spectator' (Pye 2000: 8) spatially, temporally, cognitively,
ideologically and evaluatively. In other words, point of view is 'what we
see and what the character sees' (Klevan 2005: 02). It is interesting to note
that Film Studies scholars tend to explain the difference between awareness and points of view not as a result of film dialogue, but rather from
visual information. Within this framework, distance and empathy are created by the *mise-en-scène* of differing points of views, which are reflected
through camera movements that convey the thoughts and emotions of the
characters. Characters' faces and physical gestures reveal their interiority
or inner states, as do their voices. In this monograph, I subscribe to the
view that a character's revelation of interiority is realized through facial
and physical gestures used in tandem with vocal delivery. Moreover, I claim
that dubbing has a direct impact on performance because what is said, and
how it is said, is inevitably altered. The next chapter develops further the
notion of performance and the related aspect of characterization, given
that performance, as a part of *mise-en-scène*, is crucial to our understanding of audiovisual narratives.

CHAPTER 2

Performance and characterization

We may well be rewarded for concentrating on a performer as they *merely* turn a street corner, sit in a chair, touch a wall, move around a bedroom or carry a bunch of flowers. Fresh aspects of even familiar films emerge when we attend to gestures, postures, expressions and voice – and how they are situated. (Klevan 2005: preface)

2.1 Introduction

Performance in a filmic context can be defined as 'what the performer does in addition to the actions/functions she or he performs in the plot and the lines she or he is given to say. Performance is how the action/function is done, how the lines are said' (Dyer 1979: 151). Additionally, actors' performances also give us access to characters' feelings and thoughts and as such contribute to the 'revelation of the interior states of characters' (Murray Smith 1995: 151). Both of these definitions of performance mention actors and characters and it can be seen that performance and characterization overlap. Andrew Klevan explains this succinctly:

[O]n film, characters have no existence apart from the particular human beings on screen, and no life apart from the particular performers who incarnate them. Character and performer are inextricably intertwined; they coalesce. (2005: 4)

In this chapter, I examine characterization and performance in more depth, with a focus on voice, in order to explain why it is important to investigate both in audiovisual translation.

2.2 Studying performance

2.2.1 Defining performance

From a semiotic perspective, signs of performance include facial expressions, voice, gestures, body postures and movements, items of clothing and the use of lighting (Dyer 1979: 151). Props, décor and lighting have already been examined in Chapter 1; in this chapter, therefore, the emphasis will be more on facial expressions, gestures, posture and other movements, since these constitute a semiotic system in their own right (Baldry and Thibault 2006: 2002–3).

As the meaning within a performance is conveyed through body movements and gestures (Dix 2008: 19 and Phillips 2005: 35), studying performance relies on kinesics, defined as the way communication is achieved through body language (Birdwhistell 1970). Seen from this angle, the visual focus of a scene proves very important when analysing audiovisual materials. For instance, we can focus on the gaze of actors as well as how characters look at each other or at the audience (Kress and Van Leeuwen 1996: 121–2 and Baldry and Thibault 2006: 201). There is also an oral facet to performance, which is mainly conveyed through voice, e.g. intonation or a character's pitch. Whether we are dealing with visual or aural/oral elements, it must be noted that, in the same way as there are different words at our disposal when we construct sentences, there are different ways of performing movements (Baldry and Thibault 2006). This will be given further consideration in Chapter 4 with the presentation of my multimodal method. Moreover, Richard Dyer (1979/1998) argues that the way we read performance signs is bound both culturally and historically. Context is therefore crucial to our understanding of a performance. This is a fascinating statement which resonates in the translation context of this study; in dubbing, *how* things are said is inevitably changed, meaning translation can be seen to have a direct impact on performance.

Dyer's seminal book *Stars* (1979/1998) studies performers as 'stars', looking more specifically at how audiences perceive films because of the 'stars' who act in them. Dyer's book has been particularly instrumental to my understanding of how performance and characterization connect and his work will be referred to in more detail in *2.3*. For the time being, it is sufficient to emphasize that *Stars* is one of the few books that focuses on the perception of performances, and since its publication, the emphasis of performance analysis in Film Studies has shifted more towards 'acting' and the impact of various acting techniques (e.g. vaudeville, Stanislavsky or Method techniques). More recently, however, Andrew Klevan, in his book *Film Performance: From Achievement to Appreciation* (2005), has focused on performance as another element of a film's 'style', enabling me to establish a strong link between performance and *mise-en-scène*. Klevan's title is also indicative of an emphasis on the interpersonal function of performance, as he claims that:

> the achievement of the performer and the appreciation of the viewer are united, and there is a similarity between the performer's art and the viewer's task. They mirror each other's effort. (2005: 7)

In Chapter 1, I looked at films in terms of experience. There is a similar emphasis in Klevan's work, as he advocates that we 'concentrate on individual scenes or sequences' in order to be 'responsive to their unfolding' (ibid.) and, quoting Charles Affron, to 'savor the delight of their rhythms and rhymes, the flow of their contours' (Affron 1997: 7). Klevan is therefore not the only scholar to argue for a 'greater sensitivity' to film performance (2005: 15); it is also evident from the works of Lesley Stern and Georges Kouvaros (1999), Affron (1997), Perkins (1999), David Thomson (1967) and Stanley Cavell (1996). The act of describing a film becomes even more important in this context; indeed:

> [D]escription is a *question* of how to bring into existence, how, in the course of analysis, to evoke for a reader that lost object [...] Ideally we would like to write in such a way as to bring the film into imaginative being for the reader, so that she views it in the process of reading. In reading she becomes a film viewer. But we would also like to offer a persuasive interpretation based on attentiveness to the object, on detailed and accurate rendition. (Stern and Kouvaros 1999: 7–9)

Drawing on Stern's and Kouvaros' work, Klevan explains that one of the biggest challenges when describing films is to put into words what we are seeing on-screen, since what we 'evoke in words a medium that is primarily visual and aural, and *moving* (Klevan 2005: 16, his emphasis). Describing scenes is a process of 'fictionalisation', and this 'fictional charge' needs to be conveyed to viewers or readers; otherwise, they will not experience the totality of the experience. This is the second main challenge when describing films.

In Chapter 1, we saw how dissecting films may result in us overly deconstructing the whole and becoming disengaged from the material. However, if we want to argue for the complexity of films, this is a challenge that we must accept and deal with. In order to overcome the second challenge, we must try to explain what is unfolding in front of our eyes and convey the 'fictional charge' of the material if we wish to do justice to the performances, i.e. it is 'only if we evoke the "fictional charge" of a film [that] we will be meeting the spirit in which the film performers move before us' (ibid.). The saying goes: 'A picture paints a thousand words', and anyone attempting to describe scenes from audiovisual material must bear this complexity in mind when trying to translate visual elements into words. In the present book, I will provide detailed description of sequences in an attempt to capture the visual, oral and movement-based aspects of my material, all the while keeping these challenges in mind. Moreover, as must be noted from the outset, there is an innate subjectivity within film description; description and interpretation are difficult to dissociate. As Klevan notes: '[T]he prose endeavours to evoke the films and interprets them at the same time' (ibid.: 105). Subjectivity is therefore inherent to film analysis and should not deter us from analysing audiovisual material in detail.

Klevan analyses sequences from ten of Hollywood's 'Golden Age' films in order to present a 'method for sustaining attention to a performance' (ibid.: 103). He considers various aspects of performance, including body posture, items of clothing, facial expressions and the use of lighting. His method 'requires that we slow down, stop, and dwell, so that we can savour the intensity of interaction, an intonation or an expression – the reverberations – and reflect [on] the resonance' (ibid.). I find this feature of his work particularly inspiring, and as we shall see in Chapter 4, 'savouring' the text, experience and pleasure are all integral analytical parts of my own method for analysing characterization through performance.

Additional accounts of performance can be found in the field of theatre studies. David Graver (1997), for instance, writes about the actors' bodies and the manner in which they signify on stage. Graver explains that:

> [T]heories of theatre commonly claim that actors exist both as characters in a drama and performers on stage. Clearly the actor's presence on stage is not unified and fixed, but can its ontological shimmer be adequately explained by a simple division between character and performer? [...] The arguments suggest that the actor pretends to be a particular character while remaining his/her real self or that the actor represents a character while presenting his/her performance. But what exactly is the distinction between artifice and reality or between presence and representation? (1997: 221)

Graver's account of performance is interesting in that it places actors' performances into a socio-historical framework and raises questions about the identity of characters, performers and actors. His perspective enables us to situate the bodies of actors at the centre of performance and consider the visual aspect of performance in more detail.

2.2.2 Bodies and performance

Milly Williamson (2005: 41), in her discussion of the sympathetic vampire, notes that an actor's body is 'a central site of signification'. She is speaking in the context of melodrama, and explains that 'the possession of a physical flaw can evoke innocence and victimhood' (ibid.). Although this is a very specific context, her statement can be extrapolated to a more general view in which bodies as semiotic signs constitute very important aspects of generating meaning, even if different genres and types of films will have different ways of 'using' actors' bodies to convey specific messages.

Hence, actors can be seen to embody characters; Graver claims that, in order to do so, they use seven 'forms of corporal presence' (1997: 233) – namely, 'characters, performers, commentators, personages, members of socio-historical groups, physical flesh, and loci of private sensations' (ibid.: 222). Not all of these elements will be developed here; what interests me most is that Graver is concerned with the various ways in which actors' bodies generate meaning:

[I]n looking for the worlds in which the actor establishes a corporeal existence
we are looking for more than just worlds in which the actor has meaning. We are,
rather, looking for worlds in which he or she has a body. More than just an object
or image, a body has interiority, exteriority, and autonomy. A body's interior hides
its unseen, volitional mechanisms, the motivating forces that drive its observable
behaviour. A body's exterior presents its image to the world, but this image is not
self-contained. It is marked, at least in part, as consequent in appearance or activity upon the character or developments of the body's interiority. Finally, although
bodies exist within particular contexts and communities, they also have a significant
degree of autonomy. (ibid.: 222)

This quote highlights that characters only exist because of the actors who
embody them and that bodies generate meaning in complex ways. Echoing
Dyer on the cultural and historical importance of performance, Graver
emphasizes that an 'actor's simultaneous construction of a representational
and a performing body is contextualized within cultural history' (ibid.:
225), i.e. we know actors both from their previous roles and from the 'public
circulation of stories about the[m]' (ibid.: 226); for instance, those that are
published in the press. The way performances are understood is therefore
highly interpersonal. Crucially, then, performances are not fully realized
if they do not have an audience. Graver explains that an 'audience projects
upon the figure that they see [on stage] what they know (or think they
know) about the life and career of the actor'. He calls this an actor's 'personage body', which is:

> not the real person behind the interpreter who is behind the performance who
> is behind the character. Personage status is not a foundational reality but simply
> another way of representing oneself or, rather, a way of representing oneself within
> a particular distinctive domain. The interiority and exteriority of personage are both
> open to scrutiny. Depending on the material from which personage is constructed,
> the interior of this body can be composed of personal history, public gossip, or a
> performing career. The exterior of personage is composed of distinctive physical
> features, typical gestures of vocal tones, the marks of personal history or the ghost
> of past performances. (ibid.: 226–7)

Graver adds that, in the case of celebrities, 'the interior of personage is
assumed to be much greater and more intriguingly complex than the audience could know, and the exterior is fetishized as a means of communing

vicariously with the life hidden within' (ibid.). Marilyn Monroe, whom I have previously written about (Bosseaux 2012), is a good example of the effect of a personage body, as 'one might see in' her 'body certain gestures repeated from role to role or the ghost of a particularly famous and successful former part' (Graver 1997: 226).

Dyer and Graver echo each other in their discussion of the way in which actors signify. Indeed, when writing on character construction, Dyer also points out that spectators or audiences make assumptions on characters 'beyond the definite information supplied' about them (1979: 132), relying on other sources of information. Dyer emphasizes that, due to 'star identification', the truth about characters is usually undermined by the truth about the actor playing him/her (ibid.: 141). Likewise, Graver also makes a parallel between an actor's personal life and their acting:

> One might [...] note the differences between the image of the actor projected on movie screens and the image he or she creates on stage. One might look for harmonious or jarring connections between incidents in the star's life and the incidents portrayed in the drama. (1997: 226)

What this highlights is that our understanding of a performance is influenced by the context of the films, television series and documentaries we watch due to the real personalities of the actors featured in them. We can therefore rely on other pieces of information in order to fully understand the context of a performance, i.e. paratexts such as reviews, magazines and blogs, by seeing what stories are associated with actors and considering whether these impact on our conception of their personage.

Actors' bodies, their interiority and exteriority are therefore central to performance and interesting parameters of identity to consider when analysing characters' performance. As Graver puts it, an actor's corporal identity is:

> linked to race, class, or gender and constructed within the socio-historical discourse of culture. This body's exterior consists of physical features deemed significant by custom and prejudice. These features might include skin colour, sex, posture, accent, dialect, gait, or hand gestures. (1997: 227–8)

By putting the emphasis on actors' bodies, I want to draw attention to the complexity of performance and characterization and highlight how they

are multi-layered and therefore challenging to tackle in translation. We
will now consider in more detail how performance and characterization
can be analysed in audiovisual materials.

2.3 Performance as characterization

Characterization – the way characters are created on-screen through actors'
performance, speech, voice characteristics, facial expression, gestures,
camera angles and character gaze – is a topic that has received little attention in Film Studies. Even when it has, this has mostly been in relation to
the 'golden age' of Hollywood cinema, e.g. in Dyer's *Stars* (1979, re-edited
in 1998), perhaps the most significant point of reference on the topic. This
influential work *Stars* explores the phenomenon of stardom from socio-
logical and semiotic perspectives, advancing that the way viewers perceive
films is influenced by the stars playing roles within them.

Dyer questions the way in which stars signify their character and examines the notion and construction of *character*. He establishes a parallel
between characters in fiction and in film, explaining that 'characterization in film approximates to or tries to be like the novelistic conception of
character' (1979: 116). He then presents ten 'signs' that 'viewers latch on in
constructing characters' (ibid.: 120–32), including audience foreknowledge,
names (and their connotations), character speech (both what they say and
how they say it), gestures (as indications of personality and temperament),
actions ('what a character does in the plot', ibid.: 128), structure (of the narrative, its function and the role of the characters within it) and *mise-en-scène*
(including colour, framing and the placement of actors). Although Dyer
focuses specifically on stars, these 'signs' or elements can most certainly be
used to analyse the way characters in audiovisual materials are constructed.
In the context of translation, the visual parameters of appearance, objective correlatives, gesture, action, structure and *mise-en-scène* will remain
unchanged. However, the connotations of these semiotic signs may change
from one culture to the next. Moreover, through dubbing, characters'

names and speech will vary along with the audience's foreknowledge of the actors, the actors' 'personage bod[ies]' and the themes and associations of the audiovisual material itself. As such, it is worth wondering what happens to the message in its entirety once the material is translated, for even though the gestures, actions and *mise-en-scène* remain intact, the screening context is different.

Considering audience foreknowledge and the possible associations viewers may have also brings to light the issue of intertextuality. According to Fiske:

> The theory of intertextuality proposes that any one text is necessarily read in relationship to others and that a range of textual knowledges is brought to bear upon it [...] Intertextual knowledges pre-orient the reader to exploit television's Polysemy by activating the text in certain ways, that is, by making some meanings rather than others. (1987: 108)

In an article on the American TV series *Xena: Warrior Princess* (Syfy 1995–2001), Sarah Gwenllian-Jones (2003: 186) points to the series' references to other texts and explains that 'intertextual references weave multiple exterior meanings of the fabric of a single text'. This is important for my research, given the claims that viewers of *Buffy the Vampire Slayer* are regularly invited to draw on their knowledge of cultural aspects – and more particularly their knowledge of specific genres, e.g. musicals – in order to understand the intertextual references of the series (Chapter 6). Stafford (2007: 83) also emphasizes that our understanding of a film presupposes knowledge of other films, while Lemke (1985) goes even further in considering a broader sense for intertextuality when he advances that films generate meaning in relation to other 'texts' such as TV programmes or books. All in all, this perspective on intertextuality as well as the various elements presented in Chapter 1 reinforces the notion that meaning is a multi-layered process and that the complex fabric of visual texts makes film texts challenging to read even before we start thinking about the translation process.

Returning to the ways in which characters generate meaning, one important parameter to take into consideration is body language. Proxemics are essential to understanding characters' feelings and their relationships with other actors or characters. If, for instance, two characters are sitting close to one another on a sofa, this will convey something intimate about their relationship. However, if one of them is situated on the edge of the frame while talking to someone standing on the opposite side, it will most likely mean that they are not close or that they may be experiencing problems. This is a very important aspect to consider: it is not only the dialogue but also the visual clues that tell us about characterization and relationships. In addition to this, different types of shots will also communicate how characters may feel towards one another: when two actors are having a conversation but are not framed together in a two-shot, for instance, it normally shows that they are in opposition to one another or that they are not united.

Therefore, every gesture is important; 'legs and feet casually kick[ing] up from the knee' (Klevan 2005: 53) when a girl is on the phone with a friend talking about a boy that she may like, or a man 'looking downwards while brushing some cigarette ash from his jacket' (Smith 2007: 220) as he tells a woman how he feels about her. As mentioned previously, characterization also refers to the interiority of characters, and visual elements help us understand the inner lives of the protagonists whom we are watching interact. Klevan illustrates this process when commenting on the specific physical placement of actors in scenes. He describes a scene in which a man, a husband/father, is not taken seriously by the rest of the family and is placed in the background of the scene. Klevan explains that 'the performer need not openly acknowledge his *position*; he remains appropriately subdued, and maintains his mild-mannered persona, but the film does not subdue the significance of his exclusion' (2005: 53). Words and visuals therefore work together to convey meaning and audiences will rely on both to get a comprehensive vision of the message. I have mentioned previously that dialogue has been neglected in Film Studies, with non-verbal elements considered to be more significant. In melodrama, for instance, Peter Brooks explains that words:

> however transparent as vehicles for the expression of basic relations and verities, appear to be not wholly adequate to the representation of meanings, and the melodramatic message must be formulated through other registers of the sign. (1995: 56)

Therefore, extreme physical conditions such as 'mutedness', 'blindness' and 'paralysis' will be used instead of words – or in addition to them, in the case of the latter two – to 'represent extreme moral and emotional conditions' (ibid.). There is an interesting contrast between analyses in AVT studies, which have significantly overemphasized words, and Film Studies, which have placed the emphasis on non-verbal elements. My work should therefore be seen as an attempt to bridge the gap between these two fields, as although I shall still take linguistic elements into consideration, I will primarily highlight the importance of non-verbal elements in dubbing.

It can be seen that characterization and performance are intrinsically linked, a fact Klevan makes explicit when he explains that:

> attending to the moment-by-moment movement of performers also enhances our understanding of film characterization. It encourages us to a character's physical and aural detail and reminds us, because we are prone to forget in our literary moods, of their ontological particularity in the medium of film. A living human being embodies a film character. (2005: 7)

Since actors embody and perform characters, we cannot talk about characterization without reference to actors' performances. My claim in this book is that translation impacts on characterization and further situates performance as a key component of 'film style' (Klevan, 2005). I follow Klevan's method, as presented in *2.2.1*, focusing on individual scenes being 'responsive to their unfolding' (2005: 7). In his interrogation of the connection between actors and characters, Klevan investigates performers':

> position and perspective (the relationship of the performer to the camera, and their position within the shot), place (the relationship of the performer to location, décor, furniture, and objects); and plot (the relationship of the performer to narrative developments). (2005: preface)

For instance, when dealing with position and perspective, Klevan analyses Charlie Chaplin's specific performance in the last sequence of the film *City of Lights* (Charles Chaplin 1931), which is marked by the themes of blindness and sight. In this final sequence, Chaplin and the (formerly blind) flower woman (Virginia Cherill) are about to be reunited upon his return from

prison. When describing the scene, Klevan takes into consideration various aspects of *mise-en-scène*: the different types of shots (close-up, medium
shot, over-the-shoulder shots), the framing, the movement of the camera
and the actors' gestures and facial expressions:

> [T]he turn of his [Chaplin's] head towards the window, and towards her, is now
> charged, and the relationship between performer and camera refines the theme of
> blindness and sight: for example, turning to see (for Charlie), coming to see (for
> the flower woman) and preparing to see (for the viewer). The two performers are
> now brought closer and closer together, in deliberate and careful stages. (2005: 23)

This method of description brings to light the details of *mise-en-scène*
and performance that must be taken into consideration when analysing scenes in both original and translated material. The visuals richly
convey the film's theme through elements of *mise-en-scène*, e.g. body
gestures and their intensity, as well as direction and pace. Body language
(proxemics and kinesics) is an important parameter when it comes to
understanding characters; visual clues, not just dialogue, tell us about
characterization and character relationships. As *City of Lights* is a silent
film, there is no mention of voice or sound in Klevan's account. However,
voice and dialogue are important parts of *mise-en-scène*, even if they
have been under-represented in Film Studies. For instance, Susan Smith
(2007) demonstrates the importance of delivery when discussing Charles
Jourdan's vocal style in *Gigi* (1958). She explains that his 'groping delivery
of the word "But ... But ..." appears like an attempt to console himself as
he begins to contemplate the advantages arising from a different, more
mature Gigi' (2007: 188). Dialogue and visuals work together to create
a polysemiotic whole, which may be altered depending on translation
choices and choice of voices. As we shall soon see, voice covers linguistic
as well as paralinguistic elements such as vocal register, timbre, tempo
and volume. Although Klevan mentions vocal manner, the tone of words
(2005: 33–5, 76) and the importance of using special/repetitive vocabulary (ibid.: 34–5, 28), these references to actors' voices are limited in
comparison to other criteria such as camera movement or types of shot.
In the next section, I consider voice in more detail since this is central to
performance and to my study of dubbing.

2.4 Voice

This section reviews different accounts of voice analysis with the aim of demonstrating that voice is integral to an individual's or character's identity. Voice has been studied from various angles with an emphasis on psychological and philosophical considerations. For instance, philosopher Malden Dolar (2006) argues there are three ways of understanding voice: first, as 'a vehicle of meaning', secondly as 'a source of aesthetic admiration' (2006: 4) and thirdly 'as an object that can be seen as the lever of thought' (back cover). Dolar investigates the uses of voices from different points of view, including linguistics, metaphysics, physics, psychoanalysis, ethics and politics. As such, his work has been very influential to my understanding of what voice is and what it represents. My discussion will also rely on works from Film Studies as well as Sound Studies to emphasize the materiality of voices, explore the different types of voices relevant to my work (e.g. voice as an organ, voice as a presence, etc.) and claim that voice is an integral part of identity paving the way for more consideration of the choice of voices in dubbing.

2.4.1 Voice as identity

When air travels to our lungs we are given a voice that defines who we are. Indeed, according to Dolar:

> We can almost unfailingly identify a person by the voice, the particular individual timbre, resonance, pitch, cadence, melody, the peculiar way of pronouncing certain sounds. The voice is like a fingerprint, instantly recognisable and identifiable. (2006: 22)

Even though the status of voice and identity has scarcely been studied in Film Studies, studies in the field of neuroscience have shown that 'faces and voices are rich in information on a person's identity (i.e. idiosyncratic features, such as gender, age and body size, that lead to unique identity) and affective state (e.g. emotional, motivation)' (Campanella and Belin

2007: 535). The authors review studies of 'face-voice multimodal integration with a focus on affective perception and person identification' (ibid.)
and provide evidence that voice is part of our identity since it 'carries useful
indexical cues allowing information to be derived on a person's unique
physical features, such as gender, age and body size' (ibid.: 538).

Further evidence of voice as identity can be found in literature presenting advances in synthetic speech. More and more people with speech
disorders are being given the opportunity to have their own unique voice, as
opposed to one standard synthetic voice, and their reactions to this change
in their lives provide valuable testimonies linking voice to identity. For
instance, Alix Spiegel, a journalist and science correspondent for National
Public Radio (NPR), explains that 'when a person speaks, two things are
happening. First, the source of speech comes from the voice box, which
vibrates to produce sound. Then, the mouth shapes those sounds into
speech' (2013: online). However, those suffering from speech disorders are
not able to transition from the first step to the second, and speech scientists
have been working to find a solution to this problem. Spiegel interviews
Dr Ruta Patel, a speech scientist at Northeastern University, about her
work on synthetic speech. Patel explains that even for 'people with speech
disorders', the 'source' of the sound, i.e. their voice, is actually 'preserved'
and that this is 'where the melody is – [that's] where someone's identity is,
in terms of their vocal identity' (ibid.). Although synthetic speech systems
have existed for many years, there is only a limited number of voices available. In addition, some users prefer not to use them as they do not feel that
the voice(s) represent them (ibid.). In order to create more personalized
voices, Patel has been working with children with speech disorders to '(re)
construct' their voices. The process is simple: she records them making
an 'ahhhhh' sound from which, by means of a computer program, she can
'determine their pitch, the loudness, the breathiness of their voice [and]
the changes in clarity' (ibid.). After doing this, she uses 'a recording of the
voice of what she calls a "healthy donor" – for example, the voice of a child
who is roughly the same age as the child she's trying to help – and gets them
to say a large number of words' (ibid.). This enables her to get 'samples'
of the sounds they produce when they talk. She then combines that voice
with the pitch, breathiness and other characteristics of the child with the

speech disorder. The article focuses on the case of a teenage girl for whom Patel constructed a personalized voice. Spiegel interviews the girl along with her mother, who had never heard her daughter's voice until Patel created one for her. The article reports on the emotions the mother and daughter experience upon hearing the (re)constructed voice; the mother is moved to tears and plainly states: 'You need a voice' (ibid.). Her words emphasize how important having a voice is to her daughter's identity – without the voice, something had been missing; with the voice, the mother has her daughter back, so to speak.

Voice can therefore be seen as an attribute of someone's personality, and since dubbing changes an actor's voice, it is worth considering what happens to the identity of characters in translation – specifically in dubbed versions. The previous paragraph made reference to voice descriptors such as 'pitch' and 'breathiness', which will be explored further in the next section.

2.4.2 Describing voice(s)

According to Dolar, we are 'aware of the voice' through accent, intonation (the melody of speech) and timbre:

> [F]or the particular tone of a voice, its particular melody and modulation, its cadence and inflection, can decide the meaning. Intonation can turn the meaning of a sentence upside down. It can transform it into its opposite. A slight note of irony, and a serious meaning comes tumbling down; a note of distress, and the joke will backfire. (2006: 21)

These parameters therefore need to be taken into consideration when describing voices. It is fair to say, however, that voice studies remains a rather under-researched field within Film Studies. Major studies on voice started in the 1980s within a psychoanalytical framework, a prominent example being Chion's *The Voice in Cinema* (1982, translated into English in 1999). Chion examines the power of the human voice and 'the special relationships that inhere between the voice and the cinematic image' (1999: xi). Interestingly, most of the work done on the cinematic voice has been gender-based and 'concerned with the difficulties associated with the woman's attempt to speak in mainstream film', with the 'notable exception of Maria DiBattista's book *Fast Talking Dames* (2001)' (Smith 2007: 196). It has been said that women in film function as a fetish in Hollywood cinema, as 'Hollywood requires the female voice to assume similar responsibilities to those it confers upon the female body' (Kaja Silverman 1988: 38–9). Breaking away from the gender-based or psychological angles, recent studies on voice have focused more on practical aspects using detailed film analysis. For instance, Susan Smith (2007) is interested in 'vocal release' – moments when the actors convey a particular feeling – and offers a close reading of actors' vocal responses examined in parallel with the text's visual images. Smith considers the male cinematic voice and focuses on male characters' interiority, an interesting turning point given that interiority had previously been synonymous with femininity in work from scholars like Silverman (1988). In particular, Smith looks at 'the creative possibilities and effects that may arise in those cases where the male's struggle to speak manifests itself in the form of some quite literal impairment to his voice' (2007: 198). I will return to Smith's work on voice and vocal release in *2.4.4*, as this has been particularly influential for the purposes of my book. First, however, let me define voice further.

What characters say and how they say it is a dimension of performance that can broadly be described as 'voice quality', usually defined as 'the permanently present, background, person-identifying feature of speech' (Crystal 1991: 376). From a linguistic perspective, voice quality can be described in terms of 'tempo', the rate at which we speak; 'pitch', the musical note of a voice; and 'volume' or 'placement', the location of voice in the body. Voices can also be described more 'impressionistically', using affective terms such as 'sad', 'jovial' or 'cheerful', i.e. a person or a character with a high-pitched voice could be described as anxious or excited. Klevan, for instance, describes Irene Dunne's voice using terms such as 'breathy' and 'slightly creaky' (2005: 33–4); she is 'gleeful, naughty, mocking' (2005: 34). In a similar fashion, Susan Smith (2007) writes about 'gentle' rhythms, 'elegiac' tones and 'romantic' or 'nurturing' qualities of voices. 'Impressionistic' adjectives can be used alongside what could be called a more objective set of vocabulary to describe the actual sound, i.e., 'high' and 'breathy' in Klevan's example.

In order to describe voices, I have relied in particular on the work of Theo Van Leeuwen (1999), who has developed a semiotics of sound in his book *Speech, Music, Sound* by focusing on what sounds communicate in different contexts and material. Van Leeuwen uses a vast range of material: films, classical music, television series and popular music. What I found particularly useful in his work was his discussion of the 'semiotics of voice quality and timbre', the distinctive quality or property of a complex sound (or tone) from the point of view of what he calls 'experiential meaning potential' (ibid.: 140). In other words, drawing from Van Leeuwen's work, we can claim that sounds (including voices) can be used to generate meaning and consequently establish relations between characters and the audience.

Van Leeuwen explains that sounds have emotive and expressive qualities (ibid.: 128): sounds 'express', 'represent' and 'affect us'. For instance, the way a voice is used can communicate distance or intimacy between actors or characters or between characters and audiences. Intimacy is usually conveyed by a soft whispering voice, while at the other end of the spectrum, loudness will express distance between characters; the louder the voice, the more distance we can assume there to be. Audiences can therefore perceive a personal, formal or public relationship between characters based not only on the way they use their voices, but also the words used and the visual information.

Various modifiers can be used to describe voices, i.e. the impressionistic or affective adjectives mentioned and used by Klevan and Smith. Voices can be described as, for instance, high/low, soft/loud, tense/lax or breathy. However, 'sound qualities are not pairs of binary opposites but *graded* phenomena' (ibid.: 130). Voices are not merely high or low; they can range from maximally low to maximally high. Moreover, the 'meanings of these sound qualities are also graded' (ibid.). Van Leeuwen further emphasizes that there are problems linked to the way we talk about these meanings. The first problem is that adjectives are used to qualify voices and 'the same component of sound quality may attract many different adjectives' (ibid.). For instance, a 'tense' voice may be called 'metallic', 'sharp', 'clear', 'piercing' or 'strident', depending on the commentator. Secondly, and similarly to how the activity of describing and interpreting a film cannot be fully separated, the 'descriptive and evaluative' often mix when it comes to describing voices or sounds. There are associations or connotations attached to sounds; for instance, it is generally seen as 'good' for a voice to be 'bright' and 'clear' (ibid.). However, the adjective used is context-dependent and it may be that using a clear or loud voice is not appropriate, e.g. in an intimate context.

Van Leeuwen therefore establishes a 'social semiotics of sound quality' (ibid.) in which context must be taken into consideration before any interpretations are made; this is something I shall also bear in mind when analysing my own material. It may also be an opportune moment to emphasize that using impressionistic adjectives is a subjective endeavour. Some academics have found this problematic, e.g. Shingler (2007: online), who notes that there is a need to develop a more precise and shared set of terms and concepts for analysing and describing speaking voices in order to avoid being subjective. I do not, however, view such a development to be necessary, having found using descriptive and impressionistic vocabulary in tandem with one another to be a useful tool in my attempt to describe voices. Douglas Pye's point of view has also provided reassurance in this endeavour:

> In our experience of the dramatic arts we often need to speak not just of the story, the characters, or what a work signifies, but about the attitudes, feelings and values with which it is imbued. Part of the problem for criticism is that such things are difficult to pin down. What we are trying to describe or evoke can feel almost intangible, more like a gravitational field the work generates than an aspect of the work itself. Language tends to reflect this difficulty: the words we use most commonly to evoke these phenomena (atmosphere, mood, tone itself) in themselves suggest how elusive they seem. Correspondingly, responses to tone can feel subjective, as though its intangibility left us floundering in personal response in comparison to discussion of other, somehow more substantive, dimensions of meaning. Yet experiences of tone, in film as in language, are real enough to shape our understanding profoundly, while the inherently social nature of language and movies means that, however difficult we may find it to articulate them, these are not experiences that confine us in our own subjectivity: more often than not our grasp of tone is shared to a significant extent by others. (Pye 2007: 74)

Describing voices, then, much like describing films, proves itself to be a challenging task because of interpretation and subjectivity. An additional source of difficulty is that, according to Dolar, we are not trained to hear voices. He points out that:

when we listen to someone speak, we may at first be very much aware of his or her voice and its particular qualities, its color and accent, but soon we accommodate to it and concentrate only on the meaning that it conveys [...] The voice is the instrument and the meaning is the goal. (ibid.: 15)

In my attempt to create a model to analyse performance in audiovisual products, I have trained myself to listen and describe voice by reading material on vocal training and even taking part in a voiceover training course. By doing so, I have gained the necessary expertise to listen to, savour and analyse sound events. Dolar also explains that there is an underlying belief that 'voice should not stray away from words which endow it with sense; as soon as it departs from its textual anchorage, the voice become senseless and threatening' (ibid.: 43). In other words, 'usually one hears the meaning and overhears the voice, one "doesn't hear [the voice] well" because it is covered by meaning' (2006: 4). My work places much emphasis on paralinguistics, as I argue that there has been an overemphasis on linguistics in Audiovisual Translation studies. I am curious to see what happens if we concentrate not only on linguistic meaning but also listen to the words: their sounds, tone, accents or melodies. Bearing in mind the inherent difficulties when describing and analysing voices, I have tried to go beyond words to hear the voices of the actors. The method introduced in Chapter 4 certainly focuses on achieving this. Moreover, since singing 'brings the voice energetically to the forefront, on purpose, at the expense of meaning' (Dolar 2006: 30), I will consider both spoken and sung words in my analysis.

Finally, Van Leeuwen claims that sounds convey emotions and feelings, and in order to develop his 'social semiotics of sounds', he 'go[es] beyond the adjectives themselves and consider[s] what the sounds actually are' and 'how they are actually materially produced, and with what range of meanings and values they can therefore potentially become associated' (ibid.: 130). This proves particularly significant to my research. I will devote more space in Chapter 4 to Van Leeuwen's work on describing physical voices, where I will examine key sound qualities that can be used to analyse performance and characterization in original and dubbed products. In the following section, I continue my overview of how voice has been described in the specific context of film analysis.

2.4.3 *Analysing voice in films*

In film analysis, the way Klevan approaches scenes – i.e. with reference to voice – is particularly interesting from a translation point of view, since in dubbed versions *what* is said and *how* it is said will be changed. Moreover, as we shall see, it is not only about 'voice' and 'vocabulary' but also how the various elements of *mise-en-scène* and performance interact and combine to make meaning. Let us consider, for instance, four short sequences initially analysed by Klevan (2005).

The first one is from *Sons of the Desert* (William A. Seiter 1933), starring Stan Laurel and Oliver Hardy. In this film, Stan and Ollie lie to their wives so that they can go to the 'Sons of the Desert' convention. Ollie pretends to be ill and a doctor prescribes a cruise to Hawaii. The boat on which they were supposed to be travelling sinks and so Ollie and Stan have to face their wives and tell the truth. Klevan analyses a sequence in which Ollie and Stan talk about the whereabouts of Ollie's wife:

> Stan and Ollie sit down at the table, on which Ollie taps his fingers with impatience and anxiety. He taps out a basic rhythm, and an apparently peripheral and unconnected action – Stan placing his hat on the table – is perfectly timed to cause the sound that produces the final beat. Inquiring about his wife, Ollie asks 'I wonder where she is?' and Stan replies, 'Maybe she went out.' Ollie replies with exasperation, 'I know she went out, but what I'd like to know is, where did she *went*?' While chastising Stan for the obvious Ollie makes a glaring grammatical mistake, but this itself is too conspicuous to adequately account for the humor. 'Go' may be the correct usage, but 'went' is more appropriate to the rhythm of his speech – and to their exchange: it completes the repetition of 'went' ('Maybe she *went* out', 'I know she *went* out', 'where did she *went*'), and cannot avoid crowning the welter of 'w's ('wonder', 'where', 'went', know', and 'where'). As Hardy vocally accentuates the final 'went', he also nods his head and jabs his finger, enhancing and justifying the fluency of his rhythm while further impressing his clumsiness. (2005: 28)

As we can see from this extended description, Klevan discusses the actors' performance through their use of humour, repetitive vocabulary, manner of expression and rhythm. His explanation also includes a description of the actors' gestures and expressions to show how distance is negotiated in the scene. Visual and oral elements are both examined, as these combine to generate meaning and contribute to the actors' performance. If we were to analyse this scene in its dubbed version, the major divergence from this description of the original would be in terms of the oral dimension: what the new voices sound like and how the dialogue has been translated. Furthermore, we would have to establish whether the combination of translated oral elements and visuals convey similar meanings to the target language audiences.

Another example worth considering is a scene from *The Awful Truth* (Leo McCarey 1937), a movie telling the story of a couple going through a divorce, Lucy and Jerry Warriner (Irene Dunne and Cary Grant), each of whom decides to sabotage the other's plans to remarry. Klevan describes the way Irene Dunne utters her lines as she comments on the faulty door separating her bedroom from that of her soon-to-be ex-husband:

> Her words fall gently and quietly, to almost a murmur, and this undemonstrative address gives room for the ambiguity to breathe. Indeed, Irene Dunne's voice *is* breathy, and slightly creaky, as if it were being gently stretched by the wind (her voice quietly quivering in the draught, perhaps, which drifts through the bedrooms on this windy night). It makes her sound dreamily faraway – nearly lost yet lulling. (2005: 33–4)

As one can see, Klevan comments not only on what she says but *how* she says it – her vocal delivery – and how this fits in with the other elements of the scene. By drawing a parallel between her voice and the sound of the wind, we can see how the oral elements (both human and natural sounds) combine to make meaning. And if we were to study a dubbed version of this scene, we would have to consider how the individual elements of the performance have been negotiated in translation and what the effect is on the target language audience.

Klevan also analyses another scene in which Jerry and Lucy's lines provide interesting material for a performance analysis. The dialogue is as follows:

LUCY: Well, I mean, if you didn't feel the way you feel, things wouldn't be the way they are, would they?
JERRY: But things are the way you made them.
LUCY: Oh no. They're the way you think I made them. I didn't make them that way at all. Things are just the same as they always were, only you're just the same, too, so I guess things will never be the same again.

[And a little later ...]

JERRY: You're wrong about things being different because they are not the same. Things are different, except in a different way. You're still the same, only I've been a fool. Well, I'm not now. So, as long as I'm different, don't you think things could be the same again? Only a little different. (2005: 34)

What is interesting in this sequence is that Jerry and Lucy both repeatedly use the same words, i.e. 'goodnight', 'same', and 'different', albeit to mean different things:

> [T]he repeat of identical words ('goodnight', 'same', and 'different'), each time variously moulded, sustains the tenor of suggestiveness (Dunne conducts her vocal variations exquisitely with flitting eyelids and floating eyebrows). It also gives coherence and consistency to the style of the performances (and the sequence). The use of 'same' and 'different' is necessary for the characters' covert negotiation, but it is also an analogy for their style of performance: different inflections are given to the same words rather than delivering distinctly different words. (ibid.: 34–5)

Everything in this scene is important: the words, their delivery, the facial expressions, the make-up and the positioning of the actors in separate but conjoined rooms. All of these elements combine to create the performances, and if this scene were to be dubbed, attention would need to be paid to each of them – including the specific words as well as the way they are pronounced – so that the 'tenor of suggestiveness', or feel, is maintained in the target language versions.

Finally, when considering performance in terms of plot and the 'relationship of the performer to narrative developments' (2005: preface), Klevan writes about Joan Bennett's performance in Fritz Lang's *Secret Beyond the Door* (1948), a film telling the story of a woman married to a man with an emotional disorder. Although the plot of the film 'could be regarded as obvious, crude and even banal' (2005: 73), this is not the case with Bennett's performance, which Klevan describes in the following terms:

> During threatening moments, as she waits to discover the secret beyond the door, Bennett does not simply collapse her internal feelings into sufferings or distress. Her vocal delivery is deep and breathy, rounded and smooth, and never high-pitched. Sensuously rhythmic, it modulates, caresses and nurtures even her most

anxious thoughts. She contains the turbulence as if relishing her passion on the verge of release. The voiceover allows her to keep thoughts courteously to herself while she impolitely whispers: eagerly murmuring, illicitly, close to the viewer's ear. (2005: 76)

Klevan's description or interpretation puts the emphasis on the musicality of Bennett's vocal delivery, highlighting her pace, timbre and pitch, as well as how her voice manages to convey a range of feelings. These paralinguistic parameters, which are so closely linked with emotional states (see, for example, the theoretical work devised by Juslin and Sloboda 2001), supplement the given dialogue and become a signifying agent of meaning. Their inclusion is integral and interactive. This description shows once again that, when studying a sequence, various elements combine to generate meaning and that singling out vocabulary along, as has been done in many AVT studies, does not do justice to the complexity of the multimodal audiovisual message.

When analysing scenes, then, every physical and oral element matters. Movements may often be given priority in Film Studies due to their visual immediacy, but both audio and visual movements need to be recognized. From a translation perspective, it is very important to bear the nature of the dialogue in mind when creating dubbed versions, as well as the vocal delivery attached to the words. Of course, since languages work differently and different types of voices will have different connotations, consistent delivery across cultures will not always be possible. My point, however, is not to advocate perfect equivalence; rather, I am trying to deepen awareness regarding the way audiovisual materials generate meaning and the complexity of the dubbing process.

Although Klevan does make reference to vocabulary and tone in the above examples, it is fair to say that he seldom does so in the rest of his book. However, his approach to scenes does mention voice, and his work is particularly pertinent for interrogating the effect of translation on films and other audiovisual material. Klevan's work highlights how the various elements of performance interact to generate meaning, and his attentive descriptions, combining the visual and the oral, have greatly informed my work. My multimodal analysis will focus on the vocabulary used in tandem with the actors' style of performance, with a particular emphasis on vocal delivery; this is because voice itself (incorporating vocal tone, timbre, dynamic and pace) and what is said will both change in dubbing, which will have a potential, perhaps notable impact on characterization. It is also important to bear the subjectivity of interpretations in mind when analysing voices. Different conclusions may be reached depending on who is doing the analysis. When Smith (2007) analyses Spencer Tracy's performance in *Father of the Bride* (1950), she focuses on his vocal delivery, the quality of his voice and the vocabulary he uses when talking about his soon-to-be married daughter. Smith quotes – and challenges – James Naremore (1993: 97), who had spoken of a father's opposition to his daughter's wedding in Freudian terms:

> A Freudian reading of the kind alluded by Naremore might, of course, construe Stanley's denial of Kay's womanhood here as a sign of possessiveness born out of a reluctance to admit to this daughter's grown-up sexuality and attractiveness to other men. Yet the very measured, thoughtful, understated nature of Tracy's vocal delivery does much to impart a maturity of reflection and a sense of integrity and dignity with regard to his character's feelings for Kay that seem ill catered for by readings based on the idea of the unruly, impassioned paternal jealousy. (2007: 173)

Whether one agrees or disagrees with these two interpretations will depend on how one approaches the material. I find Smith's alternative reading more pertinent, particularly as it demonstrates that incorporating an analysis of an actor's voicework and tone can throw a very different light on the material. Once again, we are shown that, if we wish to get the full picture, various components or parameters need to be taken into consideration when analysing performance. Like Klevan, my research argues for a 'greater sensitivity' to film performance (2005: 15), an angle also found in the works of film scholars such as Smith (2007), whose fascinating work on moments of 'vocal release' is examined next.

2.4.4 Vocal release

Smith focuses on the 'cinematic contribution' of voices and their sung, spoken, verbal and non-verbal aspects (2007: 164). Acknowledging 'the capacity of the human voice to bring a quality of feeling and texture of meaning to the medium of film that [it] may not be possible to convey through the visuals alone' (ibid.), Smith sets out to examine how an 'actor's voice actually sounds in the precise context of a particular film and the richly varied, often highly subtle ways in which its distinctive character-istics may be used to shape the poetics of the text in question' (ibid.). She offers a close reading of actors' vocal responses ('diegetic vocal releases', 2007: 167), which she examines in parallel with the text's visual images in order to demonstrate what films set out to communicate. She focuses on moments of 'vocal release'; verbal disclosures or vocal/verbal outbursts, moments when the actors convey a particular feeling through their voices – feelings which are in line with the overall storyline.

Smith describes at length voices in sequences from Hollywood films: their tone, pitch, timbre, what these voices convey and how they convey various feelings. For instance, she looks at the way female and male actors' voices are used to convey particular emotions and symbolize various states. She specifically investigates male anxiety and frustrations linked to the growing up of the respective daughter characters in both *Father of the Bride* (1950) and *Gigi* (1958),[1] as well as Pam Greer's maternal and nurturing voice in *Random Harvest* (Mervyn Le Roy, 1942) when she helps Smith (Ronald Colman) to heal from the trauma of the war (2007: 210–24).

When discussing *Love Me or Leave Me* (Charles Vidor 1955), Smith explains that when Ruth Etting (Doris Day) sings to Johnny Alderman (Cameron Mitchell), her 'would-be-lover', it is:

> the stark contrast between the overall banality of the mise-en-scène and the rich texture of Day's singing voice that ultimately makes this moment so profoundly moving: the drab emptiness of the recording studio comes to embody a quality of emotional barrenness and desolation to Ruth's life that her singing now begins to challenge and defy. (2007: 163)

---

1   This work also links in with her previous work on musicals (2006), e.g. she argues that songs and music in the musical *Gigi* are used to convey deeper feelings of male anxiety than in *Father of the Bride.*

Smith's description highlights the importance of examining visual and aural elements in unison, and we are reminded once again that it is the way voice combines with *mise-en-scène* that gives full meaning to the performance.

In terms of examples of specific voicework, Smith studies moments of 'vocal release' in, for example, *Mr Smith Goes to Washington* (Frank Capra 1939), explaining how the actor James Stewart's 'habit of speaking in a slow, stumbling, hesitant way had certainly become a recognized part of his performance repertoire by this time' (2007: 199). By casting Stewart instead of Gary Cooper, 'Capra was able to exploit a feeling of vulnerability arising out of the tremulous nature of this actor's voice and the hesitant manner of his phrasing' (ibid.: 199). This statement resonates with Graver's and Dyer's works on celebrities mentioned previously; audiences, including casting directors, construct ideas of actors in light of the information that they have on them. By reminding us how difficult it is to separate actors' real personas from the characters they play on-screen, Smith sheds a little more light on the various layers of characterization present in audiovisual materials and the challenges brought about by translation.

Smith emphasizes that James Stewart received medical help to achieve an optimum level of 'hoarseness' in his voice. For Smith, voice is to be understood not only as 'vocal performance', but also in its figurative sense, as a medium of expression:

> [I]n feeding into the whole suspense surrounding whether Jefferson Smith will manage to hold out for long enough to be able to clear his name, [it] is something that finds its most extreme form of realization in the losing sequence where Stewart's character's finds himself on the verge of both vocal and physical collapse. (2007: 199–200)

His voice is raw, deprived of its 'broader tonal range and colouring'. In order to explain its effect, Smith draws on Roland Barthes' concept of the grain of voice. For Barthes, the grain of voice is 'the materiality of the body speaking its mother tongue' (1977: 182); it is 'the body in the voice as it sings, the hand as it writes, the limb as it performs' (Barthes 1977: 188). Van Leeuwen notes that post-structuralist authors such as Barthes are known for having 'reintroduced the materiality of the sign' and reinstated 'the affective dimensions of language and music' (1999: 128), and this is precisely what happens when we listen to voices: the grain affects us as listeners, being 'something that is brought to your ears in one and the same movement from deep down in the cavities, the muscles, the membranes and the cartilages' (Barthes 1977: 179).

Barthes developed this concept of the grain of the voice in relation to vocal music and 'made a crucial distinction between voices that have "grain" and those that do not in order to understand the pleasures of listening to voices in which traces of the performer's body can be heard, inscribing a certain texture or even roughness to the voice' (Shingler 2007: online). It is the 'precise space (genre) of the encounter between a language and a voice' (1977: 181). To listen to the 'grain' is to listen to our 'relation with the body of the man or the woman singing or playing and that relation is erotic' (1977: 188). We are reminded that physical and verbal elements combine to generate meaning and that voice is, as Dolar claims, central to our understanding of identity.

Drawing on Barthes, Smith explains that voice is the 'ultimate site of intersection and negotiation between the body and language' (2007: 205). Therefore:

> [...] in the physical effort and struggle that Stewart's rasping, forced-through-the-throat style of delivery conveys, one could argue that much of the significance of the actor's performance lies in his ability to restore a sense of the *bodily* origins and integrity of the voice to the *discursive* realm of the senate chamber as Jeff proceeds to expose a congressman so habituated to using his own voice in the service of linguistic manipulation and cover-up to a more emotionally direct, visceral way of speaking and feeling. (2007: 205)

Smith describes Stewart's voice as 'an aural equivalent of sand paper', one which 'scratches and scrapes away Paine's outer armour' (ibid.). By bringing to light the 'visceral texture and bodily grain of voice' (ibid.), Smith reminds us of the power of sounds and associations, which has encouraged me to think more deeply about what happens to a voice and its 'grain' in dubbing.

Indeed, a link to dubbing can easily be made when Smith comments on the musicality and masculinity of Robert Donnat's speaking voice in *Goodbye, Mr Chips* (Sam Wood 1939). She writes that 'the gentle rise and fall in pitch as he moves effortlessly and without a pause through his sentences help[s] to confirm the emergence of a much more emotionally assured, revitalised form of masculinity' (2007: 228). As his character gets older, he is 'able to combine the rich, warm tones and cello-like timbre of his voice with a much higher, more musically ascending key' (ibid.). She also alludes to his Northern accent, quoting Barrow (1985: 12, in Smith 2007: 229): 'a voice made more beautiful in timbre by the trace of a Northern quality it never quite lost'. She also comments on Bing Crosby's voice in *Going My Way* (Leo McCarey 1944), in which Crosby plays Father Chuck O'Malley, an Irish priest. In one scene, he sings a lullaby to an older priest, 'introducing a slightly wavering quality into some of his higher-note renditions of certain words and syllables' (Smith 2007: 233). This is known as 'upper mordent' and is Crosby's 'signature vocal technique' (Giddins 2001: 11 in Smith 2007: 233):

> This technique is a well-recognized hallmark of Crosby's singing style and one that, in revealing something of this singer's Irish immigrant roots, finds what is surely one of its most lyrically apposite and poignant expression here. (ibid.)

Smith's descriptions highlight the significance of accent in these actors' vocal deliveries, while these references to accents (Scottish and Irish) and inflection of pitch bring about issues of characterization in the original film and its translated versions, as these are parameters that will inevitably change.

Finally, it must be noted that Smith's technique is to draw consistent parallels between the action (e.g. suspense, romance), the use of voice (or style of delivery) and the actors' gestures and positions on the screen, e.g. the unsteadiness of James Stewart's voice being matched with, respectively, his shaking hands and Greer Garson's voice:

> The exact staging of this part of the closing sequence is especially important in under-standing the regenerative force with which Garson's voice becomes endowed at this point. For while we as audience are now privileged with a shot showing her arriving at the gate and calling out 'Smithy?', the cut to a shot showing Colman standing at the doorway of the cottage with his back to Garson, then turning around on hearing her refer to him by his former name, makes clear the ability of this moment to re-enact the earlier nature of their first encounter, as he once again becomes aware of her in the form of a voice whose bodily source lies somewhere outside his frame of vision. (2007: 223)

Or consider her discussion of the burgeoning relationship between Greer Garson and Robert Donat in *Goodbye, Mr Chips* (Sam Wood 1939): 'As Chipping becomes more pensive again, the film shifts to a closer shot of the pair as Donat exclaims with a deepening ache to his voice: "It must be the altitude!"' (2007: 227). Likewise, as Donat, a retired headmaster dying, is lying in bed:

> The last word of this final line[2] is stretched out masterfully by Donat in the form of a slow, contented sight that testifies, even at the moment of death, to the lasting effect of Garson's vocal rhythms on this character. (2007: 229–30)

Once again, we are reminded that the various elements of *mise-en-scène* combine to generate meaning and that they should not be considered in isolation but as part of the whole.

Finally, something interesting occurs when we combine 'vocal release' and what Klevan calls a 'moment of significance' (2005: 61). Analysing *There's Always Tomorrow* (Douglas Sirk 1956), Klevan describes a brief moment between Barbara Stanwick (Norma Miller) and Fred MacMurray (Clifford Groves), during which she removes Clifford's apron:

> [A] gesture of handing out becomes one of reaching out; and her deftness at removing the apron only identifies the gesture of yearning. A swift moment of affinity quickly becomes one of distance. We know nothing of their past at this moment, and for its length the film discloses little concrete information (no flashbacks, for example). The film does not provide a direct presentation, or explanation, of a past that is too potent and too indistinct. The performers provide more indirect, yet appropriate ways of communicating their characters' past. Stanwick economically expresses a life's regrets in the gesture [...] Clifford's move away from Norma has a similar effect to Marion's moves away from him: as Clifford and Norma realise a moment of significance it is already moving away from them. (Klevan 2005: 61)

Moments of vocal release therefore work together with moments of significance, wherein voice and gesture seamlessly combine to generate meaning. Moreover, one can see that a short visual moment needs to be described at

---

2   His final line: 'But you're wrong. I have. Thousands of them. Thousands of them. And all the boys ...' is in answer to a comment that it is a pity he did not have children.

length in order to capture its full fictional charge. It is for this reason that short scenes will be described in great detail in my own analysis (Chapter 6).

2.5 Conclusion

This chapter has shown that voice is a defining element of identity and an integral part of performance and characterization. By considering material from Film Studies, it has become obvious that voice is an important parameter of performance analysis. Dolar explains that voice 'is not part of linguistics' and that 'it is not part of the body either' (2006: 72–3). In other words, a voice 'floats [...] at the intersection of language and the body' (ibid.: 73) and acts as 'the link which ties the signifier to the body' (ibid.: 59), 'hold[ing] bodies and language together' (ibid.: 60). For Dolar, voice is what bodies and languages have in common; it is their missing link. However, 'if there is no voice without a body' (ibid.), where does this leave us when we perform dubbing?

This is why voice will be a major component of my analysis of original and dubbed products. The works reviewed in this chapter have also shown that, when studying performance in audiovisual texts, we engage with the material in terms of 'experience', i.e. in terms of our relationship to both actors and characters. It is through performance that an audience experiences characters' point of view, their inner states, thoughts and emotions, and thus gets an impression of who they are. This impression is conveyed through camera movements and both facial and physical gestures, all of which generally remain intact in translation. However, what cannot remain intact in dubbing is the quality of voices and the relationship between the parameters of performance discussed so far. What I argue in this book is that the way characters are experienced depends on, or is informed by, the way actors perform these characters. I consider performance to have an interpersonal function, and my multimodal model will attend to various modalities related to (actors') performance. Before introducing this model, I shall first examine the dubbing process and discuss its possible effect and impact on performance and characterization.

CHAPTER 3

Dubbing

3.1 Introduction

Even though 'very little research has been done' in audiovisual translation (AVT) (Díaz-Cintas 2004b: 50) in comparison with other translation genres (such as literary translation), the past ten years have nevertheless seen an increase in AVT studies. There now exists a healthy amount of studies on AVT modes, including dubbing, subtitling, voiceover and accessibility practices, as illustrated in Chaume (2012) and Pérez-González's recent book (2014). Research in AVT and dubbing has been very varied, featuring works on translational norms or conventions in the target culture (e.g. Goris 1993; Karamitroglou 2000), the translation of ideological and cultural elements (e.g. Nedergaard-Larsen 1993; Martínez-Sierra 2009, online; Santamaria 2001; Pedersen 2012; Richart Marset 2012), the translation of humour (e.g. Zabalbeascoa 1993, 1996a, 1996b, 1997, 2005; Vandaele 2002; Chiaro 2006; Martínez-Sierra 2008) or dialects (e.g. Hatim and Mason 1990 and Dore 2009). In recent years, multilingualism has also become a much discussed topic (e.g. Corrius 2008; Díaz-Cintas 2011; Martínez-Sierra et al. 2010 and de Higes Andino et al. 2013; O'Sullivan 2008) as has censorship (e.g. Merino et al. 2005; Ranzato 2011 and 2012). The history of audiovisual translation, including dubbing, has also been discussed at length (e.g. Chaume 2012, Ivarsson 2002, Izard 1992, and Gottlieb 1997). This chapter reviews specific studies related to dubbing in order to contextualize my work on performance and characterization. In the first part, the emphasis is placed on dubbing practices, synchronization and the agents involved in the dubbing production chain. The second section then focuses more particularly on the language and sound of dubbing, leading the way

to the final section, which is dedicated to the uncanny, i.e. my specific
contribution to theorizing the effect dubbing has on viewers.

3.2   The specificities of dubbing

3.2.1   A short overview of dubbing practices

Dubbing has been used and studied for many years all over the world,
as illustrated in Chaume (2012: 6–10), who presents what he terms the
'global map of dubbing' in Europe, Asia, the Americas, Africa and Oceania.
Dubbing is 'one of the oldest modes' of AVT whose 'origins can be traced
back to the late 1920s' (Chaume 2012: 1). Indeed, it is when 'written language on screen in silent movies' in the form of intertitles was introduced
'to accompany the iconic representation of images', that 'translation becomes
essential to the full understanding of filmic narration' (2012: 10).[1] The
silent era lasted from 1895 until the end of the 1920s, although it was in
fact never fully silent as it was common to have intertitles along with, at
times, a commentator – or 'spieler' in the US – narrating from behind the
screen and on occasion even translating the intertitles. Translation was
therefore present as early as the silent era, although as Ivarsson notes: '[I]t
was relatively easy to solve the translation problem. The original intertitles
were removed, translated, drawn or printed on paper, filmed and inserted
again in the film' (1992: 15). In the late 1920s, dialogue began to be introduced into films. Those with partial dialogue were called 'part-talkies' and
those with full dialogue 'talkies'; the first full talkie, *The Lights of New York*
(Brian Foy), was released in 1928. However even before this, translation
was deemed important by famous directors; for instance, 'as early as 1923,
David W Griffith noted that only 5 per cent of the world's population then

---

1   See also Abecassis (2008) on silent films and talkies.

spoke English and rhetorically wondered why he had to lose 95 per cent of his potential audience' (Chaume 2012: 11).

Thus, when talkies appeared, they prompted the need for different types of translation, from the translation of intertitles to dubbing and subtitling – initially into French, German and Spanish (Izard 1992). In each of these cases, translation formed part of the post-production process. As noted in Chaume (2004a and 2012), foreign audiences did not react positively to translation and in the 1930s, a new solution was introduced: multiple film versions. Translation became an integral part of the production process; the same director would make the same film in two or three different languages (e.g. French, German and Spanish) using the same actors, although on occasion the actors might be changed if additional languages were involved. The Joinville Studio in Paris, for instance, was founded by Paramount in 1930 for that very purpose. One can imagine that such a venture proved very costly and after a few years, when dubbing and subtitling techniques had become more developed, the translation of films was once again relegated to the distribution process, where it remains to this day. I will now examine in more detail the type of research that has been performed in the field of dubbing, with a focus on constrained translation and synchronization.

3.2.2 *Synchronization*

Dubbing is an example of constrained translation, i.e. there is more than the linguistic code to take into consideration. It is therefore not surprising that much of the initial research into dubbing in the late 1980s predominantly emphasized media constraints in dubbing, particularly synchronization (e.g. lip-synchronization). Indeed, as emphasized by Chaume (2012: 66), synchronization 'is one of the key factors' in dubbing; in its broadest sense, it is understood as the process of 'matching the target language translation and the articulatory and mouth movements of the screen actors and actresses, and ensuring that the utterances and pauses in the translation match those of the source text' (2012: 68).

Synchronization is not merely a concern for dubbing – it is also an integral part of original AV products, in which context it is called sound post-synchronization. Sound in films is usually not natural, i.e. the background noises that can be heard are usually recorded after the film has been shot. In most cases, this is done by Foley artists who recreate ambient sounds in a realistic way, e.g. breaking a glass to recreate the sound of a window being smashed. There are also examples in film history in which the voices we hear on-screen are not coming from the actors; I explain in Bosseaux 2012, for instance, that Marilyn Monroe does not actually sing all of her songs in *Gentlemen Prefer Blondes* (Howard Hawks 1953). Régine Hollander (2001) also comments that the way post-synchronization is carried out can have an impact on the semantic content of scenes, explaining that in the dubbed French version of *Natural Born Killers* (Oliver Stone 1994), there are scenes of characters arguing which are rendered more explicitly than in the original version, where the voices were mixed with sound effects (ibid.: 83). This is because adapters work with an international version or track which only has music, sound effects and background noises (Chaume 2007). Consequently, they can only work on the dialogue and not the rest of the soundtrack, which would include songs or background noises such as a TV channel playing while characters are speaking. Therefore, when comparing original and translated AV products, we should not forget that sound is reworked in a film's final mixing and thus not idealize the way voices sound in the original.

Returning to the matter of sound in dubbing, there are three types of synchronization: *lip or phonetic synchrony*, *kinesic synchrony* and *isochrony*. The first one, *lip or phonetic synchrony*, consists of 'adapting the translation to the articulatory movements of the on-screen characters, especially in close-ups and extreme close-ups' as well as detailed mouth shots (Chaume 2012: 68). The second, *kinesic synchrony*, is 'the synchronization of the translation with the actors' body movements' (ibid.: 69), while the third, '*isochrony*', corresponds to the 'synchronization of the duration of the translation with the screen characters' utterances' (Chaume 2012, drawing from Whitman-Linsen 1992: 28). The three different types have been discussed at length in the field – see, for instance, Agost (1999), Chaume (2004c, 2012), Chaves (2000), Fodor (1976), Goris (1993), Luyken et al. (1991), Mayoral et al. (1988) and Whitman Linsen (1992) – and so I shall not (re) define these further but rather emphasize that synchronization will be an important parameter in my analysis when comparing originals with their dubbed versions.

Lip-synchronization, i.e. matching labio-dental and bilabial consonants or open vowels in close-ups, will therefore be considered when discussing vocabulary choices and their potential impact on characterization. In terms of close-ups, for instance, Chaume notes that 'phonetic equivalence overrides semantic or even pragmatic equivalence: it is much more important to find a word with a bilabial consonant than to find a synonym or a similar word in the TL' (2012: 74). Chaume also explains that these choices should be made without affecting characterization or plot (ibid.: 75), something that we shall consider the possibility of achieving in authentic dubbing situations in my case studies. When it comes to *kinesic synchrony*, it may be that a kinesic sign (i.e. body language) is being performed as the character is speaking. If the translation needs to be shortened and certain words are considered redundant, these may be substituted or omitted, which could have an impact on performance and characterization. Ideally, changes in semantic meaning should not affect 'the overall meaning of the film, or the character's personality' (Chaume 2012: 72); again, we shall see how this is handled in my case studies. Finally, when trying to achieve *isochrony*, certain vocabulary choices could end up having an impact on characterization if, for instance, they carry negative connotations.

Another type of synchronization worth mentioning is 'character synchrony' (Whitman-Linsen 1992) which corresponds to the expectations of the target audience in terms of what a voice may sound like. Chaume comments that, 'in general, a child actor cannot be dubbed by an older male voice; a woman's voice must sound feminine; and the "baddie" must sound grave and sinister' (2012: 69–70). However, real life practices may not make it possible to give due consideration to these parameters, e.g. legal restrictions on children working. Chaume explains that character synchrony falls more under the remit of dramatization than synchronization and is 'the exclusive concern of the dubbing actors and the dubbing director' (ibid.: 70). As dramatization is closely related to performance, issues related to character synchrony will therefore also be discussed in my case studies.

Finally, it is important to mention the notion of genre when discussing synchronization. Indeed, the extent to which synchronization is achieved depends on the genre and type of audiovisual material. Chaume emphasizes that a 'thorough application of all synchronization types is required for the *television series* genre, although the degree of perfection is not as high as that demanded by the big screen' (2012: 76). In an earlier article, Chaume also explained that films 'demand a highly polished synchronization at all levels', since:

> producers, distributors and exhibitors are fully aware that the success or failure of a dubbed film depends on its synchronization [...] from labial consonants and rounded or spread vowels, to pauses and syllables, and even facial movement synchronization with the on-screen characters. (2004c)

Bearing this in mind, it will be interesting to see how the various types of synchronization in the French version of the television series *Buffy the Vampire Slayer* have been handled and whether there is an impact on performance and characterization.

This section has briefly mentioned dubbing actors and directors. We will now consider the various agents and aspects of the dubbing process in order to further illustrate the incredible translation challenges posed by AV products.

3.2.3 *The various agents and aspects of the dubbing process*

Dubbing involves the work of many agents: translators, dialogue writers, dubbing directors, actors and sound engineers. Chaume highlights how 'Western European dubbing workflows' follow a specific 'production chain' (2012: 29): TV stations or distributors, dubbing companies, translators (who produce a rough translation), dialogue writers (and sometimes dubbing assistants), dubbing directors, voice talents (also known as dubbing actors, dubbing artists or dubbers) and sound engineers. Chaume presents these various agents with a view to sensitize students in particular to the numerous aspects of dubbing from a career perspective. Since I am more interested in agents in terms of their potential impact on vocal performance and character perception, I shall focus more particularly on agents directly related to sound and acting, starting with dubbing directors.

Historically, dubbing directors have been responsible for choosing the professional actors or voice talents who lend their voices to original actors. Chaume emphasizes that '[v]oice selection is a crucial task and for many professionals, the success of a dubbing largely depends on the right choice of voice talent' (ibid.: 36). However, it is never possible to fully control the reactions of viewers and it is not uncommon to read criticism online or in the press regarding dubbing choices. For instance, Chaume explains that the Italian version of *True Grit* (Joel and Ethan Coen, 2010) has attracted criticism due to the fact that, in the original film, Matt Damon's character mumbles for the remainder of the film after sustaining an injury to his tongue; in the Italian version however, his voice remains unchanged, thereby losing his idiolect in translation.

Directors also assist voice talents throughout the dubbing process, e.g. by giving them acting directions and telling them what happens in the film (voice talents do not have access to the whole film before they begin shooting, only to the loops they are involved in). Directors therefore 'guide' the voice talents:

> through the film, instruct them on the plot of the film and on their particular character, tell them what intonation they need to use in each sentence and how to interpret each take or loop, and finally reject or approve the recorded take. (ibid.: 36)

Voice talents thus work under the supervision of dubbing directors, as do sound engineers. Although there will be different agents and procedures depending on the country involved, Chaume concedes that the differences between countries are minimal (2012: 29–37) and that, generally, dubbing directors are responsible for 'view[ing] the film with the written translation and check[ing] whether lip-sync, kinesic synchrony, isochrony [...] and oral discourse [...] have been taken into account' (ibid.: 31).

Voice talents record their takes in a dubbing booth, usually working alone or two at a time. This means that the film dialogue will be shot with one talent in one booth and another in a separate booth, with 'no turn-taking and no answers to their questions, or no questions to their answers' (ibid.: 36). This practice is bound to have an impact on performance and dramatization. Indeed, how can emotions be fully conveyed if the actors do not interact with one another? Chaume also adds that the process is a 'continuous series of stops and starts, rather than a theatrical performance' (ibid.: 37). When the recording is finished, the sound engineers 'reassemble' and 'edit' the tracks, which have been dubbed separately (ibid.). They are responsible for synchronizing the new dubbed tracks with the international track and the original images.

Directors therefore perform a similar role to that of a film, TV series or theatrical director, and they have the power to modify the initial translator's and dialogue writer's words as they see fit. For instance, if 'a particular word or sentence does not convey the appropriate (semantic or pragmatic) meaning for a particular occasion' (ibid.: 36), they can retranslate it on the spot. It can also happen that dubbing actors change lines of dialogue if they feel that they do not fit the style of their acting. Engineers also have their say when it comes to making changes to the translation. One can see from this short account that the fact that dubbing involves so many participants clearly makes it a mediated process: voice actors are guided throughout and the various agents have the capacity to make changes to what the translators and dialogue writers have produced.

As one of my aims is to elaborate a model for studying originals alongside their dubbed versions, the rest of this section shall focus further on the aspects of the dubbing process that prove particularly relevant to this goal. Chaume (2012) distinguishes six aspects or 'priorities that must be taken into account in a standard dubbing with the concept of ideal receiver in mind' (2012: 15). These criteria are acceptable lip-sync, credible and realistic lines of dialogue, coherence between images and words, loyal translation, clear sound quality and acting (ibid: 15–20). Chaume is concerned with audience satisfaction and understanding, both of which depend on how well these six criteria are navigated: 'the absence of these conventions, because they are predictable and conventionalized, jeopardizes the accurate transmission of the message, in terms of both information and aesthetics' (ibid.: 20). Like Chaume, I am also concerned with these six criteria, and when comparing originals with their translated versions, I will be referring to dubbing constraints and the resulting products in terms of synchronicity, linguistic choices and visual elements.

As mentioned previously, it is fair to say that sound quality and acting have been under-researched in AVT and Film Studies, perhaps because such studies go beyond the actual work of translators. One of my aims is therefore to contribute to this neglected area of research; as my work focuses on the impact of dubbing on performance and characterization, I shall examine the criterion of 'acting' to show how important this is when it comes to dubbing. To echo the words of Chaume, I will consider the 'transmission of the message, in terms of both information and aesthetics' (ibid.: 20) from the perspective of performance and voice.

Even though studies on sound and acting have been scarce, Whitman-Linsen and Chaume have, however, commented on the issue of over-dramatization. For instance, Whitman-Linsen explains that in dubbing:

> role interpretations are overdone, over dramatic, overladen with emotion. The voices sound phony and theatrical and out of keeping with body expression. Everyday conversations are enacted as if they were dealing with tragic deaths of family members and the outbreak of atomic wars. People just do not speak like dubbers seem to imagine they do. (1992: 47)

Similarly, Chaume comments that:

> by convention, dubbing actors and actresses – voice talents – are required to perform in such a way that they sound neither faked (overacted) nor monotonous (underacted). Overacting is without a doubt one of the factors that also cause the viewer to cross [their] tolerance threshold […] Voice talents, in their enthusiasm to dramatize the target text dialogues, or perhaps also because of their origins and training in the theatre, sometimes emphasise intonations and pronunciations to such an extent that if we hear a conversation from any big screen or television film, without knowing where the sound is coming from, we immediately know that they are cinema or television dialogues, and not real conversation. (2012: 19)

When discussing 'sound quality', Chaume also comments that, in dubbing, 'the volume of the voices is also higher than in normal speech, to facilitate greater comprehension, i.e. there is always a fairly high volume and clear voices with tight articulation' (ibid.: 18). Moreover, 'certain sound effects such as reverberation are used in cases in which the characters have their backs to the camera or are at a distance, to create the effect of a slight echo' (ibid.). These statements reinforce my previous assertion that sound in film is not natural and is the result of the work of sound (recording and mixing) engineers. Chaume adds that viewers have been 'conditioned to accept that s/he is watching a film and that in general, s/he will be listening to voices in stereo and with a clarity alien to real-life situations' (ibid.: 19). I shall therefore bear in mind Whitman-Linsen and Chaume's comments and see if my analysis of voice sheds new light on their criticisms. In the following section, I will consider studies on dialogue and voice in order to further contextualize the specificities of my research.

3.3 Discourse and voice

3.3.1 Dubbed dialogue

Chaume explains that:

> what sets the linguistic code apart in audiovisual texts is that in films, television series, cartoons and certain advertisements, we are dealing with a written text that must seem oral and spontaneous. (2012: 100)

As one can see from this quote, dubbing is considered to be a very specific type of discourse. In Chapter 1, I touched upon fictional dialogue from the point of view of Film Studies. I will now rely on AVT scholars' work in order to explain how fictional dialogue is conceived from a dubbing perspective. Dubbed dialogue is a 'combination of linguistic features used both in spoken and written texts' (Chaume 2012: 81, drawing from Remael 2000; Chaume 2004a; Pérez-González 2007), although it can be seen more specifically as a simulation of spontaneous speech (Franzelli 2008: 225) as it mimics speech by using 'task stress' (Dechert 1984: 224) such as false starts, repetitions, ellipsis, pauses and interruptions. However, this orality is an illusion; it is 'préfabriquée' (Tomaszkiewicz 2001: 381) as it is 'actually planned, or as we might say feigned, false, *prefabricated*' (Chaume 2012: 82). This is because dialogue comes from a script 'written to be spoken as if not written' (Gregory and Carroll 1978: 42). This situation has also led scholars to talk about dialogue as 'secondary speech' (Remael 2003: 227).

As seen in the previous section, dubbed language has a specific sound to it; it does not sound like original dialogue. It 'does not correspond to the way normal people talk' (Whitman-Linsen 1992: 118) and in some instances, characters have been described as 'speak[ing] like printing pages' (Rosa Assis 2001: 216). The term 'dubbese', first coined by Maria Pavesi (1996), is now widely used to talk about dubbed language in particular as a 'culture-specific linguistic and stylistic model for dubbed texts' that is 'similar, but not equal to real oral discourse and external production oral discourse (i.e. original target-culture films, sitcoms, etc.)' (Chaume 2012: 87). Pavesi was the first to identify dubbese and many other scholars have since followed her lead, including Chaume (2004a), Baños-Piñero (2006), Marzà and Chaume (2009) and Freddi and Pavesi (2009).

According to Chaume, (dubbed) dialogue writing must meet the following three requirements: 'creating the effect of natural, credible and true-to-life dialogue', 'complying with lip-sync' and 'promot[ing] a balance which avoids overacting and underacting when dubbing actors perform the dialogues (i.e. avoiding cacophonies, etc.)' (2012: 88). These three criteria are not always met, however, a situation which Chaume refers to as the burden of dubbing, since it was 'consolidated at a time when imitating real spoken language was completely unacceptable' (2012: 91). Nevertheless, as Caillé points out, the ideal is that dubbing realistically conveys the 'content' of the human voice that is to be taken seriously by audiences. According to him, lip-synchronization should not be the sole important aspect to consider when dubbing, as it is only really necessary in the case of close-ups or big close-ups; rather, the emphasis should be on the rhythm, sensitivity, anger and tenderness conveyed by the original. Therefore, a dubbed version should endeavour to keep the 'savour' or taste of the original voice, since 'if the voices of actors are judiciously chosen, if the dubbed text is judiciously translated, if it moves or entertains, we have succeeded' (1960: 107, my translation). I find Caillé's emphasis on voice, and therefore performance, truly refreshing. Among other things, what this quote highlights is that, although translating linguistic elements and lip-synchronization are both important in dubbing, the choice of voices is one of the crucial factors in terms of audience appreciation. This leads me to a discussion of voice in the context of dubbing.

3.3.2   Voice and characterization

In his influential book *The Voice in Cinema* (1999), Michel Chion looks into the power of the human voice and 'the special relationships that inhere between the voice and the cinematic image, gendered voices in films, screams, the absence of voices, and technologies of the voice' (1999: XI). Although dubbing is not his primary concern, Chion comments that:

> the work that especially American actors devote to vocal accents and timbres also allows them to reassert their identity as actors, to show that they are not just blank canvases for makeup, but that they can reinvent and master their craft through technique, the body and voice. (1999: 172)

By associating body and voice(work), Chion establishes a clear connection between identity and voice, thereby reinforcing an understanding of voice as identity as seen in Chapter 2. Chion explains that one consequence of 'voicework' is that audiences come to identify a voice with a specific actor. However, he adds that, when American films are dubbed into French, 'there is no longer the same dubbing-actor's voice used for each film of a star' (1999: 172). Indeed, '[o]nly for movie stars in the classic sense – stars who always play themselves, like Arnold Schwarzenegger or Sean Connery – do French spectators get to hear the same dubbing voice from film to film' (1999: 173/4). Whitman-Linsen (1992) also explains that well-known actors are usually dubbed by the same dubbing actor over periods of 30 years. Consequently, audiences who watch dubbed films as opposed to subtitled versions do not hear the same voices and will become aware of dubbing as a practice: '[T]he audience becomes aware of the voice as an entity distinct from the body, even when it comes from the very center of the image' (ibid.: 173). According to Chion, the source of the sound is normally understood to be what is seen on-screen – something which dubbing changes drastically. Drawing from Jean Renoir, Chion (1985: 74) explains that 'accepting dubbing is like ceasing to believe in the oneness of the individual' (*'Accepter le doublage, c'est cesser de croire à l'unicité de l'individu'*). Indeed, in dubbing, the original body is separated from her original voice, even if dubbed films give the illusion that the voice and body are working together.

In relation to Barthes' concept of 'grain', and in the context of my work on performance and characterization, this seeming contradiction prompts another question: is a character's specific meaning lost in the dubbed version of a film? In the French context, for instance, it is not uncommon for actors' voices to change from film to film. The American actress Julianne Moore has had at least three voices (Isabelle Gardien, Cécile Paoli and Ivana Coppola) since the beginning of her career, as has Marilyn Monroe (Claire Guibert, Mony Dalmès, Madeleine Briny and Claire Declerc, who provides her singing voice in the dubbed version of *Gentlemen Prefer Blondes*). It is difficult, however, to comment on the significance of such changes in greater detail, since to my knowledge no studies have been carried out on the way audiences perceive voices and the change of voices.

Indeed, voice and characterization have only been investigated sporadically in AVT, although some aspects of voice have been mentioned in studies investigating geographic and social accents in dubbing, highlighting the fact that rendering those is a thorny endeavour. For instance, Armstrong and Federici (eds, 2006) and Federici (ed. 2009) have compiled a solid collection of articles dealing with the challenges of regional, social and idiolectal varieties of language. Examples include the works of Ilaria Parini (2009), who explains how Italian-speaking gangsters or *mafiosi* are sometimes dubbed into Sicilian for Italian audiences; Taylor (2006), who comments on the 'neutralising effect' in some of the dubbed works of British director Ken Loach; and Dore (2009), who reflects on the Italian dubbing of *The Simpsons*, discussing the use of dialects in the translation of the first series.

Voice is also mentioned in Nigel Armstrong's examination of sociolinguistic and linguistic patterning in *The Simpsons* and its dubbed French version (2004). Armstrong discusses the use of accents, cultural transposition and voice quality, concluding that voice quality transfers closely from English to French because 'its physicality lends it universal properties' (ibid.: 108). In his study, this proves particularly true in the case of Marge Simpson, whose hoarse voice is described as 'permanently present' and 'person-identifying'; a symbol of the fact that she is tired and harassed by her role in the family. Armstrong further comments that:

[h]oarseness is a voice quality that transfers successfully across the two languages of interest here, as it conveys characteristics of much the same sort in English and French. This is perhaps because hoarseness in this particular context has a very concrete, physical base in the reality of Marge's situation: we can imagine her raising her voice a good deal to make it heard above the ambient noise produced by children and inadequate husband. Such physicality transcends cultures (or at least cultures that tolerate a raised voice in such contexts) and hence translates directly. (2004: 106–7)

Armstrong also explains that Homer's pharyngeal voice and slow rate of speech serve to portray him as 'not the most gifted' of human beings. Armstrong's descriptions of voices are reminiscent of accounts by Dolar, Smith, Van Leuween and Klevan in that they emphasize how much a voice is part of a character's personality.

Régine Hollander (2001) also considers voice when she compares the dubbed and subtitled French versions of Oliver Stone's *Natural Born Killers* (1994). She comments on the speech of the characters, their accents and how these are used for characterization, claiming that 'interpreting a film and characterization also depend on what is transmitted by the accents of actors and the way they express themselves' (2001: 84, my translation). Woody Harrelson, who plays Mickey, adopted a Southern accent for the purpose of the film, which is used to situate him both socially and geographically. In the dubbed version, Hollander points out that the voice of the actor playing Mickey is 'neutral', leading to a loss in signifying character details. She also discusses syntax and expressions, such as when 'don't' is used instead of 'doesn't' to portray the colloquialism of his speech. Hollander explains that the choice of the adapters (and subtitlers) to drop the negation in French is a poor one because this happens quite regularly in spoken French (2001: 84). She concludes that, in general, there is a loss in characterization in the dubbed and subtitled versions and that it is impossible to convey in another language the network of associations evoked by the dialogue, images (and visual effects) and sound in the original film (2001: 79). On the whole, Hollander feels that that both versions 'fail to transmit a network of intricate cultural references' (2001: 79, my translation) and are 'particularly ineffective' (2001: 86, my translation) in rendering these elements, although the dubbed version does greater justice to the original than the subtitled one. Even though Hollander's discussion revolves around the outdated subtitling vs. dubbing debate and can be very critical at times,[2] what interests me in her work is her emphasis on the difference between the 'properties' or 'characteristics' of original voices. As such, she prompts us to think about what is an 'appropriate' choice of voice for a dubbed version. A dubbed voice changes pitch, articulation, class, regional context, colloquialisms, individual turns of phrase, timbre, educational levels and other suggestions of cultural positions and capabilities. It is thus worth wondering to what extent viewers engage differently based on changes in voice.

Nolwenn Mingant (2010) also mentions voice in her analysis of the French dubbed version of Quentin Tarantino's *Inglourious Basterds* (2009). Mingant sets out to 'look at the codified relationship between a film and its audience, the issue of voice texture, and how dubbing may result in a loss of narrative and thematic construction' (2010: 713). However, even though she uses the word 'loss', her approach is not simply to criticize the work of the dubbing team; she consistently highlights the difficulty of the task and brings to light examples of creativity. In her own words, her article is more an 'interrogation' of the 'complexity' of dubbing and a reflection on its role in the French system. Like Sofía Sánchez Mompeán (2012), Mingant emphasizes the fact that dubbing involves a double suspension of disbelief. She claims that 'the notion of willing suspension of disbelief is central to the cinematic art. It is part of a pact with the audience [...] the audience tacitly accepts' (ibid.: 713) what is shown to them on-screen at face value. In the dubbed version, this suspension of disbelief is doubled as it 'now requires that most of the characters should speak French' (ibid.: 715). She explains that 'French spectators routinely accept to twice suspend their disbelief, passing over the discrepancy between nationality and language' (ibid.: 717). Indeed, if cinema creates an illusion, dubbing

---

2   Indeed, she writes that 'the nature of the exercise given to adaptors already condemns them to imperfection, inexactness and lacunas' (2001: 86, my translation), even though she acknowledges that choices are restricted by constraints; she gives examples of good choices made by adapters in relation to bilabials (e.g. p-b-m), fricatives (f-v) and labiodentals (2001: 85–6). Moreover, no mention is made of the working conditions for subtitlers or other agents of the translation process.

creates 'the illusion of an illusion' (Caillé 1960: 108), something I shall bear in mind when discussing the effect of dubbing in *3.4*.

In *Inglourious Basterds*, foreign languages are used as 'shortcuts to characterize the protagonists' (ibid.: 724) and Mingant presents an interesting reflection on what dubbing does and what audiences expect from it. As such, her interpersonal perspective makes her work particularly useful for my own analysis. Moreover, Mingant's study not only focuses on translation problems and possible losses; she also draws our attention to the fact that the ability of certain actors to speak multiple languages facilitated the dubbing process. Indeed, Christoph Waltz, Diane Kruger and Mélanie Laurent were all capable of providing their own dubbing, therefore maintaining the quality of their voices and ensuring 'the quality and logic of the[ir] performances [was] fully maintained' (ibid.: 721), a statement which resonates with my interest in dubbing and performance.

When it comes to the 'texture' of voices, Mingant is concerned with tone, accent and 'giving the right texture' (ibid.: 719). In *Inglourious Basterds*, Tarantino presents a collection of language variations: 'British English vs. American English, Southern American English vs. Boston American English, Munich German vs. Frankfurt German' (ibid). When translating, then, what is important is not only *what* the actors or characters say but *how* they say it. When considering this dimension, Mingant focuses on the texture of the dialogue, with an emphasis on accents and how these are rendered in French, e.g. Diane Kruger exaggerating her German accent in English and Brad Pitt using a Southern accent. She is concerned with characters' elocution, intonation and pronunciation, as well as how difficult it was to render these in French. These paralinguistic elements are key when describing voices and will also form part of my analysis.

One final important contribution Mingant makes with her work is her point that, when translating accents, there are 'two traditional strategies' in French dubbing: 'the tendency to neutralize accents, and the recourse to speech registers as a compensation strategy' (ibid). My own case studies shall consider whether these two strategies have been applied. Furthermore, Mingant comments that, due to this neutralization, 'most Hollywood male actors tend to have the neutral voice of a man in his late thirties' (ibid. 22). She mentions the example of Jean-Pierre Michaël, who dubs Brad Pitt and has also provided the voice of, variously, Keanu Reeves, Jude Law, Christian Bale and Ben Affleck. What this means is that a French voice talent is used or hired to dub multiple American, English or Spanish actors. One original voice and body in the original entail two, three or four bodies, all with the same voice, in a variety of dubbed versions. This could prove confusing for viewers, something which I shall also bear in mind when discussing the effects of dubbing.

Moreover, there is the question of whether these new voices are really appropriate for the bodies that they inhabit, something Daniel Meyer-Dinkgräfe (2007) alludes to in an article on the various phases of the dubbing process in Germany, when he comments that:

> a 'good' voice is necessary for an actor to be successful in dubbing; 'good' in this context means several things: the actors need to be able to use their voices effortlessly [...] In questions of doubt, the dubbing voice tends to match the appearance of the original actor more than the original actor's voice. For example, in the television series *Magnum P.I.* (1980–8), lead actor Tom Selleck's voice is unexpectedly and uncharacteristically high in pitch compared with the actor's masculine appearance, while the German voice of Norbert Langer is much lower in pitch and thus fits the actor's outward appearance better (Wehn 1996: 11). The dubbing voice thus has to be both appropriate for the original actor and it should appeal to a wide range of listeners – even if the character portrayed by the original actor is unpleasant, the dubbing voice must convey unpleasantness without offending the listener. (2007: online)

This quote highlights the difference between the 'characteristics' or 'properties' of original and dubbed voices. We are left to wonder whether or not Magnum's German voice was an appropriate choice. But what does an 'appropriate' choice consist of? More generally, we are left to wonder what happens to voices in dubbed versions and to what extent the dubbing actors' voices fit the original actors' appearance. Can viewers be expected to engage differently based on changes in voice and pitch? The answers to such questions clearly impact on the way viewers engage with the audiovisual product, and these are issues which will be considered during my analysis.

Intonation is another topic that has received very little attention in dubbing, even though there has been a sizeable contribution on the notion of dubbing as prefabricated discourse. Work by scholars such as Chaume (2012), Marzá and Chaume (2009), Whitman-Linsen (1992) and Baños and Chaume

(2009) have all commented on the important role of prosody and paralinguistic elements; there remains, however, a lack of actual empirical studies
on intonation. A notable exception is Sofía Sánchez Mompeán (2012), who
investigates the naturalness of tonal patterns in the Spanish version of *How
I Met Your Mother* (CBS, 2007–14). Mompeán considers paralinguistic as
well as prosodic elements to find out whether or not the 'intonation patterns
adopted in dubbed versions can have an impact upon the naturalness of the
final outcome' (2012: 10). To do so, she studies the pitch of sentences in the
dubbed version of the US sitcom, in spontaneous speech and in a Spanish
domestic production. She concludes that intonation is more often than
not overlooked and that there is a 'close resemblance' (ibid.) between 'dubbing intonation and reading intonation, which tends to hinder naturalness
dramatically' (ibid.). Mompeán focuses on the 'credibility and naturalness
of fictional dialogues' (ibid.: 13). Her interest in the consequences of using
a wrong tonal pattern 'which could bring about a change in the meaning
of a whole utterance' (ibid.) demonstrates the importance of investigating
not only what people say but how they say it. I agree with Mompeán that,
in dubbing, we are not only dealing with words but also with paralinguistic elements and prosodic features such as intonation, rhythm, timbre and
volume, all of which will be used in my analysis. Finally, drawing on Perego
and Taylor (2009), Mompeán also highlights that the 'limited number of
dubbing actors does not suffice to provide a colourful repertoire of tones,
necessary to convey all kinds of voices and sound convincing' (2012: 2). This
statement reflects Mingant's opinion regarding the neutralization of accents
in French dubbing and is also something to bear in mind in the analysis.

   Other studies alluding to character perception are Palencia Villa
(2002) and Ramière (2004). On the one hand, Palencia Villa considers
'characterization' in terms of character credibility and explains that this
credibility is 'strongly related to the sonorous interpretation of the text'
and that it 'depends on the film's voices and their semantic content' (2002).
She concludes that dubbing has not modified this in her corpus, and it
will be interesting to see in my own work whether the change in voice has
impacted on character credibility. Ramière (2004), on the other hand,
looks into the perception of fictional characters and their interpersonal
relationships in *A Streetcar Named Desire* (Elia Kazan 1951) and its French

dubbed and subtitled versions. She concludes that the translation of elements of modality, and also of the phatic and emotive functions, may lead to changes in the way the audience perceives the characters, e.g. whether we feel they are more straightforward or vulgar. She also highlights some slips or shifts in register and comments on the tone of voice of one of the characters, as well as certain elements of the non-verbal codes (actors' performance, décor and music). She concludes that, in the French version of *A Streetcar Named Desire*, the dubbing process has entailed changes related to the perception of the characters, some of them radical. However, she does not fully integrate these elements into her analysis, which is something I claim must be done in order to get a more comprehensive picture of characterization through performance in dubbing.

Finally, although the focus of Valeria Franzelli (2008) is on subtitling, I find her work interesting in the context of my own as she looks at how anger is subtitled in three films (two films in French subtitled into Italian and one Italian film subtitled into French) and focuses on facial expressions as a sign of anger. Franzelli describes the linguistic features characterizing anger in her corpus and how these have been translated (2008: 222). She claims that, even though there are differences between cultures in their visualization of anger – facial expressions of anger being 'cultural constructs' – there are correspondences and similarities between Italian and French (ibid.: 224). She also refers to voice and 'prosodic universals' among occidental people. Franzelli emphasizes that acoustic elements do not have a universal value and that the same prosody (rhythm, stress, intonation of speech) can have different significations (2008: 224–5) in different languages and cultures. As such, her study demonstrates the importance of considering not only words in AVT but also acts of mimicry, gestures and linguistic expressions. I am interested in seeing if the perception of characters in my own corpus is affected when words relating to politeness or other expressions conveying anger or vulgarity have been omitted in dubbing. Having examined the specificity of dubbed dialogue and highlighted the potential for studies on voice and characterization, I can now move on to the effects dubbing has on viewers using Freud's concept of the uncanny, thus contextualizing further my claim that dubbing can (and does) affect characterization and performance.

3.4 The effect of dubbing: The uncanny

According to Freud, the uncanny, a translation from the German word *'unheimlich'*, literally meaning 'un-home-like' or 'not of the home', is a 'province' which 'belongs to all that is terrible – to all that arouses dread and creeping horror; it is equally certain, too, that the word is not always used in a clearly definable sense, so that it tends to [evoke] whatever excites dread' (1919: 1). Freud's seminal concept has permeated many discussions in various academic fields from literature (e.g. fairy tales and the Gothic), film (including animation) and genre studies (e.g. horror and fantasy), as well as architecture, contemporary art, technology (including robotics and artificial intelligence), philosophy, sociology and religion. I will begin by defining the uncanny and then explain how this can be applied to dubbing.

3.4.1 'Defining' the uncanny

According to Freud, the uncanny is 'that class of the terrifying which leads back to something long known to us, once very familiar' (ibid.). In this sense then, the uncanny is related to what is 'new' and 'unfamiliar'. However, not every frightening new thing is uncanny: 'something has to be added to what is novel and unfamiliar to make it uncanny' (ibid.: 2). Freud explains that the factors 'turn[ing] something fearful into an uncanny thing' are 'animism, magic and witchcraft, the omnipotence of thoughts, man's attitude to death, involuntary repetition and the castration-complex' (ibid.: 14). The most evident example of the uncanny for Freud is the automaton, since such figures raise 'doubts whether an apparently animate being is really alive; or conversely, whether a lifeless object might not be in fact animate' (ibid.: 5).

To illustrate the effect of the uncanny, Freud's discusses Hoffman's tale of the Sandman, in which children are robbed of their eyes. The story includes a doll called Olympia with whom the main character, a human being, has fallen in love. In this story, one of the main sources of the uncanny is intellectual uncertainty, which in this particular context refers back to knowing whether or not 'an object is alive or not, and when an inanimate object becomes too much like an inanimate one' (ibid.: 8–9). Another example is that of the 'double' or '*Der Doppelganger*', with all of its connections with reflections in mirrors, shadows, guardian spirits etc. (ibid.: 9). For instance, during her descent into madness in *Black Swan* (Darren Aronofsky 2010), Nina Sayers (Natalie Portman) keeps seeing her distorted image in mirrors or strangers, along with strangers who look just like her. These encounters with her double create further anxieties for Nina and the audience alike, both of whom are trying to understand what is real and what is not real. Mulvey also points out that major sources of uncanniness are 'death, dead bodies, the return of the dead, and spirits and ghosts' (in van den Oever 2010: 201). It is therefore easy to see why the uncanny has been used to discuss reading and viewing experiences related to horror stories and films, e.g. Rosemary Jackson's *Fantasy: the Literature of Subversion* (1981) and Robert Spadoni's *Uncanny Bodies: The Coming of Sound Film and the Origins of the Horror Genre* (2007).

Other uncanny situations include moments when we think about someone whom we have not seen in a while, only to receive a letter from them the same day, or else running into the same person repeatedly in different contexts over a short period of time. We think that such events are uncanny, strange; that there must be a meaning beyond the coincidental. But Freud, in fact, would say: 'It is only this factor of involuntary repetition which surrounds with an uncanny atmosphere what would otherwise be innocent enough, and forces upon us the idea of something fateful and inescapable where otherwise we should have spoken of "chance" only' (Freud 1919: 11).

Additionally, the effect of the uncanny is 'the sense of helplessness sometimes experienced in dreams' (1919: 9), or the disorientation felt when one is lost and keeps returning to the same familiar point as they try to find their way back, or when one keeps bumping into the same piece of furniture whilst looking for a light switch. Such experiences leave one with a sense of mental and spatial disorientation. The uncanny is 'an experience of estrangement, a defamiliarized sensation' (Mulvey in van den Oever 2010: 189). To put it simply, the uncanny is the result of the familiar being defamiliarized, something I find very applicable to what it is that dubbing does: a familiar body, a foreign actor, speaks with a voice that is not their own, or a familiar voice is heard coming from a body that belongs to someone else or does not belong to the speaker.

Although I am more fascinated by the effect itself rather than the reasons behind the feelings evoked, it is interesting to note that, according to Freud, repressed emotions are the source of our feelings of uncanniness. He explains that the principle behind the uncanny goes back to primitive beliefs that we, as the human race, once had:

> animistic conception of the universe, which was characterized by the idea that the world was peopled with spirits of human beings, and by the narcissistic overestimation of subjective mental processes (such as the belief in the omnipotence of thoughts, the magical practices based upon this belief [...]) as well as by all those other figments of the imagination with which man, in the unrestricted narcissism of that stage of development, strove to withstand the inexorable laws or reality. (Freud 1919: 12–13)

According to Freud, we have all gone through such a stage on an individual level, and 'none of us has traversed it without preserving certain traces of it which can be re-activated, and that everything which strikes us now as "uncanny" fulfils the condition of stirring those vestiges of animistic mental activity within us and bringing them to expression' (ibid.) as they have 'remained preserved under a thin disguise' (ibid.). For Freud, there are actually two main reasons for uncanny experiences: 'when repressed infantile complexes which have been repressed are once more revived by some impression, or when primitive beliefs which have been surmounted seem once more to be confirmed' (1919: 17). Both of these can be connected further: primitive beliefs, i.e. magical and superstitious ideas, are related to infantile complexes.

The uncanny therefore belongs fully to the realm of perception and experience, tying this discussion back to film experience and interpretation as seen in the previous chapters. According to Mulvey, Freud's discussion of the uncanny in fact:

> revolves (from multiple perspectives) around the human mind's response to certain kinds of shocks that are, by and large, sudden and unpredictable. In this sense, the uncanny is posited on a distortion of normal, continuous, and significantly habitual experience into something strange and frightening. (2010: 189)

The uncanny is 'tangential' (Cixous in Jackson 1981: 68); it exists 'only in relation to the familiar and the normal', i.e. 'on the edge of something else'. It is a 'relational signifier', a 'mode of apprehending' in itself (ibid.). This experience of 'estrangement involves a "double consciousness" that contains both a denial of an obvious reality and the presence of a lost, past feeling from which the present sensation emanates' (Mulvey in van den Oever 2010: 194). Therefore, when we feel something is uncanny it is actually 'nothing new or foreign but something familiar and old – established in the mind that has been estranged only by the process of repression' (ibid.). Freud attributes the 'uncanny sensation to something old and familiar that "returns"' (Mulvey in van den Oever 2010: 201). In other words, when the distinction between imagination and reality is blurred or 'effaced' (Freud 1919: 15), the uncanny comes into play.

As such, the uncanny 'uncovers what is hidden and, by doing so, effects a disturbing transformation of the familiar into the unfamiliar' (ibid.). There is a dualism in which the signification of the uncanny lies (Jackson 1981: 65). As mentioned in the previous section, there is also a dualism in dubbing, since we must suspend disbelief in order to truly enjoy watching a dubbed film. If, however, we stop and dwell, as Klevan encourages us to do when savouring performances, it is very difficult not to notice that the source of the sound in dubbing is not what is seen. In the following section, I will focus more particularly on the medium of film as an uncanny experience.

3.4.2 *The uncanny in new technologies and AV materials*

According to Laura Mulvey, 'films easily provide deformed and distorted images of the world' (Mulvey in van den Oever 2010: 196), turning the real into the uncanny since 'film is a lens-based art' with 'optical technology at its basis' (ibid.). This is why the concept of the uncanny lends itself so easily to describing the effect cinema had on viewers when it first appeared. Annie van den Oever, for instance, explains that early cinema had an alienating impact on viewers who were 'baffled by what they saw on the screen' as they were brought 'face to face with something that was inexplicable' (2010: 186). Van den Oever compares the experience of the audience to that of the readers of Hoffman's Sandman: 'one is not sure about the ontological status of the seen. It seems that the intellectual uncertainty it triggers has a strong impact on the imagination' (ibid.). For van den Oever and Mulvey, the 'new optical medium' that is cinema is said to have '*destabilizing* powers' (ibid.: 187), like Hoffman's automaton. Cinema is seen as the 'new automaton', and this 'automaton' can be seen as a metaphor for the new 'cinema machine'; in the same way as the automaton moves and seems animate, the cinema machine creates an 'intellectual uncertainty' in viewers about the 'ontological status of the seen' (ibid.: 186). Cinema therefore 'alienated' early audiences by offering them a new experience of their familiar world from an optical and perceptual point of view, making the real strange. Van den Oever and Mulvey's observations add another dimension to Chion's statement that, in films, the source of sound is usually what is seen. As we shall see, this uncanny dimension seems to me to be applicable to dubbing.

For Mulvey, cinema is based on a paradox, with its 'allegorical relation to the automaton and to the fusion between the animate and the inanimate created by the cinematic illusion' (2010: 187). There is a 'defamiliarization of the everyday, inherent in its translation on to the screen'. One of the main reasons for this is the 'still frames, that when animated by a projector, mimic human perception' (ibid.). We go from 'filmstrips to illusion of movement on the screen' and the 'automaton that is "brought to life" (wound up, as it were) by the projector "materializes" into an image on the screen and performs beautifully, usually concealing its animate nature' (ibid.). Thus, at the time of the birth of cinema, the effect was that of unfamiliarity and uncanniness, and even though we have since moved on and audiences are used to what cinema does, Mulvey claims that what still persists to this day is the defamiliarization of the everyday.

Mulvey and van den Oever (2010) therefore emphasize that there is something magical about the way cinema functions, a feature which can also be found in Tom Gunning's work on how the uncanny can be used to describe people's reactions to new technologies. Indeed, Gunning (2003) explains that 'a series of uncanny experiences seem to cluster around technologies of communication like the telephone, or [those] of representation like the photograph' (2003: 47–8). He considers Universal Expositions at the end of the nineteenth and beginning of the twentieth century, as well as viewers' perception of what we now consider old technologies, albeit ones that were novel at the time. His discussion of the fascination with novelty and the magical effects of technological advances is framed by references to the uncanny: 'such visual and auditory novelty beckons one to enter into a new world. But once within, once past the threshold, astonishment gives way to curiosity and investigation and eventually to familiarity' (ibid.: 41). There is a 'discourse of wonder' around new technologies which 'draws our attention to new technology, not simply as a tool, but precisely as a spectacle, less as something that performs a useful task than as something that astounds us by performing in a way that seemed unlikely or magical before' (ibid.: 45).

In the same way as we may one day hear the real voice of a foreign actor and become fully aware of the dubbing process, we can suddenly become aware of how new technologies function. This is usually through 'a breakdown in equipment' which can 'tear apart acquired familiarity and assurance, creating a disaster within our second nature' (ibid.: 46). A definite parallel can be drawn with the dubbing process since it is often said that we become aware of dubbing when there is a 'breakdown' or mishap in translation; for instance, when lip-synchronization is not respected.

Gunning uses the concept of the uncanny to 'mediate between the extremes of astonishment and automatism' (ibid.: 46): 'the experience of wonder re-emerging just when rational explanation seemed to have triumphed'. The uncanny is always 'crouching, ready to spring':

> [N]ew technologies evoke not only a short-lived wonder based on unfamiliarity which greater and constant exposure will overcome, but also a possibly less dramatic but more enduring sense of the uncanny, a feeling that they involve magical operations which greater familiarity or habituation might cover over, but not totally destroy. It crouches there beneath a rational cover, ready to spring out again. (ibid.: 47)

Mulvey (2010: 194) also emphasizes the 'passive attitude' of viewers and links this 'passivity' to habituation or 'habits'. Likewise, it is not unusual when referring to audiovisual translation practices in general, and dubbing in particular, to also consider them in terms of habits. We are told that audiences from dubbing countries like Spain and France 'prefer' dubbing because they are used to it: in Spain, for instance, dubbing was imposed as a manipulation device under Franco, but is still the norm nowadays based on audience habits. For

Mulvey, the uncanny strikes particularly because we are passive audiences. This process of habituation is also mentioned by Gunning (2003: 44) in his discussions of new technologies and the process by which we become used to them. Gunning explains that we go from wonder to knowledge to habituation and automatism, with the 'outcome of this habitualization [being] to render us unconscious of our experience' (ibid.). This emphasis on habits and passivity provides a link to discuss the effect of dubbing as uncanny, since dubbing audiences are said to be habitualized and passive.

3.4.3   Uncanny encounters in dubbing

Hence, the effect of the uncanny arises when one encounters something that is familiar, albeit from an emotional or physical distance. Like the 'cinema machine' and the 'automaton', I would like to suggest that dubbing creates an intellectual uncertainty in viewers, who may find themselves wondering whose voice they are actually hearing. Drawing from Gunning, it is possible to claim that dubbing, much like new technologies, involves an 'uncanny re-emergence of earlier stages of magical thinking' (2003: 47). Indeed, as with cinema or new technologies, dubbing involves 'magical operations': a new voice is given to somebody else's body. And as previously mentioned, the audience is also passive in dubbing, in the sense that it is accepting of the new situation while suspending disbelief over the fact that someone (noticeably) foreign is speaking perfectly in the target audience's language. The feeling of alienation or estrangement arises when one accidentally realizes that the voice of an actor whom they have heard in many films is not actually their own, but that of another actor, another body; or when someone who is used to an actor's original voice discovers that this actor has, in another language, another voice borrowed from another actor, another body.

To support the argument that dubbing can be conceptualized in such a way, let us consider Driscoll's work on animation. Driscoll claims that:

> [a]nimation gives life to all inorganic things: stones speak water gestures like a human, rats get drunk [...] [N]otice how humans devolve into dogs and dogs evolve into humans. Flowers grown in winter and the dead return to life; physical objects dissolve

into air. This is the objectification of human dreams and is the revival of animism; an animism that humanity has wanted to make real since ancient times. (2002: 284–5)

With this reference to animism, one can see a clear link between animation and the uncanny. Drawing from Driscoll, Hsu (2004) explains that '[a]nimation is literally an uncanny medium' because the 'vanishing of the distinction between imagination and reality can in fact be realized through the medium of animation' (2004: 10–11). Moreover, the human voice that is used for an animated character is clearly disembodied: the inanimate object is given life through a human voice. On-screen, the spectacle is familiar: we witness the world of the characters, one to which audiences might be able to relate. However, since there are 'no human bodies shown on screen', the fact that we hear a human voice 'to some extent defamiliarizes the viewing experience' (ibid.: 11). For Hsu, the disembodied voice in animation 'serve[s] to elicit the apparition like quality of anime (or animation) to infer the medium's inherent breach with real life situations. This irrevocable disjuncture – between voice and body – emanates, again, a sense of uncanniness' (2004: 12). I believe that this conceptualization of dubbing in animation as something uncanny can also be extrapolated to interlingual dubbing. Indeed, we are left to wonder 'what body this voice normally inhabits' (Chion 1999: 23). Moreover, it can be argued that this uncanniness is exacerbated even further because a real human being has or possesses a voice that is not their own. In a way, the new voice acts like a ghost voice inhabiting or haunting the body of the foreign actor. And this voice, much like a ghost, can even move from one body to another, like that of the French actor Jean-Pierre Michaël inhabiting, at various times, the bodies of Jude Law, Brad Pitt and Keanu Reeves.

3.5 Conclusion

This chapter has shown that voice and characterization have yet to be systematically researched in Audiovisual Translation (AVT), even though scholars such as Armstrong, Hollander and Mingant have integrated these

aspects in related analyses. We have seen that dubbing has been studied
from a range of angles in AVT and that its various agents and aspects make
it a rich and complex process. I have reviewed studies focusing on voice
and touched upon the importance of translating accents. I will comment
further on the dubbing of accents in Chapter 4, as accents form part of
the paralinguistic elements of voice. Before then, however, it is important
to note that many studies focusing on accents tend to compare translated
and original versions in terms of equivalence trying to see how accents,
dialects, etc. have been conveyed in the target text and whether the connotations have been fully recreated in translation. When investigating
how characterization has been reproduced in a translated text and how
language transfer may impact on AVT products, the notion of equivalence
may be seen as a solid starting point only if one is fully aware that it is not
always possible – and sometimes even impossible – to completely recreate the associations of original texts in their entirety due to language and
cultural differences.

In order to ensure that we do not focus merely on issues of equivalence,
I have also brought in the concept of the uncanny. Indeed, the resulting
experience of hearing a voice that does not belong to the body from which
it emerges can be explained using Freud's concept. Indisputably, if we stop
and dwell on our viewing experience of dubbed films, we come to realize
that hearing an actor speak with a voice that is not their own is a fascinating,
strange and at times even disturbing experience. This uncanny feeling may
be what older audiences experienced when the telephone was invented: the
source of sound, the telephone, is not the real source of sound, the person
speaking. Hence, the telephone, animation and dubbing blur 'the categories of presence and absence' (Gunning 2003: 48) and can make us feel
destabilized and even frustrated, as was the case with some French viewers
of *Buffy the Vampire Slayer* (as we shall see in Chapter 6).

Thus, characterization or character construction in audiovisual materials can be studied by investigating character traits as well as their actions and
relationships through actors' performance, voice quality, speech and voice
characteristics, facial expression, gestures and camera angles. Characters'
point of view, their inner states and emotions are reflected through various
means, some of which will not change in dubbed products; namely, the

visual components of performance. What does change, however, is what the characters say, how they say it and the way the various elements of performance interact and combine to generate meaning. In the next chapter, specific elements of performance and characterization are presented in the form of a multimodal model for analysing the relationship between the oral and image tracks as they unfold together. This analysis incorporates parameters from cinematic modalities (such as shot composition, sound and music) as well as oral aspects of performance, paying particular attention to actors' voice quality. By studying the presentation of characters as it is constructed through performance, my work principally endeavours to answer the question: what effect can a change in voice (including, for instance, vocal timbre, accent and colloquial usage) have on performance and characterization?

The model

4.1 Introduction

My research is concerned with the universe presented in texts, which I have referred to in my previous work on literary texts (Bosseaux 2007) as the 'feel' of a text. The term 'feel', initially coined by Paul Simpson (1993: 46), can also be used in a film context to discuss elements of character perception or characterization. As Pye puts it, 'a story is capable of being told or dramatised in many ways' (2007: 29). The previous chapters have highlighted that audiovisual materials tell stories in various ways and that gestures and movements can likewise be performed in many ways. The model I am putting forward in this book will therefore consider micro-elements of the oral and visual levels of audiovisual materials as they build up to give audiences a specific image of the film world. My focus is on how performance can be affected by dubbing and particularly on its impact on a character's identity, i.e. characterization.

Subtitling, in comparison to dubbing, allows one to keep the original dialogue, including the voice quality and intonation of the original actors. At the same time, however, this 'authenticity' is partly lost when it comes to reconstructing the polysemiotic whole:

> [F]rom a semiotic point of view, subtitling – although retaining the original soundtrack and thus creating a more authentic impression than dubbing – is less authentic than dubbing. Subtitling constitutes a fundamental break with the semiotic structure of sound film by re-introducing the translation mode of the silent movies, i.e. written signs, as an additional semiotic layer. Technically speaking, subtitling is a supplementary mode of translation. (Gottlieb 2005: 21)

Gottlieb also explains that dubbing 'retain[s] the semiotic composition of the original while recreating the semantic content in another (verbal) language' (ibid.: 11). As a result, it can be expected that both dubbing and subtitling will have an impact on the way characters express themselves and how they are portrayed in different target cultures. However, as my concerns are identity and voice, my work will only consider dubbed versions.

In this chapter, I introduce the transdisciplinary multimodal model that I have designed for analysing originals and their dubbed versions. We will begin by discussing multimodality, with an emphasis on the different modes and codes to be taken into consideration in dubbing research. The three main components of the model will then be presented: the oral, visual and linguistic dimensions. The focus is on how these can be analysed individually as well as in combination.

4.2 Multimodality and AVT

According to Kress and Van Leeuwen, language:

> has always existed as just one mode in the totality of modes involved in the production of any text, spoken or written. A spoken text is not just verbal but also visual, combining with 'non-verbal' modes of communication such as facial expression, gesture, posture and other forms of self-presentation. (1996: 39)

An audiovisual text can therefore be seen as a combination of different meaningful modes; a 'mode' being defined as a 'meaning-making resource' (Kress and Van Leeuwen 2001: 15). In this context, multimodality is concerned with how various modes are put together to design a semiotic product or event. Within an AVT framework, then, multimodal analyses consider the various layers of the semiotically complex AV product and how the polysemiotic whole of the original product is dealt with or reconstructed in translation.

In recent years AVT scholars have responded to Chaume's call for multimodal analyses in his book *Cine y Traducción* (2004a) and have shown an increased interest in this form of analysis. In this book, Chaume encouraged researchers to consider linguistic elements as well as other codes from both acoustic and visual channels, e.g. iconographic codes, photographic codes and codes of mobility. However, although Chaume can be credited for initiating this call, other scholars had paved the way for such a move. Henrikk Gottlieb (1994), for instance, was the first to start a conversation on 'modes' in the AVT community when he defined subtitling as 'diagonal translation' from the spoken to the written mode, as opposed to dubbing, which is 'horizontal' translation (1994: 104–5) from the spoken to the spoken mode (e.g. interpreting) or from the written to the written (e.g. novel translation). Gottlieb also highlighted that other modes should be taken into consideration when they contribute to verbal elements, e.g. music and sound effects (ibid.). Such a conception of AV products was later adopted by other scholars across the AVT discipline, who have emphasized that films are semiotically complex in their investigation of subtitling and dubbing. In dubbing research, for example, Zabalbeascoa (1997) produced pioneering work to show the prominence of the role of non-verbal information in dubbed products. Subtitling is also now commonly seen as an example of intersemiotic translation in, for instance, Díaz Cintas and Remael (2007: 50–1), who emphasize the importance of intersemiotic cohesion and the supplementary relationship between subtitles and other semiotic systems, as well as Chuang (2006), who emphasizes that 'subtitle translation involves a multiplicity of semiotic modes which gives shape to the film text and the subtitle text' (2006: 372).

There are five modes to consider in AV materials: spoken, written, the mode of music, the mode of sound effects and that of moving images (Chuang 2006: 374). Chuang looks into how these modes interact and how the translator-subtitler can use these modes when subtitling *Farewell My Concubine* from Chinese into English. She argues that translators can omit or change words in the subtitles if these are conveyed visually by the 'moving image' (2006: 378):

> Other semiotic modes (i.e. moving images and music here) contribute their specific meanings to the process of subtitling. The translator integrates the meanings of a certain section of dialogue, moving images and music to create the meanings that make sense to the target audience as that to the source audience. (ibid.)

The emphasis is on how these five modes co-exist and how they can be used by translators. In relation to multimodality and dubbing, one work by Pérez-González (2007) is particularly interesting from the point of view of my research. Pérez-González focuses on the 'authenticity' of film dialogue and the audience's perception of the quality of a film. He applies Martin's (1992, 2000a, 2000b) systemic functional modelling of the exchange in order to study the sequential dimension of film dialogue. Drawing on Vanoye's work (1985) mentioned in Chapter 1, Pérez-González argues that there are two levels or dimensions to take into consideration when analysing fictional dialogue. The first one, the 'horizontal' dimension, 'denotes the interaction between the fictional characters' while the other, the 'vertical' dimension, refers to how characters address the audience/viewers/readers (2007: 4). These two modes are interdependent, and Pérez-González argues that 'editing and montage practices serve as a filter that selects and frames the way fictional conversation between characters is presented to its ultimate addressee, the film audience' (ibid.). This vertical level can easily be linked back to *mise-en scène* (as discussed in Chapter 1) as it is affected by editing conventions and montage practices. Both modes point to the double-layered nature of fictional dialogue and are important for the model I am developing as I am interested in the way characters relate both to one another and to the audience, as well as how to analyse the multi-layered original and its translation.

In order to study interaction at the horizontal level, Pérez-González investigates 'conversational maxims, exchange sequences, discourse markers, pragmatic connectors, non-verbal and prosodic variables' (ibid.: 5). He presents a case study based on the English and Spanish versions of four scenes from Sidney Lumet's *Twelve Angry Men* (1957) and advances certain criteria for the choice of the text: 'dialogue as narrative resource', 'dialogue and characterization' and 'dialogue and visual resources' (2007: 12–13). Fictional dialogue is thus a major component of analysis as it is instrumental in explaining the storyline and in constructing the characters' personas or profiles. Moreover, the way dialogue is presented visually through camera work, i.e. how the audience is placed in relation to the characters, is also of primary importance.

Pérez-González uses Martin's functional model to look at 'exchanges', i.e. a series of conversational turns delivered by two interlocutors; most particularly, he employs Martin's notion of 'telos', which is defined as the projected culmination of the purpose at hand (2007: 25). Pérez-González comments on various occasions on the 'interpersonal' dimension of dialogue for the purpose of characterization, for instance. This interpersonal dimension is also prominent in my research, as I am interested in the effect dubbing has on the way audiences perceive characters. Pérez-González reveals a range of 'interpersonal shifts' in his data, defined as changes 'between the relations that characters develop with each other through conversation in the source language and the social relations that the same characters develop in the target dialogue' (ibid.: 16). These shifts are at the level of structural units (turns), communicative units (moves) and syntactic units (sentences). Within such a framework, Pérez-González is able to show that 'naturalness is sequentially construed by the characters through the conversational interplay of mood and appraisal telos on the fictional place' (2007: 34) and that 'the translation of conversation triggers off shifts from appraisal (in the source text) to mood telos (in the target text)' (ibid.).

Like Pérez-González, I am in favor of studying entire film sequences by looking at both horizontal and vertical levels of interaction. Moreover, I argue that the oral and visual channels must be taken into account systematically when considering 'the dialectics between the horizontal and vertical dimensions of the target dialogue vis-à-vis its source counterpart' (ibid.: 12).

AVT research therefore generally conceives of films as being semiotically complex products made up of various modes above the linguistic level. There are various studies showing the particularities of the AVT process although it is fair to say that the linguistic dimension has been given prominence. For instance, there are many studies on dubbese in Spanish and Italian which claim that the language used in dubbed versions is unnatural (e.g. Romero-Fresco 2004 and Pavesi 2005). My claim, drawing from Chaume, would therefore be that, in order to be comprehensive in our analysis, we need to consider other modes beyond the linguistic. There is still a lot of scope for more studies to be written explaining how these modes interact to create meaning and how translation may affect performance or characterization. Recently, Jeremy Munday put it succinctly when he explained that some of the:

linguistic features that are 'lost' in the film may be compensated by visual elements on
the screen [...] In view of this, one line of research that would be well worth following,
and which would benefit from interdisciplinary work within translation and film
studies, is the relation between the visual and the subtitles to attempt to determine
the strategies adopted by subtitles as they evaluate the possible compensatory value
of the image on the screen. (2006: 34)

Although Munday is concerned with subtitling, his call for more interdisciplinary work focusing on a convergence with Film Studies in order
to understand how the visual and the written combine to generate meaning proves important in the context of my own work as it supports my
multimodal endeavour. My method will therefore emphasize the various
film modes and their interrelation and interaction in order to understand
how these modes work together and ultimately shed more light on the
complexity of the dubbing process. My primary objective in this book is
to elaborate a multimodal model that examines an audiovisual product
beyond just the linguistic code, i.e. one that also includes other cinematic
codes, such as aspects of the cinematography (e.g. camera cuts). In order
to account for the whole of the semiotically complex AV product, fictional
dialogue will be investigated through spoken and sung dialogue, both of
which are instrumental in allowing viewers to make sense of the storyline
and in constructing the characters' personas. I will now examine the various modes and codes of AV products in more detail.

4.3   From modes to codes of the multimodal text

Chaume highlights that 'one of the first commandments of audiovisual
translation' is that 'the screen, not the original written text, is the script.
We translate what we hear in the clip, not what is written in the script'
(2012: 102). It follows that:

> [t]he true nature of audiovisual translation is code interaction. Problems arise when
> we hear, or hear and see, simultaneously, two or more signs that refer to each other.

In the case of two signs transmitted by means of different codes in the acoustic channel, either the soundtrack or the track containing the dialogues can be modified. (ibid.: 107)

As mentioned previously, multimodal texts are composed of five modes (spoken, written, music, sound effects and moving images). One can see that these modes can be further grouped into two categories: the visual, including moving images and the written components, and the oral, incorporating spoken, music and sound effects. The linguistic code, which is part of a text's acoustic dimension, has been studied extensively in AVT research. There are, however, also paralinguistic features in addition to vocabulary choices, such as silences, sighs, pauses or laughter, as well as discourse markers (e.g. 'huh') and interjections (e.g. 'oh'), all of which must also form part of our analyses as they give us valuable information about the characters' world, e.g. how they feel. The visual dimension has been overlooked, despite the fact that Chaume argues that visuals are more important than words because 'the interpersonal meaning conveyed by a discourse marker lost in translation can frequently be understood by simply looking at such signifiers as the on-screen characters' faces, position, or distance' (2012: 110). In a multimodal analysis, then, the various modes of AV products should be analysed together since the message is conveyed through all of them. The five modes are made up of specific codes, and it is to these I now turn.

There are many codes transmitted through both the acoustic channel (linguistic, paralinguistic, musical, special effects and sound position) and through the visual channel (iconographic, photographic, mobility, shot type, graphic and editing codes). I will be focusing on those most relevant to my own research.[1] Chaume (2004, 2012) argues that the *iconographic* code is the 'most relevant code transmitted via the visual channel' (2012: 110). It is composed of *icons, indices* and *symbols*. Icons are 'signs or likeness that stand for an object by signifying or representing it either physically or by analogy' (ibid.); images and characters, for instance are signs. On the other hand, indices 'represent their objects regardless of whether or not

---

1   For a full discussion of these codes, see Chaume 2012, chapter 6.

they resemble them, but only by virtue of real connections or [a] relationship of contiguity with them (such as the relationship between smoke and
fire)' (ibid.). Finally, symbols are signs 'referring to the objects they sub-
stitute by convention, like the representation of Earth by a globe' (ibid.).
Chaume is most interested in these aspects as they are the ones dealt with
by translators. He argues that these may need to be verbalized in translation, although the 'general norm [...] is usually not to make them explicit'
(ibid.), respecting AVT constraints. Chaume uses these descriptions to
emphasize the complexity of AV translation, explaining that 'when there
are images accompanying words', translating becomes more difficult as
'translators have to negotiate the message and need to be aware more than
ever of issue of coherence, between images and words' (ibid.). We shall see
in my own case studies how such complexities are handled by the French
adapters of *Buffy the Vampire Slayer*.

The second code to be taken into consideration in AV products is
the *photographic* code, which includes colours and lighting. As seen in
Chapter 1, colours have a conventional meaning and each one may have
particular associations in certain cultures. For instance, if a joke is made
that refers to a particular colour, this may prove to be a source of difficulty
for translators if the colour does not have the same connotations or associations in the target language or culture. Moreover, since lighting usually has
a narrative value, translators should ideally have some knowledge of its possible attached meaning. I will refer to the photographic code in my analysis
in terms of lighting and colours and their effect on *mise-en-scène* as well
as on the 'atmosphere' and 'the meaning of certain dialogues' (ibid.: 174).

The *shot type* code is also of paramount importance as shot types (e.g.
close-ups, extreme-close-ups, long and medium shots or pan shots) have an
impact on translation choices in terms of synchrony. Shot types are important narrative devices and also dictate lip-synchronization, e.g. in the case
of close-ups and extreme close-ups. Chaume (2012: 114) identifies three
important codes in lip-synchronization: the linguistic, mobility and shot
(or planning) codes. When translating, one ought to consider the meaning of the words uttered – part of the linguistic code – as well as the shot
type, i.e. shot type code, and the *mobility* code, which includes proxemics
signs, kinesic signs and the screen characters' mouth articulation' (ibid.: 115).

Alongside the shot type code, the mobility code will undoubtedly form part of my analysis as it is concerned with body language, which – as we have seen in Chapter 2 – is a crucial aspect of performance. Types of shots (e.g. the position of the character within the shot and their relation to the audience) and the distance between the characters will, for instance, dictate whether or not isochronic synchronization must be complied with. The way *distance* is negotiated in dubbed versions will also be considered to see the effects of characters speaking from a distance. I will also pay attention to translation coherence when it comes to the rendering of kinesic signs, as well as to mouth articulation to see if it is respected in the dubbed version, e.g. do 'mouth openings and closing coincide with the target utterances'? (ibid.: 175).

The *linguistic* code will form part of my model, whereby I will use Systemic Functional Grammar to frame my discussion. However, since a large number of studies in AVT have focused on the linguistic code, this will not be the primary focus of my model. Naturally, I will consider vocabulary items and their meaning, but I will place more emphasis on the phonetic level as well as paralinguistics, since the focus of my study is on voice and what actors sound like. The *paralinguistic* code will therefore be extensively investigated; for instance, I will consider whether or not the 'primary qualities of the voice expressed by the timbre, pitch, volume, rhythm and loudness' or 'nasality or moaning, whispering, breathing control' (2012: 173) of original voices have been taken into consideration in the dubbed text. Moreover, 'physiological and emotional reactions, such as laughter, weeping, sighing [and] panting' (ibid.), along with silences and pauses will form an integral part of my analysis as I see whether they have been rendered in translation and, if so, how. The *sound position code* will also be integrated, as I will bear in mind the difference between diegetic and non-diegetic sound – as well as on and off-screen sound – and how they are dealt with in translation. Moreover, since one of my case studies is a musical, the *musical code* will also be taken into consideration; for instance, in the case of songs that are important for plot development, we shall see whether and how they have been translated and what happens to, for instance, rhyming schemes, stresses and the number of syllables.

The final code worth investigating in the context of dubbing is the *syntactic* code, which can also be referred to as *montage* or *editing*. Editing, as seen in Chapter 1, determines how a story is told or put together. When making decisions, translators should ideally consider the film as a whole, as another scene could be used in order to legitimize a choice. Chaume argues that, in a film, 'the way images flow and follow one another is meaningful and motivated' (ibid.: 176). Therefore, when the associative aspect of the images from the original film is significant, we shall see how these have been dealt with in translation.

Hence, it is vital to go beyond the linguistic code and consider the semiotic interaction of other cinematic codes. That is why I have included a substantial amount of works from both Film Studies and Sound Studies in this book, enabling me to discuss both visual and vocal elements. Chaume (2004 and 2012) also emphasizes the importance of 'being conscious of the filmic codes involved in audiovisual texts', which is 'extremely helpful, especially when the linguistic code is the only code that can be manipulated in any way' (2012: 118). Even though Chaume's approach is mostly didactic, he nevertheless gives some consideration to dubbing research, explaining that, though there are many articles, theses, research projects and books in AVT, 'some of these works are only concerned with the texts' linguistic codes, and a few have reflected on the other semiotic codes that weave together the source and the target text' (2012: 158). To remedy this, Chaume presents an 'integrated' model for analysing audiovisual materials, combining a DTS framework as well as a semiotic angle (2012: 161–77). This model:

> focus[es] on understanding audiovisual texts as multidimensional texts that convey information through different meaning codes, both linguistic and non-linguistic […] and attempt[s] to describe the main translation problems that an audiovisual text can pose for the professional by showing a list of potential translation problems and a list of related questions. The answers to these questions will reflect the tendencies of regularities of translation, the norms of audiovisual translation (and translation for dubbing) within a community in a given time. Once the model has been applied to translations, and norms have been identified, feedback can be introduced into the model to enlarge or modify it, and extend its use to other corpora and communities. (2012: 162)

There are two levels in the model. The first level, the 'external level', is concerned with 'professional issues, historical aspects, and communicative and reception issues related to the translation brief', as these 'factors condition, a priori, the different decisions the translation will take throughout the process' (2012: 165). The second dimension is concerned firstly with translation problems related to all types of translation and secondly to 'problems specific to audiovisual translation' (ibid.). In addressing Chaume's concerns, my work shall be seen to complement the 'external level' of Chaume's model.

The factors that have informed my work are historical factors, such as when the source text (ST) and target text (TT) were released, the situational and cultural context of the ST and TT, whether or not the director has given some thought to the translation process[2] and the identity of the director and the translators. Where possible, professional factors will also be considered, e.g. which dubbing company took on the work, whether the version under analysis is a redubbing, whether a subtitled version exists and the working conditions for the translator (e.g. deadline, fees, the material at their disposal, copyright and whether the translator had received training). In terms of communicative factors, I consider it important to identify clients, addressees, the communicative context, the channel of communication (for instance, a DVD of a cinema release implies certain conventions) and the genre and meaning codes (e.g. the meaning of special types of shots). Finally, in terms of reception, the following information will be included in the analysis: the appropriateness or acceptability of the dubbing performance and lip-sync compliance.[3]

Chaume considers these elements to be useful for macrotextual analysis, providing a 'solid grounding and a true descriptive methodology' (2012: 170) in preparation for a microtextual analysis. He then introduces the second part of his model, the internal level, as well as some specific general

2   Although it is not common for directors to be involved in the translation of their films, there are nevertheless examples of directors – such as Stanley Kubrick, Quentin Tarantino and Ken Loach – who are well-known for their contributions to the choice of titles or translation strategies for their films.

3   For Chaume's complete list see 2012: 167–9.

translation problems. I would agree that it is important to study linguistic elements, such as contrastive linguistics problems, register and dialect issues, pragmatic nuances and semiotic entities (ibid.: 170–1). However, these need to be contextualized by a thorough audiovisual analysis including 'music, sounds, images, movement and lighting' (ibid.: 171) so that these elements are not solely considered from a linguistic perspective. As I have argued throughout, dialogue and signs interact with one another, and my model will place the emphasis particularly on voice and the relation of the body to the voice to see if and when there are changes in performance and, subsequently, characterization.

Like Chaume, my model has:

> a semiotic component that differentiates it from other linguistic or literary models of analysis. Research in audiovisual translation […] requires an ability to understand texts as whole, to understand the interaction between information and interpersonal meaning conveyed through the different meaning codes and channels of communication, and to assess the influence of the visuals on the dialogues and vice versa. (ibid.: 176)

Indeed, codes interacting can create 'extra meaning' (2012: 172), e.g. an emphasis or a contradiction, and this can in equal parts constrain and aid translators when it comes to making choices. Chaume's research strand is more concerned with identifying 'norms, patterns of behaviour, or recurrences observed in the translation' (ibid.). As has been explained in this section, my work does include some of these elements, but they are treated from a different angle. I am more concerned with voice as identity and with understanding the consequences of the choice of voice talents. My research is therefore not designed to find norms, although my conclusions could be used by others to tease out norms. Moreover, previous work on translation norms may be useful in establishing the target cultural expectations of the dubbed TV show under analysis.

My research therefore complements Chaume's attempt to bridge a gap between Translation Studies and Film Studies by incorporating film elements to a translational analysis. My analysis will therefore determine the meaning of codes in the original and dubbed versions, and the way these interact with the dialogue will be scrutinized to see the impact on performance and characterization. Having examined modes and codes, I can now turn to the model itself, beginning with voice analysis.

4.4 Voice analysis

4.4.1 Voice descriptors

The following paragraphs will examine the physicality of voices and the key sound qualities that are to be considered in my performance analysis, inspired principally by Van Leeuwen (1999), whose work was introduced in Chapter 3. Van Leeuwen focuses on the semiotics of sounds, including voices, and is concerned with what sounds and voices convey. His work has therefore been very useful to me in terms of understanding how voices sound and how they can be described, and acts as the source of most of the technical vocabulary contained in this book. Two other works with different scopes and target audiences also permeate this section: that of Chaume (2012) and Alburger (2011). Whereas Chaume considers voice from a translation-related angle and is concerned with the profession and craft of dubbing, Alburger writes in the context of voice acting and aims his book at those who wish to forge a career in the voice acting business. Chaume's angle is therefore different from that of Van Leeuwen, as the former seeks to describe voice from the point of view of translation; for instance, he is interested in how professional translators can signal paralinguistics to dubbing actors. Alburger, meanwhile, offers tips and exercises for training one's voice with a view to becoming a professional voice talent. I also wish to note that I have myself taken part in a voiceover course in order to better understand how voice acting works. The following sections therefore draw from the works of these two authors as well as my own voiceover training experience, all of which have greatly informed my understanding of voice and helped me create my methodology. In Chapter 3, I mentioned that voices could be described from a linguistic perspective in terms of pitch, tempo or volume. I will now examine these

voice descriptors in greater detail, with particular emphasis on their associations and the meaning they can be said to convey.

4.4.1.1 Pitch

Pitch, the musical note of a voice, can be further defined as the 'degree of
highness or lowness of a tone' and 'the quality of a sound governed by the
vibrations producing it' (Oxford English Dictionary). Since my multimodal
analysis endeavours to emphasize the importance of the performative aspect
of sound, I will first examine pitch as a paralinguistic element – that is, a
non-verbal element of communication.

Pitch can be further described in terms of *range* and *level*. The range
of a pitch can be defined as the limits between which the pitch is produced (for instance, between the two extremes of 'high' and 'low'). There
is therefore a notion of evolution or change in pitch range, which is why
it is usually associated with 'pitch movement'. Van Leeuwen explains that
the 'melodies' of speech 'can be ascending, rising in pitch, or descending,
falling in pitch' (1999: 103) and that 'whether ascending or descending,
melodies can move in large or small intervals, large strides and energetic
leaps, or restrained measured steps' (ibid.: 105).

In terms of meaning, different pitch ranges have various 'semiotic
force[s]'. According to Van Leeuwen, a 'wide pitch range' can express 'excitement', 'surprise' or 'anger', while a 'narrow pitch range' may convey 'bore-
dom' or 'misery' (ibid.: 106). Indeed, the 'wide pitch range allows us to give
vent to strong feelings, whether excitement or shock, of grief or joy', but the
'narrow pitch range *constrains* the expression of strong feelings, whether as
the result of [a] "stiff upper lip" attitude, or because of modesty or tiredness, or because we are paralysed with fear' (ibid.). Therefore, pitch range
is a scale that can run from 'monotone (the absence of pitch variation) to
a maximally wide pitch range' (ibid.: 172). Although differences in pitch
ranges can be explained at the level of the individual (e.g. because of our
vocal cords and lung capacity), they are also situational: different cultural
contexts, time periods and social groups can be said to have an influence on
the way people speak. Van Leeuwen comments that, for instance, 'American
English has a narrower pitch range than British English' (ibid.: 106), which

will be important to bear in mind when comparing the American and British voices in *Buffy the Vampire Slayer*.

The level of pitch is also important to incorporate in voice analysis since:

> speakers adopt different pitch levels for different sound acts. Like the other aspects of pitch, pitch level relates to vocal effort. The higher the pitch level, the greater the effort needed, the more the voice is, literally and figuratively 'keyed up'. The lower the voice, the more relaxed, and, literally and figuratively, 'low key', it will sound. (ibid.: 107)

The related notion of volume must also be taken into consideration. In terms of the physical, someone raising their voice 'usually increases both loudness and pitch' (ibid.: 108); think of male hard-rock singers, for instance, most of whom have high-pitched voices, are loud and usually thought of as assertive. As Philip Tagg explains, 'the loudness and grain' of male rock singers 'also bear greater resemblance to shouting, screaming or (at least) calling than to talking' as 'the dominant character of vocal delivery in rock is one of effort and urgency' (Tagg 1990: 12). Van Leeuwen also comments that there are different associations depending on the bearer of the high-pitched voice: 'when high-pitched voices are softer and more intimate', they are usually associated with 'small people' and soft low-pitched voices with 'large people' (Van Leeuwen 1999: 107). Consequently, gender stereotypes and particularly stereotypes of femininity are often related to the pitch of voices, i.e.:

> In the movies, women stereotyped as the 'innocent, vulnerable girl next door' seduce us with a high, childish voice (Marilyn Monroe), women stereotyped as dark and dangerous temptresses seduce us with a sensuous, low voice (Lauren Bacall), in their speech as well as in their singing. (ibid.: 109)

Pitch range and level will therefore form part of my multimodal analysis since vocal sounds must be studied in context; both in their physical context, that is, who is making the sounds, and in the context of the sentences, scenes and films or TV series in which they appear. As the voice parameter is changed in dubbing, the context of utterance as well as the special context are altered. This makes vocal analysis all the more interesting to study

in both the original and translated versions. Let us now consider further
specifics of voice texture through a discussion of vowels and consonants.

4.4.1.2 Vowels and consonants

Different dimensions need to be taken into consideration when describing voices and sound qualities. This section examines the specificities of
vowels and consonants in order to understand more fully the mechanics
of their pronunciations. In terms of vowels and the way they are formed,
the first feature that must be mentioned is that they are either 'closed' or
'open'. Closed vowels represent a 'blockage of the airflow', whereas open
ones result in a 'relatively free flow of energy and various forms of constraints' (Van Leeuwen 1999: 146). Moreover, vowels are 'multidimension-
ally determined, in a way which is based on the position and movement
of the tongue during their articulation' (ibid.). The 'dimension' of vowels
must therefore be taken into consideration when discussing form.

There are three aspects of dimension to take into consideration when
describing vowels. The first one is *frontality*, which corresponds to the
place in the mouth where vowels are formed. This can be at the front of
the mouth, for instance /i/ in 'heed' or 'big', or at the back of the mouth,
such as when the tongue moves backward in the mouth when saying /a/,
e.g. in 'part' or 'hard'. As Van Leeuwen is concerned with what different
sounds mean, he identifies metaphorical extensions to frontality relating
to distance, e.g. the respective deictics 'this', formed at the front of the
mouth, and its counterpart 'that', formed at the back, a difference also
present in their French equivalents 'ici/là-bas'. The second dimension is
that of *height*, which relates to the position of the tongue in the mouth.
There are two positions, high and low, the difference between which can
be seen when one pronounces 'up and down' and 'here and that'. The last
dimension, *aperture*, relates to the extent to which the mouth is opened or
closed. Specifically, aperture is the 'difference between vowels pronounced
with the mouth comparatively closed and the oral cavity consequently
comparatively small, for example, /i/ in "heed" and /u/ in "hood", or with
the mouth comparatively open and the oral cavity therefore much larger',
e.g. /a/ in 'hard' (ibid.: 147). Let us consider the example of /o/ and /u/

as rounded vowels in English; this is, in fact, a question of aperture. In a dubbing context, the way vowels are formed is of importance as words in translation will not have automatic one-to-one 'shape' equivalents, and one cannot expect voice actors to pronounce words in the exact same way as they were uttered in the original.

Consonants, meanwhile, can be listed according to three qualities. The first one is *place*, i.e. where they are made or articulated in the mouth. The second is *manner*, referring to how they are made. The third one is *voicing*, which refers to the presence or absence of vibration in the vocal cords. Voicing corresponds to the difference between 'consonants which have "tone", so that they can be "sung" and achieve a certain loudness' and 'consonants which do not have "tone", and are always quiet with near-silent release of air' (ibid.: 147). The voiced consonants are /l/, /m/, /n/ and /v/, while the unvoiced or voiceless consonants are /h/, /f/ and /s/. With unvoiced consonants, the voicing starts after the release of the consonant. However, if they are voiced, the voicing commences as the consonant is being released, or just prior. Van Leeuwen notes that, in many languages, the words for silence and stillness often begin with an unvoiced /s/ (ibid.: 147). This association between consonants (or vowels) and the meaning that they convey may not always be automatic, but as writers and poets do indeed employ assonance and alliteration to achieve this effect, it can be argued that such associations can be used when comparing originals with their translations – albeit cautiously, particularly when languages do not belong to the same family.

When it comes to *manner*, we find that there are three ways in which consonants may be formed. The first type is that of *plosives* (or stop-plosives) which involve a physical blocking of the airstream and a sudden release in a 'small explosion of sounds' (ibid.: 148). Plosives can be voiced or unvoiced (or voiceless). The voiced plosives are /b/, /d/ and /g/, with /b/ articulated frontally, /d/ in the middle and /g/ in the back of the mouth. There also three voiceless or unvoiced plosives: /p/, / t/ and /k/, the former being placed frontally, the intervocalic /t/ in the middle and /k/ in the back of the mouth. Voiceless consonants are articulated with a puff of air, e.g. the bilabial /p/, where the lips literally bounce off one another. Van Leeuwen comments that plosives are 'apt for expressing things that are sudden, unexpected, or explosive' (ibid.). Moreover, as with all the key qualities of sounds presented in this section, there is a gradation of sound; some voiced plosives operate on a large scale, as in 'boom' or 'bang', while other unvoiced plosives operate on a smaller scale, e.g. the 'pitter-patter' of rain (ibid.).

The second type of consonants, *fricatives*, are so called as they produce friction when the sound is made. In terms of the physical effects, the airstream is constricted, resulting in a narrow passage from which the air may come out, thereby causing friction. As with plosives, there are two types of fricatives: unvoiced or voiced. Unvoiced fricatives are the consonants /f/, /th/ (e.g. in 'thing'), /s/ and /sh/. The voiced fricatives are /v/, /th/ (as in 'those'), /z/ and /zh/ (as in 'Jasmine'). Van Leeuwen explains that the consonants themselves are associated with friction, e.g. with huffing and puffing. Two other consonants, /l/ and /r/, can be added to this list as they are closely related to fricatives (ibid. 148) in that they both 'include a degree of constriction'. According to Van Leeuwen, /l/ is the 'most *gliding, fluent* and *flowing* of fricatives' (ibid., his emphasis); it is a '"frictionless fricative", in which the air glides over a surface rather than [...] meet[ing] with a friction and scrapes, grates, hisses and so on' (ibid.: 150). On the other hand, /r/ can be seen more like a 'semi-vowel' in 'red' and 'road', whereas in 'scrape' or 'train' it has a more 'grating' friction (ibid.: 148).

The final type of consonants are grouped together under the term *nasals* and comprise /n/, /m/ and /(si)ng/, all of which are voiced and resonant. No fundamental obstruction is involved as these are being formed, meaning the 'air can flow through the nose' (ibid.: 149). The mouth remains closed so that the sound is actually 'kept inside'; it is therefore not completely uttered, as with a hum, a murmur or a mumble (ibid.). For this reason, Van Leeuwen associates nasals with non-committal reactions. In addition to these three categories, Van Leeuwen also adds that of the *semi-vowels* /j/ (as in 'yacht') and /w/ (as in 'wolf'), since these two consonants are fully voiced and do not restrict the airflow.

The type and dimension of vowels (e.g. height and frontality) and consonants (e.g. plosive and nasals) will thus be used in my analysis to describe the words and sounds as they are performed in the original and dubbed versions. Van Leeuwen emphasizes that the 'greatest semiotic potential' of vowels and consonants 'derive[s] from the way they are articulated – from the vowels' dimensions of frontality, height and aperture, and from the way they are combined' (ibid.: 150). This proves significant in the translational context of this book, as dubbing will inevitably change the way vowels and consonants are produced. The original actors' mouth movements will remain the same but the dubbing languages will have different ways of articulating the translated words, particularly as languages differ structurally. Moreover, the less the languages have in common, the greater the differences will be.

My purpose in this book is not merely to dwell on the differences between the ST and the TT, but rather to emphasize the complexity of the dubbing process through the elaboration of a model for comparing the versions. My understanding of translation in general is that full equivalence can never be reached given the myriad of constraints and elements to be taken into consideration. Finally, I must emphasize that not all of the technical vocabulary listed in this chapter can be integrated in each and every case, as this will be dependent on the case study in question. Let us now consider further the sound and voice qualities which will be used in my analysis.

4.4.1.3 Voice qualities

According to Van Leeuwen, the quality of voices can be described using seven criteria: tension, roughness, breathiness, loudness, pitch register, vibrato and nasality, all of which follow a graded process and can be described using two opposing adjectives. When referring to the first one, *tension*, the two contrasting adjectives used are *tense* and *lax*, with each at the opposite end of a binary scale. As noted previously in my examination of pitch, sound and voice description always undergo a process of gradation. Tension is therefore described on a scale ranging from maximally tense to maximally lax. As for the physical effects, Van Leeuwen explains that, 'when you tense the muscles of your throat', your voice 'becomes higher (lower overtones are reduced, higher overtones increased), sharper, brighter and more tense' because 'the walls of the throat cavity dampen the sound less than they would in relaxed state' (ibid.: 130–1). The opposite occurs when you 'open your throat and relax your voice', i.e. your voice 'becomes more relaxed and mellow' (ibid.: 131). In terms of associations and perception, the sound 'resulting from tensing not only *is* tense, [it] also *means* 'tense' – and *makes* [one] tense' (ibid.). The context or situation will therefore add another dimension or 'colour' to help understand what this tension actually conveys. Consequently, tension may, in different contexts, mean 'aggression', 'repression', 'excitement' or simply the feeling one has when one must 'speak up' in public (ibid.). Drawing from Ivan Fonagy and Klara Magdics (1972: 286), Van Leeuwen comments that vocal tension can express a wide range of emotions, including 'fright', 'scorn', 'sarcasm' and 'anguish' (Van Leeuwen 1999: 131).

The second voice or sound quality relates to *roughness* and its counterpart *smoothness*, with the related adjectives being *rough* and *smooth*. There is also a graded element, this time from maximally rough to maximally smooth. Van Leeuwen explains that a 'rough voice is one in which we can hear other things besides the tone of the voice itself – friction sounds, hoarseness, harshness [or] rasp' (ibid.: 131). All of these adjectives can be used to comment on the tone of the voice itself as well as the irregularities of a voice. The opposite of roughness is the 'clean, smooth, "well-oiled" sound in which all noisiness is eliminated' (ibid.: 132). Van Leeuwen comments that roughness 'is more audible in lower pitches', and is therefore 'more easily heard in male voices' (ibid.: 132). He also adds that its meaning 'lies in what it is: "rough"' (ibid.). Consequently, a rough voice will be easily linked to a rough appearance, i.e. the aforementioned example of the voice of a hard-rock singer. Similarly, the smooth voice is the 'vocal equivalent of a polished surface' and 'immaculate tuxedos' (ibid.). Let us not forget that the context of enunciation is also important here and that roughness may be valued differently in different cultural contexts.

The third voice quality is *breathiness*, a term used to describe voices in which the breath mixes with the tone of the voice. There are different degrees of breathiness and it is usually associated with softness and intimacy. Like all sounds, breathiness also derives meaning from its context and could convey either excitement or fear. For instance, Marilyn Monroe's voice is very well known for its breathiness, which communicates sensuality and erotic appeal.[4]

The fourth quality, *loudness*, as well as its counterpart *softness*, employ the two adjectives *soft* and *loud*, which are likewise graded from maximally loud to maximally soft. Loudness is associated with the need to cover a particular distance, be it physical or social, whereas softness is associated with intimacy and confidentiality. As with all of the other qualities, the meaning of softness or loudness is context-dependent; for instance, depending on the context, loudness could convey dominance and power while softness could be used to communicate intimacy or, contrariwise, to threaten someone.

The fifth element, *pitch register*, employs the two adjectives *high* and *low* and is similarly graded. Van Leeuwen explains that register is 'the scale from the very low "in the chest" voice to the very high voice (falsetto for men)' (ibid.: 134). In music, low and high voices are also referred to as 'chest voice' and 'head voice'. In terms of associative meanings, 'because men's voices are on average lower than those of women and children, the meaning of high and low relate to gender (and age) in complex ways' (ibid.: 134). Just like pitch level (as examined in *4.4.1.1*), pitch register can also be associated with size, whereby small things usually make high noises and large ones low. Pitch register is therefore related to loudness, as louder voices tend to be high in pitch. Its meaning is also context-dependent and it is generally associated with issues of power and status: e.g. men use 'higher regions of their pitch range' for assertion and domination (ibid.). Men will speak low in order to try to give a dominant impression, whereas women 'use the lower end of their pitch to be assertive' (ibid.). Van Leeuwen comments that women are presented with the dilemma of either having a low and soft pitch register, which is usually associated with assertiveness and intimacy and can invoke the 'dangerous woman' stereotype, or else having a high pitch (thus running the risk of 'belittling' themselves) and being loud (thus being assertive), which can invoke the 'shrill and strident fishwife' stereotype (ibid.). One can see once again how certain sound qualities carry specific connotations

---

4   See, for instance, Konkle (2008), Banner (2008) and Bosseaux (2012).

which would need to be taken into consideration in the context of translation, particularly as cultures are not homogenous and the connotations
vary from one country or region to the next. It is also worth mentioning
that pitch is not only associated with gender but also ethnicity; Chaume,
for instance, mentions that black people are identified with a 'deep voice'
(2004a: 190).

   Vibrato, a sound quality often associated with emotionality and loss
of control, is the sixth criterion and also one of the contrasting adjectives
used, the other being *plain*. Van Leeuwen explains that a voice could be
plain and unwavering (firm, but also emotionless, dull or bland) or possess a kind of 'grain', i.e. have a 'regular or irregular wavering, warbling,
vibrating, pulsating, throbbing, rumbling and so on' (ibid.: 134). As seen
in Chapter 3, Barthes hypothesizes that the voice of an actor can be said
to possess a remnant of the actor's body in its grain. In this context, the
sound quality of vibrato can be used to describe the grain of the voice; the
traces of the physical can be heard in the voice in the form of a vibrato. Van
Leeuwen claims that vibrato, as with the other qualities, 'means what it is':
the 'vibrating sounds literally and figuratively *tremble*' (ibid.) because of
the emotions they convey, e.g. love. If we were to talk about film music,
strings would be an excellent example of vibrating sounds used when emotions are running high, particularly in Hollywood cinema soundtracks.
Once again, the context will dictate how these sounds are interpreted.
For instance, the unwavering voices in a church choir could be seen as a
parallel to the unwavering faith of the singers, and the emotions or impres-
sions resulting from listening to this would be dependent on the audience's feelings towards religion; if they do not believe in God, they may
hear a bland performance, but if they are believers, they may instead hear
a firm one (ibid.). The possibility of interpreting a vibrato sound in such
drastically different ways once again highlights the subjectivity inherent
in any analysis. It is important to note that, when interpreting the results
of my case studies, I consulted a certain amount of information (such as
blogs and fan testimonials) but did not design a survey to obtain more
informed opinions as to what the voices were generally thought to convey
in the originals and dubbed versions. This is because my emphasis was not
primarily on interpretation but rather on elaborating a model for analysis

and on the theoretical apparatus behind the model, even if the analysis has uncovered interesting results.

The final element, *nasality*, refers to 'sound[s] produced with the soft palate lowered and the mouth unblocked, so that the air escapes both via the nose and via the mouth' (ibid.: 135). Van Leeuwen indicates that this is a complex sound quality to write about in terms of associations, as nasality judgements are very much linked to value judgements. He further explains that the languages, dialects and singing styles that people usually refer to as 'nasal' are those that they do not like. Nasality is related to tension, which explains why 'pinched and nasal tones pervade many of the sounds of pain, deprivation and sorrow' (Lomax 1968: 193). Nasality can be heard in 'moaning', 'wailing' and 'screaming' (Van Leeuwen 1999: 136), and can also be linked to inhibition and (sexual) repression since it is used in situations of stress or when we must control or restrain ourselves.

I will therefore use these seven sound qualities when analysing my corpus in order to determine how the voices sound and what it is they convey in the original and translated versions, bearing in mind that '[e]very sound is a *bundle* of different qualities' (ibid.: 145). Indeed, 'sound quality is multidimensional', with every sound quality being a combination of different features, all helping to 'define what the sound quality presents or represents' (ibid.: 140). In practice, this means that my analysis will incorporate these sound qualities as well as descriptions of consonants and vowels as they combine to generate meaning. Van Leeuwen further explains that:

> a voice is never only high or low, or only soft or loud, or only tense or lax. The impression it makes derives from the way such features are combined, from the voice being soft *and* low *and* lax *and* breathy, for instance – and of course also from the context in which this voice quality is used – from who uses it, to whom, for what purpose and so on. (ibid.: 129–30)

Moreover, these features have different semiotic values, while there are also nuances to take into account in the context of both the original and the translation. It is therefore important to consider all these elements together in the context of the words, sentences and narratives in which they appear.

Words achieve their full meaning in context, and since we are dealing with films, it is also necessary to take the visual context into consideration. This is why my model also considers visual aspects, as will be dealt with in *4.5*.

This examination of voice and sound qualities has emphasized that voices convey emotions and that sound has an emotive power. For instance, when describing the voice of rock singer Steven Tyler from Aerosmith, one can say that it is 'rough, loud and high' and that its timbre resembles 'shouting and even screaming': the '[r]esonance is produced almost entirely in the throat and the mouth' (ibid.: 137). On the other hand, a female rock star like Cyndi Lauper has a soft and warm voice with an open throat and a relatively low pitch, e.g. in her song 'True Colours'. Her voice uses the resonating chambers of the chest and comes from the breast and the heart. Drawing on Shepherd, one could qualify her vocal performance in terms of the 'woman as emotional nurturer' (1991: 167–8). Furthermore, the 'provenance' of sound and voices is crucial when describing voices because 'when a sound travels its meaning is associated with the place it comes from' (ibid.: 139), i.e. from the heart in the case of Lauper and the head in the case of Tyler. We will now examine provenance further.

4.4.1.4 Locating the voice

Thus far, voice has been described in terms of how sounds are made and what they convey, but it is also fundamental to understand voice in terms of where it comes from in the body. This is the notion of placement, which is defined as the location of the voice in the body (Alburger 2011). Voice is understood to be generated from various parts throughout the upper body and head. For instance, voice can come from the chest, wherein it will usually be low, or from the head, wherein it will be high or falsetto. The voice can take on even more specific provenances in the context of this latter category; if coming from the face, the voice can be produced from the top of the head, behind the eyes, at the top of the cheeks, at the front of the mouth, under the tongue, from the nose, in the throat or from the front of the throat (Alburger 2011). In terms of the upper body, the voice can come from as low as the diaphragm, right up to the stomach and chest.

All of these locations will produce a different sound, though arguably in some cases there is only a slight variation, such as the difference between the top of the head and the eyes. This difference may also be much more marked, however, such as that between the chest and the head. Moreover, depending on the placement or location, the pitch will be different too; for instance, if sounds come from the abdomen/stomach or the chest, the pitch will be low(er) than if the voice were placed in the face, the throat or the eyes, where the pitch will be high(er). The way vowels and consonants are produced, as seen in *4.4.1*, is therefore also linked to placement; think in terms of aperture and height.

Each of these body locations will thus have an impact on the sound produced and result in different sounds or pitch characteristics: a voice will sound nasal if coming from the nose, breathy if it is generated from the back of the throat, bright or clear if uttered from the top of the cheeks, raspy or husky if from the throat and strong if coming from the diaphragm. Moreover, every movement of the mouth and tongue as well as the amount of air taken in will contribute to generating a different sound.

Additionally, the notion of placement also relates to the way we open our mouths. Van Leeuwen explains that:

> we can speak with closed or open jaw – the latter is a key contributor to the distinctive timbre of Indian and Pakistani English. We can speak with retracted, 'pursed' lips or with protruding, 'pouted' lips – a feature of 'little girl speech'. (1999: 142)

Mouthwork has implications in dubbing: what to do if a character has a lisp, an accent or tight lips? Should this be taken into consideration in translation? Can it always be reproduced whilst retaining the same connotations? We shall examine how all of these aspects of provenance are negotiated in translation.

Another type of provenance can be identified through accents. Chaume (2004a) emphasizes the importance of dialectal variety in the context of dubbing, while in the context of characterization there can be no doubting the fact that accents play an important role in the construction of characters, which I will consider in terms of the opposition between British and American English in my analysis of the French translations of *Buffy the Vampire Slayer*.

The next section will examine other aspects of voice that complement the aforementioned sound qualities. Before doing so, however, it
is important to re-emphasize that the model I present in this book is not
intended to be prescriptive nor to criticize the works of translators, but
rather to provide a tool for comparing and analysing in order to highlight
the challenges of reconstructing meaning in a dubbing context. Indeed,
when replacing one voice with another, the link between the body and
the voice is deconstructed. The previously-mentioned characteristics will
therefore be altered not only because different actors are producing the
sounds, but also because languages work in different ways and a one-to-
one matching or equivalence of words and sound cannot be expected in
translation.

4.4.1.5 Other meaningful aspects

Notions of *tempo*, *rhythm* and *volume* are also important ones to bear in
mind when analysing sounds and voices, as these contribute in to particular types of voice. *Tempo* refers to the pace of speech, which may be fast,
slow or moderate. For instance, the American actor Chris Tucker is well
known for the fast pace of his speech in *Jackie Brown* (Quentin Tarantino
1997) and *The Fifth Element* (Luc Besson 1997), as is the case with Joe
Pesci in *Goodfellas* (Martin Scorsese 1990). Additionally, tempo may vary
throughout actors' performances depending on the scene or film in which
they are starring.

Related to tempo are the notions of 'durational variation' and 'dynamic
range' (Van Leeuwen 1999: 173–5), which address, respectively, the degree of
duration and the loudness of a sound event. For instance, when we lengthen a
word it is usually to convey a particularly emotion, as when we say 'craaaaazy!'
with a 'wide durational range' (ibid.: 174) to show that we are excited or angry.
On the other end of the scale, there can be a short durational range, i.e. when
words are shortened by using contractions on verbal forms or words, as in
'vamp' for vampire or 'innit' for 'isn't'. Dynamic range refers to the varying
degrees of sound 'from *pianissimo* to *fortissimo* to the use of just one degree
of loudness throughout the sound event' (ibid.: 175). It must also be noted

that different loudness levels can convey different emotions, ranging from fear to excitement.

Emotions can also be communicated through *rhythm* and *volume*, both of which are complimentary to tempo. Speech can be smoothly flowing, plodding, melodic, staccato, syncopated or rushed; the volume may be loud, soft or varied (Alburger 2011). Drawing from Fonagy and Magdics (1972), Van Leeuwen explains that, whether spoken or sung, melodies and the paralinguistic element of intonation 'express emotions' (1999: 94). Joy, for instance, can be expressed through a 'wide pitch range at high pitch level' with a rising melody, a lively tempo and glides in pitch (ibid.: 95). On the other hand, tenderness may be communicated through a voice at 'high pitch level but with narrow pitch range' with a descending melody that is 'undulating', a medium tempo and a 'soft, slightly nasal and labialized voice' (ibid.). Surprise may be conveyed with a medium tempo and a breathy voice, a 'voice suddenly glid[ing] up' (or up and down) to a high pitch level, and then fall[ing]'. The extent of the fall will depend on the degree of the surprise (ibid.: 96). Finally, anguish may be characterized by a breathy voice, a 'voice at mid-pitch level' with 'extremely narrow pitch range', i.e. constrained or restricted, with the melody of the 'pulsed syllables ris[ing] about a semitone and return[ing] to mid-high level where it becomes so to speak paralysed' (Fonagy and Magdics: 1972: 289) (ibid.).

Sounds and melodies can therefore be said to convey or express emotions, and Van Leeuwen goes even further by stating that he believes that melodies not only express feelings of:

> tenderness, they also and at the same time *caress*, they do not only 'express scorn', they also and at the same time *mock*, they do not only 'express longing', they also and at the same time *plead*. (1999: 97)

Thus, they are *sound acts* (ibid.), just like fricatives provided friction and plosives were explosive. This understanding of how sounds work may be debatable and I certainly do not mean to suggest that there is always a one-to-one matching of sound to emotion. However, I find Van Leeuwen's perspective fascinating as the performative quality of sounds and voices can allow us to see them as an integral part of a character's performance. Indeed, interiority is conveyed through voices, words and sounds, and Van Leeuwen further comments that:

> the sound 'caress' may be realized by a certain choice of melodic means (voice at high pitch level; narrow pitch range; slightly descending and undulating melody); but also and at the same time by certain rhythmic choices (for instance a medium tempo); by a choice of 'social distance' (soft, hence, close); and by certain choice of voice quality [...] (slightly nasal, labialized). *Change any of these, and the sound act will also change – change the voice quality of the aural 'caress' to nasal, tense and loud, and the melody might be better described as sounding like a whining complaint'.* (ibid.: 97–8, my emphasis)

This proves incredibly significant in the context of translation, as shall be seen in my own case studies. The experiential quality of sound is crucial to my understanding of dubbing, since it is only by pronouncing words that they take on their full meaning; one must '[t]aste them on the tongue to "unlock the metaphors", as Schafer puts it, [and] to explore the rich potential of speech sounds' (Van Leeuwen 1999: 149).

4.4.2   From voice analysis to film analysis

This section has introduced the various voice descriptors or paralinguistic elements that will be used in my analytical model, such as pitch (movement, range, level), tempo, melody, breath, rhythm, phrasing, tone, articulation, inflection and placement. These descriptors have been shown to be interdependent, as they all 'combine in different ways to make their contribution to the realization of sound acts' (Van Leeuwen: 110–11). Moreover, it is important to consider paralinguistic elements as they can change the meaning of the words uttered by actors: a different tone or pitch, a rise in volume or a change in intonation can transform the underlying meaning of an utterance. As Maya Angelou aptly puts it: 'Words mean more than what is set down on paper. It takes the human voice to infuse them with shades of deeper meaning' (1969: 82).

When reviewing studies of voices in *Chapter Three*, I mentioned 'impressionistic' adjectives that could be used to describe voices in films. These adjectives refer, in fact, to the attitude or the tone of voice. This section has highlighted that it is extremely difficult to dissociate sounds from the meaning that they convey or are thought to convey. The adjectives that researchers choose to describe voices in singing or speaking are irrefutably subjective, as they are chosen based on someone's experience and understanding of these words, i.e. consider how Van Leeuwen describes voices as 'soft, smooth and well-oiled, or rough, raspy and cracked [...], wails, groans and other vocalizations' (ibid.: 127). Van Leeuwen also contrasts Madonna's voice in *Like a Virgin* and *Live to Tell*, claiming that she 'uses her voice quite differently' (ibid.: 150). In the first song, she has a 'high, "feminine" voice and she combines this "little girl" voice pitch with a more hardened sound, quite tense and strident, bearing the scars of abuse and betrayal' (ibid.: 153). In the second song, her voice is 'less high and less tense, lower, more relaxed, more sure of itself as well as softer, breathier and warmer. Only after a while do an occasional vibrato and increased tension add the strength of relived emotion to some of the key moments' (ibid.: 153–4). In my analysis, following the example of Van Leeuwen, I will describe the 'arsenal of vocal devices' that actors use, such as 'moans, grunts, wails, shouts, gliding pitches, [...] clear enunciation of words, clear, clean phrasing, [...] glides or slides to and from pitches' (ibid.), bearing in mind the inherent subjectivity of my attempt. However, as explained previously, this does not undermine the main goal of my research, which is to create a model for analysing performance and characterization in original and dubbed products, with an emphasis on the complexity of the dubbing process.

Moreover, when reading literature on voice – particularly in the field of voice coaching (Alburger 2011) – the advice is centred around the notion of pleasure. We are told, for instance, to take our time and relish the sounds. This is reminiscent of the emphasis on pleasure in the works of Dyer (1993) and Klevan (2005), and the final section of this chapter will therefore focus on pleasure as an important criterion of my method. Finally, since we are talking about sound, let us not forget that silence is also an important part of sound, and that pauses are significant as they can be perceived as narrative silences (Chaume 2004a: 190).

I will now examine the visual elements I will be using in the analysis of my material. First, however, I would like to emphasize the fact that different languages have different vowels and consonants. The method I am putting forward here uses English as a source language and French as a target language, and although it is transferrable to other languages, it must be borne in mind that there are structural differences between languages[5] and that when applying the method to other language pairs, some refocusing may and will be necessary.

4.5 Film analysis

This section takes up where Chapters 1 and 2 left off, further explaining the topics of space, the positioning of the camera and framing in order to demonstrate how scenes from audiovisual material can be analysed in both the original and translated versions.

The following figure, taken from 'The Grammar of Television and Film' (Daniel Chandler ©1994–2015, online), summarizes the major types of shots to be taken into consideration when analysing the various elements of *mise-en-scène* as they unfold:

Figure 1: Shot sizes © David Chandler. Reproduced with permission.

5   In French, for instance, 'syllabicity' is more important than 'syllabic stress' (as opposed to English) (Low 2005), while English 'has many closed vowels and frequent clusters of consonants at the beginning or end of words' (2005: 193).

One can see from this table that there exists a variety of shot sizes, from extreme long shots (XLS) to extreme close-ups (XCU), and that there is a drastic change in focus between different sizes (e.g. from XLS to XCU). Taking long shots (LS) as an example (also called establishing shots as they are used to set a scene), the subject or the actor will be shown as part of a wider background, with the focus not on the actor but on the setting surrounding them. In XCU, however, the only focus will be a character's facial features, almost to the point of alienation. Big close-up shots (BCU) take us slightly further away from the actor or character's specific facial expressions in order to let us see more of the face and of the background, while in a close-up (CU), the actor/character's face, head and upper body appear as the lower frame passes just beneath the shoulders. If a character is shot in a CU, what is being emphasized is their face and facial expressions, with the background just about visible. These shots prove the most problematic when dubbing, since lip-synchronization will be very much in focus and under the audience's scrutiny.

There are three types of medium shots (MS), from medium close-ups (MCU) to medium long shots (MLS) and the intermediary medium-shot or mid-shot (MS). In MS, the actor and the setting are given equal consideration, with their hand and arm gestures visible as the 'lower frame passes through the waist' (ibid.). In MCU, the subject's head and shoulders can be seen entering the frame as the lower frame passes through the chest. As one can see, the subject's face is more in focus and the background is given less importance than in MS and MLS. We then move from MLS, where the legs begin to become visible, to LS, in which the whole body (including the feet) are featured in the shot and facial expressions are less visible; the actor/character is no longer the focus of the scene. For these reasons, LS and XLS are the easiest to handle in dubbing.

In addition to shot sizes, directors have at their disposal a series of types of shots to introduce actors and characters and convey the point of view of a scene (see Figure 2).

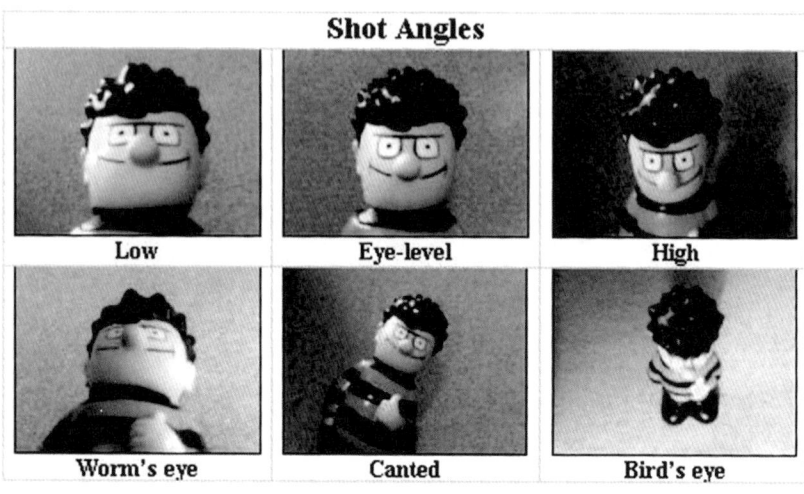

Figure 2: Shot angles © David Chandler. Reproduced with permission.

As can be seen from these images, facial expressions can be appreciated differently and may take on different meanings depending on the angle of the shot. For instance, a high shot angle can lend a sense of uneasiness to an actor/character's facial expressions, whereas the same expression at eye-level could be interpreted as a friendly one. Different genres use shot angles and sizes in very particular ways. For instance, high shots and BCU abound in horror films in order to convey fear. It is also fascinating to notice how the physiognomy of a character can be altered using various shot angles; in a low or worm's eye shot, the actor's jaws seem more prominent, whereas in bird's eye view, the face is not visible anymore and the actor appears small.

Finally, camera and lens movements also need to be taken into consideration as they can provide certain information about the character, in much the same way as the choice to use a passive voice over an active one could provide information about the speaker in a linguistic exchange, i.e. if one uses 'the door had been left open' as opposed to 'she had left the door open', the agency is different and we are presented with a different worldview. Let us consider the table below to get a better understanding of how camera and lens movements function (see Figure 3).

Figure 3: Camera and lens movement © David Chandler. Reproduced with permission.

The presentation of a character using a zoom-in or zoom-out or a ped up to a ped down will have different meanings in terms of what order the director wants us to focus on the objects in the frame. Moreover, the speed at which these movements are performed will have a considerable impact on interpretation, just as a sentence with no commas will take a shorter time to read and convey an aspect of rapidity and hurriedness to the character who is uttering it.

These movements ought to be read in conjunction with the shot sizes and angles; when zooming in and out, for instance, the focus moves from a BCU to a MS (or further) or vice versa. The focus could switch quickly from the actor's face to the background surrounding them, thereby conveying a particular disorienting effect or, if done slowly, creating the impression that the subject is taking their time. Through the use of ped up and ped down, we can switch from MCU to a CU of the actor's legs, which can have multiple implications depending on the context. If we relate this discussion to dubbing, it is obvious that different translation strategies will have to be used depending on the camera and lens movements; for instance, if there is a zoom in or a crab left to right, the mouth movements will have to be taken into consideration, whereas it will be easier to handle a conversation shown in ped up/down or tilt up/down since the face of the actor may not be at the centre throughout the exchange.

One of the main difficulties when comparing originals and dubbed versions in terms of performance is to make allowances for the fact that visuals remain the same throughout the translation process. In extreme cases, scenes could be omitted, but in that case the whole of the audiovisual material would be altered, i.e. as scenes are missing, there cannot be a discussion of how changes affect the way the visual and verbal elements combine or interact. In a dubbed product, what changes in translation is the oral or acoustic dimension; that is, the soundtrack. If the visuals then remain the same, how can we discuss the impact of translation on the polysemiotic whole? Through the elaboration of my model I am concerned with understanding how the verbal and non-verbal merge or marry to create meaning in originals and translations. An additional consideration is how much change is needed or what point needs to be reached in order for us to be able to say that performance has been altered and that we are now faced with different characters? These are not easy questions to answer and my work is not proposing to give a definitive solution as such. Rather, I would like to raise further awareness regarding the complexity of constructing meaning in audiovisual materials and of the impact dubbing has on performance, identity and characterization. In Chapter 3, voice was recognized as a major component of identity; we are who we are because of our physicality as well as the way we sound. By studying voice in dubbing, I want to try and understand whether Sean Connery and Scarlett Johansson remain Sean Connery and Scarlett Johansson when they are dubbed by French, Spanish or Arabic actors. This question is one that will permeate my work and analysis, and in order to provide an answer, my multimodal model will be used to describe voices, gestures and facial expressions through the devices used by directors to portray and give life to characters and performance. I will describe how the actors relate to one another as well as the 'perspective given to us by the camera' (Gibbs 2002: 54), as 'the image will change' (ibid.) if the camera moves. The analysis will be attentive; the material will be analysed through close watching of scenes, reading the audiovisual material scene by scene and shot by shot in order to witness how the world of the film is created, e.g. whether distance is portrayed through the use of long shots or intimacy through the use of close-ups and framing.

Having examined vocal and visual elements, I will now move on to the final dimension of the transdisciplinary method: the linguistic component.

4.6 Linguistic analysis

4.6.1 Systemic Functional Grammar (SFG)

First of all, it is important to emphasize that analysing vocabulary in AV products can be realized using any linguistic framework one is familiar with. Furthermore, since the linguistic code in AVT has been studied at the expense of other cinematic codes (Chaume 2012), I have relegated it to third position in my model, behind the visual and oral dimensions, a fact which is also reflected in the relatively small portion dedicated to linguistics in this book. That is not to say that it is not important to analyse words in AV products and their translations, but as I am concerned with rectifying an uneven situation, I will be placing more emphasis on the acoustic and visual dimensions rather than offering purely linguistic considerations. The framework I will be drawing upon to analyse words is that of Systemic Functional Grammar (SFG), as developed by M. A. K. Halliday (1994), which I have found useful in my previous research (Bosseaux 2007) for analysing originals and translations.

SFG was created in the first instance to discuss written texts. Halliday was concerned with the meaning and function of writers' motivated linguistic choices and how grammar relates these choices systematically to a wider sociocultural framework. Broadly speaking, then, SFG is concerned with the use of language and language as a meaningful form of communication. The fundamental point of departure for SFG is that, when constructing utterances, word choice depends on the situations speakers find themselves in and there is consequently a network of interlocking options to choose from at our disposal. SFG therefore places emphasis on meaning potential and intentional meaning. Naturally, deciding what is and what is not intentional is no easy task, and one must be careful not to attribute an intention without due consideration. However, when considering original and translated versions, e.g. in the case of dubbing, we can use SFG to further emphasize that translators[6] must be aware of the text's possible intentional meaning in order to convey its various semiotic layers, such as the use of intertextual elements, rhymes, quotes or jargon.

Halliday's most famous legacy is his development of an analysis of register in which register is defined as a 'configuration of meanings'. According to Halliday, there are three register variables in a text, which he describes as the *field*, *mode* and *tenor*. The *field* of a text is, in its broadest sense, what is being spoken or written about. Chaume further describes the field as the 'subject matter of an interaction' (2012: 143), giving the US TV series

---

6   This term is used to encompass all agents of the dubbing process discussed in
     Chapter 3.

House M.D. (created by David Shore, Fox 2004) as an example of the 'medical profession's field of discourse' (ibid.) in a TV show. The *mode* is concerned with the form and structure of language in the text and the way language is transmitted. In a dubbing context, one can argue that audiovisual texts 'contain all kinds of modes of discourse' (ibid.): a film, for instance, may quote passages from religious texts such as the Bible, as in *Pulp Fiction* (Quentin Tarantino 1997) or *12 Years a Slave* (Steve McQueen, 2013). Finally, the *tenor* is concerned with the writer-reader relationship or, if considering oral discourse, the 'speakers involved in the discourse' (Chaume 2012: 143). Tenor analysis might include an examination of the level of formality or intimacy between participants, something which Hatim and Mason (1997) consider in relation to the English subtitles for the French film *Un Cœur en Hiver* (Claude Sautet 1992).

Halliday further explains that these three variables are 'realised' by specific elements performing a related functional role. Consequently, there are three metafunctions or interconnected elements of meaning in texts or oral discourse to take into consideration. The first one is the *textual* metafunction and is concerned with how a text is organized; in other words, the coherence of a text. In terms of register variable, this is the *mode*, with *cohesion* the corresponding 'lexicogrammatical' element used to analyse this metafunction – one which has been much discussed in Translation Studies; see, for instance, Mona Baker's *In Other Words* (2011) for a very comprehensive account of how it pertains to translation. The *ideational* metafunction corresponds to how information concerning the world is conveyed to readers. Drawing from Halliday, Van Leeuwen comments that what 'language enables us to do is construct representa-tions of 'what goes on in the world' (1999: 189). The ideational metafunc-tion therefore deals with the way information is transmitted between the members of societies and with how meaning is represented in a clause. Its major lexicogrammatical realization is the system of *transitivity* and how participants consider themselves, e.g. as an active actor or a passive goal. Transitivity also considers the process (verb) and circumstances of sentences as well as voice, e.g. active and passive constructions. Other lexicogrammatical elements include lexis (or vocabulary), as demonstrated in Hatim and Mason (1997). Transitivity 'enables us to create different relationships between the[se] participants' (Van Leeuwen 1999: 189), while lexis 'provide[s] the terms that "stand for" the "participants", the people, place and things in the world' (ibid.). In terms of register variable, this is the *field*. The transitivity system has proved to be a useful analytic model in both stylistics and critical linguistics for analysing a text's meaning as a useful aid to understanding or identifying an author's style (see, for instance, Simpson 1993). The final metafunction, the *interpersonal*, deals with how the relationships both among characters and between the audience and the characters are conveyed. In terms of register variable, this is the *tenor*; the strand of meaning which reflects the relationship between writer and reader or between the participants involved in the communicative act. The interpersonal metafunction is concerned with the communication role that the speaker adopts (e.g. informing, questioning, persuading etc.) and includes evaluation. In English, the major lexicogrammatical realization of this metafunction is *modality*, with the use of modal verbs such as 'should', 'must' or 'may', as it is through the use of modality that we can gauge 'the speaker's judgment of the probabilities, or the obligations, involved in what he is saying' (Halliday 1994: 75). Modality is also referred to as 'the "attitudinal" features of language' (Simpson 1993: 47). Another lexicogrammatical element to take into consideration when analysing the interpersonal metafunction is that of pronouns, e.g. 'you' can be translated in many languages by different pronouns indicative of intimacy or formality, as in Hatim and Mason's study mentioned above (1997).

Halliday's work has proved useful both within and outside of Translation Studies. In AVT, for instance, SFG has been used in Taylor's study on multimodal transcription (2003), Pérez González's work on film dialogue (2007) and Baldry and Taylor's consideration of the multimodal nature of films and its impact on the strategies used by subtitlers (2004). Baldry and Taylor use multimodal transcriptions of visual and acoustic dimensions and present a method 'breaking down a film into single frames/ shots/phases and analyzing all the semiotic modalities operating in each frame/shot phase' (2004: 191). Outside of AVT, the work of Baldry and Thibault (2006), mentioned in Chapter 1, is one of the most complete studies done so far on multimodality using SFG. Beyond the linguistic level – in the field of Music Studies, for instance – David Machin (2010) works within an SFG framework to emphasize the meaning potential of visual signs:

> To continue with our example of colour, a saturated red might alone be used to com-
> municate sensuality. But if we combine that red on a design alongside three other
> highly saturated colours – yellow, blue and black – its meaning changes. Such a use
> of colours, a loud, varied colour palette, is often used to communicate vibrancy and
> fun, or could connote garishness and lack of taste, for example. Clearly in such a case
> it is not just the hue that has meaning potential but the degree of saturation. This
> meaning would have been different had the colours been all dilute as opposed to
> saturated. (2010: 8)

With this example, Machin reinforces the claim that signs do not have fixed meaning. This proves very meaningful in the context of translation; as mentioned previously, a colour might connote a particular meaning in one culture but not in another. The emphasis Machin places on meaning being dependent on the options available to us and on how important describing and classifying potential meanings proves particularly relevant to my research:

> The point is that we need first to be able to describe the available repertoire. We
> must then treat this as an inventory of potential meanings. In our analyses we first
> describe the semiotic choices found in a text or visual composition and, second,
> describe the way that meaning potentials are activated. (2010: 8)

As seen in *4.4*, Van Leeuwen (1999) is also concerned with meaning poten-
tial in the context of sound. Meaning potential is therefore an interesting starting point when analysing originals and their translated versions, and in the present book, I have drawn from previous works in SFG and AVT as well as my own on fiction (Bosseaux 2007) to argue that the way we experience film characters depends on actors' performances and other aspects of *mise-en-scène*, as highlighted in Chapters 1 and 2. Specifically, my claim is that the feel of audiovisual texts rests on visual and oral (including linguis-
tic) manifestations, which are integral parts of the original texts. Translation will change the connection between the verbal and the non-verbal and may bring about a change in the feel of the texts. My analysis will incorporate a study of voice, paralinguistic information, actors' movements, camera

shots as well as dialogue, language being just one aspect of the multi-layered communication process.

Where necessary, translators' linguistic choices will be analysed to see whether they contribute to a change in the feel of the audiovisual text as part of the polysemiotic whole. Using SFG, the feel of the original and dubbed versions can be examined through the use of modal verbs and adverbs expressing notions of obligation, possibility and permission (e.g. must, can or should) as well as perception verbs (e.g. feel, see and hear) and adverbs (e.g. maybe), all of which convey a character's views on their situation and can be interpreted as determinant factors in identifying characterization. Interpersonal relationships may also be investigated by considering the translation of the personal pronoun 'you'. There are two options when translating 'you' into French: '*tu*' and '*vous*', with the choice of which one to use depending on the relationship between the participants. Analysing translators' choices in this regard may therefore shed light on characterization in both the original and translated versions.

Another layer of the process of linguistic communication worth investigating is that of transitivity. One of the main premises behind my research is that characters have unique linguistic or oral styles that contribute to their identities; think, for instance, of Daniel Day-Lewis, who was praised for his voicework in *There Will Be Blood* (Paul Thomas Anderson 2007), and likewise Leonardo Di Caprio in *Django Unchained* (Quentin Tarantino 2013). Linguistically speaking, characters can be seen as participants with particular tendencies, e.g. that of being agentive or affected. Transitivity patterns can be used to describe the structure of processes, participants and circumstances in a verbal exchange, shedding light on the way characters experience events, something which is encoded in the sentences they utter. Elements of transitivity can help us understand the ideational aspects of characterization by showing how characters' experiences of events are encoded in the exchange. For instance, if a character uses a passive construction such as 'The money was stolen' to describe an event they themselves are responsible for, or if a character describes themselves as being passive in a particular situation, this may provide important information in terms of the narrative and development of events. The transmission of ideas is a vital component of communication, and transforming passives into actives in translation could have an impact on character construction. These linguistic elements will be examined alongside non-linguistic elements (e.g. paralinguistic information, body movements and facial expressions) to describe character profiles in both the original and translated versions in order to see what happens to characterization in dubbed products.

When it comes to incorporating the textual metafunction, discourse markers – lexical items used to make discourse coherent – may also be taken into consideration in so far as they are used to clarify speakers' intentions and what they intend to do with their words (Schiffrin 1988). There have been many studies in AVT (and particularly subtitling) on discourse markers and the necessary negotiations involved when switching from an oral discourse to a written one (see, for instance, Biagini 2010; Hatim & Mason 2000; Assis 2001; Mason 1989 and 2001; Tomaszkiewicz 2001 and 2009). The main role of discourse markers in conversations is to establish a beginning and endpoint to conversations for their participants. In the present study, discourse markers may be considered where they contribute to characterization; for instance, certain expressions or interjections ('Oh well'), these being an integral part of information management; discourse connectives ('and', 'but', 'or'); conjunctions acting as markers of cause and results ('so', 'because'); temporal adverbs ('now', 'then'); and other adverbs ('really', 'luckily') and verbal forms such as 'Y'know', 'listen', 'wait' or 'I mean', which give information about participation.

The linguistic analysis of my multimodal model will therefore include elements of Halliday's SFG with an emphasis on the interpersonal and ideational metafunctions, as I am interested in the way characters relate to one another as well as to the audience and in how the latter may construct an image or feel of the characters. Dialogue will be investigated in the case studies as it is instrumental to constructing characters' personas or profiles. Thus, alongside visual and oral elements, modality, transitivity and discourse markers will all be studied in both the original and translated audiovisual products. Additionally, linguistic elements will be analysed in the context of music, as some of my material comes from a musical. I will now examine works dealing with song and music translation in order to understand further how to handle linguistic elements as part of a vocal (sung) performance.

4.6.2 Music and songs in translation

Lyrics and music were mentioned in Chapters 1 and 2 as playing an important role in setting the mood of a film as well as for characterization. In Translation Studies, research work on the translation of songs has attracted some attention in recent years with the works of Dinda L. Gorlée (ed. 2005), Susam-Sarajeva (ed. 2008) and Helen Julia Minors (ed. 2013). These volumes testify to a growing interest in the discipline for the translation of 'singing sign-events' (Gorlée 2005, book cover), from popular songs to operas, hymns and musicals.[7]

When translating songs, the focus is generally on rendering the lyrics in such a way that they fit the music. Such a practice brings its own set of constraints, as translators must take into consideration aspects such as rhythm and rhymes. Gorlée differentiates between what is called 'logocentrism', 'a view defending the general dominance of the word in vocal music' (2005: 8), and 'musicocentrism', a 'wordless approach' (ibid.). Translating words that fit the music is particularly complex in logocentric songs (ones which focus on words). In the next paragraphs, I will give an overview of the works that have inspired my analysis of material, including that of logocentric songs.

First of all, Peter Low proposes an approach to translating songs which he calls the 'Pentathlon Principle', inspired by *Skopos* theory. Low singles out five criteria that need balancing when analysing the ST: 'singability, sense, naturalness, rhythm and rhyme' (2005: 185). Within the functionalist framework he uses, the emphasis is on the function and overall effect of the original song and its translation. Low's method offers the possibility of assessing the success of a translation by calculating an 'overall aggregate [...] on all five of the criteria' (ibid.: 203). When it comes to *singability*, Low advocates a translation technique of 'acceptable accuracy' (ibid.: 194). In this context, meaning or *sense* is still an important criterion in translation, but

---

7   Before 2005, Hewitt (2000) and Kaindl (2004) were among the few studies to look at popular music. More recently, Susam-Sarajeva (2006 and forthcoming) examines Rembetika songs and their translations into Turkish.

singability prevails in order for the singing to retain *naturalness*. Therefore, a synonym sometimes may be used even if 'it incurs some semantic loss', as it might be the best solution in terms of singability, e.g. the adjective 'tight' can be chosen over 'strict', 'with two consonants and a nice singable diphthong' (ibid.). Singability proves greatly significant in the context of dubbing, as mouth movements will dictate which consonant or vowel can be used. Low also advocates naturalness of register and word order for an 'effective communication on first encounter' (ibid.: 195). As seen previously, naturalness in dubbing is an important criterion since dubbing gives the illusion that actors speak perfectly in the target language. Naturalness can also be used to talk about the translation of *rhythm*. Low suggests that an identical syllable count in the TT is usually desirable, but that in order to achieve a natural rhythm, a syllable can be added 'judiciously' if the alternative is 'insolubly, unacceptably clumsy', and that 'an occasional [...] tweaking may be preferable to a glaring verbal gaffe' (ibid.:. 198). Moreover, syllable count is not the only parameter; the length of vowels and consonants as well as rests must also be taken into consideration. Finally, Low claims there has been an overemphasis on the importance of *rhymes* in song translations (ibid.: 198–9). He therefore advocates flexibility and suggests Ronnie Apter's terminology (1985) as a method for translating rhymes with 'rhyme's cousins – off-rhyme (line-time), weak rhyme (major-squalor), half-rhyme (kitty-knitted) and consonant rhyme (slit-slat) – alone or in a combination with other devices like assonances and alliterations' (1985: 309–10).

Although Low primarily introduced the Pentathlon Principle in order to assist translators with their task, it can also be used to describe and comment on translators' choices. Using *Skopos* theory, Low emphasizes the function of the songs and lyrics. In a similar way, I use SFG in my corpus to analyse dubbed songs, paying attention to the function of certain sounds, camera movements and words in so far as they are important for characterization. Low also emphasizes the importance of the overall effect of the translation, explaining that nothing is 'sacrosanct and must be perfectly retained', as this would lead to 'great losses elsewhere' (2005: 210). This is also relevant when analysing dubbed products: choices will have been made according to visual, technical and linguistic constraints and it will not always be possible to preserve all aspects of the original; there is, after all, no such thing as perfect equivalence. Bearing all of this in mind, I shall analyse the whole or totality of the performance both in the original and as it is reconstructed in translation.

Another work of interest when considering music and song translation is Johan Franzon's analysis of three Scandinavian translations of *My Fair Lady* (George Cukor 1964). In this work, Franzon seeks to establish which 'communicative clues may be considered relevant for the theatrical functionality of singing and which options song translators may have in the compromise between fidelity and formatting strategies' (2005: 274–5). Drawing from Jakobson (1959), Franzon identifies the translation of a musical as an example of 'creative transposition' (Franzon 2005: 264) or 'adaptation' (of target lyrics to the musical line). He considers various elements, or functional units, including utterances that signal emotions or attitudes, stage activity (such as gestures and verbal behavior) and the perceived impact of the music (ibid.: 274–5). In my own work, these fall under the interpersonal metafunction and performance (including kinesics). Franzon advocates the 'recreation of the source text qualities of rhymes, vowel sounds, semantic, stylistic, or narrative content or a little bit of each' (ibid.: 266) to create a target text that 'resembles its ST in respects relevant to its presentation as a staged narrative to music' (ibid.: 267). Franzon's depiction of the translation process emphasizes its complexity: in song translation, translators have to negotiate between various functional units creatively, while in dubbing, the additional constraint of synchronization must be added.

Finally, the translation of songs and music must be considered from a sociocultural angle. In the same way as performance is culturally and historically bound, translating songs is context-dependent. In this sense, songs can be examined using Mikhail M. Bakhtin's concept of *dialogism* (1984), as they take part in a dialogue with other texts and discourses – whether musical, verbal or visual – as well as with the genres and styles of the source and target cultures. As cultural contexts will be different in translation, it is possible to use André Lefevere's concept of 'acculturation' (1998) to discuss translation. This is how Klaus Kaindl (2005) approaches the translation of songs, which he sees as a 'socio-semiotically determined practice'. In this 'process of cross-cultural transfer', mediation is a prerequisite because the associations and references of the ST may not be shared in the same way by members of the source and target cultures (2005: 243). For Kaindl, in attempting to juggle various criteria and choices specific to song translation, the translator becomes more than ever a 'bricoleur' (a term borrowed from Levi-Strauss 1966): someone who combines the various elements (music, language, vocals, instrumentation, culture etc.) of the multi-layered text and weaves them together to form a new unified system. The emphasis is not only on the 'verbal text' but also on musical structure, instrumentation and 'vocal presentation' (Kaindl 2005: 250), all of which are elements of performance. Therefore translators are involved in the 'functional reinterpretation' of these elements (ibid.), having to choose one functional aspect over another. In his study, for instance, there are four important contextual formats: narrative, staging, presentation and musical, and he explains that the intertextual coherence of the narrative and the staging levels must be prioritized.

Many scholars therefore emphasize the 'multimedial aspect' of song translation (Franzon 2005: 262), and it is evident that a variety of elements has to be taken into consideration at different levels when translating and analysing songs. In my study, I will consider performance through visual and oral elements, including song lyrics, with an emphasis on their meaning within the storyline (e.g. plot information), rhymes and the translation of utterances that reveal emotions or attitudes. Throughout this section on linguistic analysis, the importance of translation as a process of choice has also been reiterated. All of the scholars mentioned here agree that translating involves prioritizing certain aspects over others and that personal interpretation and subjectivity inevitably come into play when making choices. Low, for instance, acknowledges the role of interpretation when he explains that his choice of 'Don't abandon me' over 'If you go away' to translate Jacques Brel's song *Ne me quitte pas* has been determined by his understanding that, at the end of the song, the woman has already left. According to Low, there are no 'ifs about it – she is already long gone – at least such is [my] interpretation' (Low 1994 in 2005: 202). One should not forget that subjectivity needs to be accounted for in any analysis since 'the position from which one speaks, whether internal or external, affects the thing spoken about' (Hermans 1999: 105). Once again, I wish to emphasize that my primary concern is to provide a tool for analysis that can be used by other researchers in AVT. My other priority is to re-establish pleasure as part of AVT analyses, since – as I shall demonstrate in the following section – viewing audiovisual products is a reflexive activity involving pleasure.

4.7 Viewing as a reflexive activity

As one can see, the attentive analysis that I put forward in this book draws on various fields. Moreover, and most importantly, it places particular emphasis on experiencing the material and not merely reducing it to its meaning components at the risk of forgetting that viewing films or television series can be and often is a pleasurable experience. In order to conclude this chapter, pleasure will therefore be discussed as a legitimate criterion for my model, drawing on Antoine Hennion's work '*Pour une pragmatique du goût*' (2005, translation 2007), in which he presents a pragmatics of music comparing it to a pragmatics of taste.

According to Hennion, taste has long been recognized in the field of Art History as something that is not separate from works of art (2007: 3), as it 'is not possible to distinguish between the two' (ibid.); what is being 'tasted' cannot be separated from who 'tastes' it. This is Hennion's pragmatics of the act of tasting – a pragmatics which aims at 'restoring the performative nature of the activity of taste, instead of making it an observance' (ibid.). Thus, tasting is understood as a performance: 'it [tasting] acts, engages, transforms, it is felt' (2007: 3).[8] I fully agree with Hennion, and while I have strived to anchor my work in various fields and to create a 'scientific' method for comparing originals with their translated versions, I strongly subscribe to the view that '[w]orks "make" the gaze that beholds them, and the gaze makes the works' (ibid.)

---

8   '*C'est une performance: cela agit, cela engage, cela transforme, cela fait sentir*' (2005: 5).

As such, in terms of being a viewer-analyser, I see myself as being what
Hennion calls an 'amateur' or 'fan'; 'the one who does something with'
(ibid.) acting and voice.

I have emphasized that describing voices is an arduous endeavour which
involves discussion of both the spoken and sung voice. Various elements
all require exploration, including timbre (vocal quality), rhythm and pace,
tessitura (vocal range), breath control, articulation (how the voice approach
the notes and syllables) and the dynamic shape of specific spoken or sung
phrases. As mentioned previously, this task is highly subjective. Some may
disagree with my conclusions on the voices under analysis and on what
the audiovisual material communicates in the original and translated versions. I accept this fact, and acknowledge that I have not relied on surveys
to corroborate the feelings I have experienced when witnessing an actor's
performance, since my main purpose in this book is to present a method
that stands at the crossroads between different disciplines and paves the
way for future research. I leave this alternative perspective to scholars from
audience studies in preference of an analysis that recognizes aesthetics and
acknowledges the pleasure that performances convey. Ultimately, my goal is
to create a multimodal method for analysing vocal performance in original
and dubbed products, and I hope that my research might inspire others to
continue developing a multimodal analysis, whatever the interpretations
and results may be.

Therefore, my analysis, in answer to Hennion's call, shall involve 'tasting' the films and TV series under scrutiny and not merely reducing them
to material scientifically chosen for analysis. This is because:

> [t]aste, pleasure and effect are not exogenous variables or automatic attributes of
> objects. They are the reflexive result of a physical, collective and equipped practice,
> regulated by methods that are themselves constantly revised. That is why I prefer to
> talk about attachments and practices, which lays less emphasis on labels and more on
> the framed activity of individuals, and leaves open the possibility of taking whatever
> emerges into account. (2007: 4)

Hennion's account of taste as a reflexive activity is also reminiscent of
Klevan's method (2005) reviewed in Chapter 3, which emphasized the
interpersonal function of performance and prompts us to savour films.

When appreciating a work of art, a film or piece of music, there is an exchange between the work and the viewer, and the key concept for Hennion is:

> reflexivity, both as central to the activity of amateurs themselves and as a method required by the sociologist in order to account for that activity [...] Saying that the musical object or the taste for wine are not given, but result from a performance by the taster – based on techniques, physical training, and repeated trials, necessarily over a period of time – is relating the very possibility of a description back to amateurs' know-how. (ibid.: 3)

Dyer, when emphasising the importance of emotional 'responses' to the stars who perform in films, writes along the same lines as Hennion and Klevan when he says:

> I feel I should mention beauty, pleasure, delight [...] We should not forget what we are analysing gains its force and intensity from the way it is experienced, and that ideology shapes the experiential and affective as much as the cognitive. When I see Marilyn Monroe I catch my breath; when I see Montgomery Cliff I sigh over how beautiful he is; when I see Barbara Stanwyck, I know that women are strong. I don't want to privilege these responses over analyses, but equally I don't want, in the rush to analysis, to forget what it is I'm analysing. And I must add that, while I accept utterly that beauty and pleasure are culturally and historically specific, and in no way escape ideology, none the less they are beauty and pleasure and I want to hang on to them in some form or another. (Dyer 1998: 162)

Pleasure was also an important factor in Barthes' concept of the grain of the voice, as examined in Chapter 3. Phil Powrie (2008), for instance, uses this concept to discuss Paolo Conte's vocal performance when singing 'Sparring Partner' in François Ozon's film 5x2 (2004). Conte's voice, he argues, is a 'gravely, world-weary' one (2008: 216) that contributes to making the song 'work empathetically' with the narrative (ibid.: 206). The 'grain of the singer's voice can affect us more immediately because it is prior to the meaning of the word' (ibid.: 219) and this experience is 'haptic, the senses merge, we can almost touch the voice; it is tactile' (ibid.). Hearing and viewing the grain of the voice are most certainly reflexive activities that effect or affect spectators.

The approaches of Hennion, Klevan, Barthes and Dyer are particularly interesting to me as I am interested in the 'feel' of the text and the potential effects of performance on audiences. Their views have therefore influenced my work and set the tone for my analysis of the material. Moreover, Hennion's account is particularly relevant to my work on body and voice since he emphasizes tasting as an interpersonal activity that requires a body and a (social) environment in which meaning is created primarily as the subject meets and mix with the object:

> It [tasting] first and foremost concerns the co-production of the body that loves and the loved object, through a collective and equipped activity. Exercise is the right word for this: the body exercises and gets used to the exercise, and on the way the word exercise slides from training to the faculty that one exercises. The more 'constructed' the gesture of a tennis player, the more 'natural' it becomes to her/him, so that the ball flies through the air much faster if she/he is relaxed. But this can be so only with the racket, the net, the court, the rules of the game, the opponent, and years of practice. No language, no nose, no taste for wine until the wine has become the object of a set of practices that place it at their centre. No ear, no musical emotion, without a music to listen to. It took over three hundred years of practices and inventions to create our way of loving music. (ibid.: 7)

Watching or viewing audiovisual material can be added to Hennion's list of reflexive activities. Films or television series can be tasted like wine, food, music or sports. Tasting films means appreciating them, loving them, and the word 'film' can easily be substituted for the word 'music' in the following quotation:

> [Tasting music] is not simply a matter of a particular piece; it passes through a multitude of mediators (Hennion 1993), beginning with the present – the sound of an instrument, the atmosphere of a hall, the grain of a record, the tone of a voice, the body of a musician –, but also in the duration of a history – scores, repertoires and styles, genres and more or less stable forms –, or for each individual – a past, works heard, moments lost, desires unfulfilled, roads travelled with others, and so on. (Hennion 2007: 7)

In the same way, watching, appreciating or loving a (dubbed) film involves many factors and actors, including translators and dubbing artists, all of who must be given thanks for making it possible for audiovisual products to travel in translation and reach countless audiences.

4.8 Conclusion

I have argued throughout that characterization can be investigated by study-ing performance through visual and acoustic (including verbal) elements. In this chapter, I have presented the multimodal model that I created for analysing factors of performance through visual (e.g. body movements), paralinguistic (voice) and linguistic cues (Systemic Functional Grammar). I will next perform an attentive film analysis of scenes, taking into consid-eration pleasure, camera position, perspective (angles), distance, colour, visual focus, kinesic action and soundtrack, as well as providing detailed vocal analyses. Moreover, linguistic aspects will be taken into consideration as part of dialogue exchanges. Even though they do not change in transla-tion, it will also be important to analyse visual elements such as camera position, angles, and distance in order to determine how the visual and the acoustic combine to create meaning and consider the impact of dubbing. The model presented is transferable and can be used with other languages and AV material. However, not all of the visual and acoustic elements that combine to create characterization described in this section may be used, as this will depend on the material and languages under investigation. In other words, researchers will have to select elements of visual and verbal performance that are relevant to their own studies. The examination of the translators' choices will aim to shed light on the effect of dubbing on per-formance and characterization. Moreover, since performance is culturally bound, any analysis must take into consideration the wider sociocultural and ideological context of audiovisual products in order to get a compre-hensive picture of the overall meaning. Thus, the next chapter introduces the material I will be using to test my model: the American TV series *Buffy the Vampire Slayer*.

CHAPTER 5

Buffy the Vampire Slayer

5.1 Introduction

The popular American television series *Buffy the Vampire Slayer* (1997–2003, 20th Century Fox) tells the story of a young American woman called Buffy Anne Summers. Buffy lives in Sunnydale, an imaginary town in Southern California, which has been built over a Hellmouth, a centre of demonic energy. In the mythology of the show, Buffy is the Chosen One, the 'Slayer'. She has a specific mission: to kill vampires and rid the world of evil forces. With the continuing help of her friends, Willow and Xander, and her Watcher, Rupert Giles, Buffy battles the forces of darkness and her own inner demons. In effect, the show deals with Buffy's transition from being a teenager to becoming a young woman. There are one hundred and forty-four episodes spanning seven seasons, each corresponding to one year in Buffy's life from the age of sixteen. We see Buffy going to high school for the first three seasons, then from season four she goes to college. Buffy dies at the end of season five and therefore 'drops out'. In season six, Buffy comes back from the dead and tries to make a living. In the final season (season seven), she works as a counsellor in her old high school. Each season is centred around one major 'Big Bad', which is 'Buffyspeak' for the evil forces which must be defeated.

In an interview with the American online humour website *The Onion*, Joss Whedon, Buffy's creator and showrunner, summarizes why he created Buffy:

> I designed *Buffy* to be an icon, to be an emotional experience, to be loved in a way that other shows can't be loved. Because it's about adolescence, which is the most important thing people go through in their development, becoming an adult. And

it mythologizes it in such a way, such a romantic way – it basically says, 'Everybody who made it through adolescence is a hero.' And I think that's very personal, that people get something from that that's very real. And I don't think I could be more pompous. But I mean every word of it. I wanted her to be a cultural phenomenon. I wanted there to be dolls, Barbie with kung-fu grip. I wanted people to embrace it in a way that exists beyond, 'Oh, that was a wonderful show about lawyers, let's have dinner.' I wanted people to internalize it, and make up fantasies where they were in the story, to take it home with them, for it to exist beyond the TV show. And we've done exactly that. (in Robinson 2001: online)

This quote perfectly summarizes *Buffy*'s essence, theme, genre and, most importantly, Whedon's intentions for the show to touch people universally. The TV series is actually a spin-off of a film released in 1992, which was not very successful. The film was written by Joss Whedon but directed by Fran Rubel Kuzui. For the TV series Whedon had more creative control as the head writer, director and executive producer. The primary goal of this chapter is to show how Whedon and the other writers of *Buffy the Vampire Slayer (BtVS)* have made the show a long-lasting success worldwide. Indeed, although *BtVS* concluded in 2003, the show is – at the time of writing – still being broadcast on US, UK and French cable TV. The series has been praised by academics and fans for its construction of believable characters and its creative language, 'Buffyspeak' or 'Slayerspeak', characterized by neologisms, humour, and slang. The following sections thus introduce the 'Buffyverse' in order to contextualize the ensuing translation analysis.

5.2 Genre

BtVS borrows from the repertory of the fantastic and also plays on a mixture of genres: 'action, horror/vampire, comedy, science fiction, the gothic, teen drama, and melodrama' (Jowett 2005: 10). The series therefore mixes the genre of fantasy and horror, but rather than traditional fantasy texts which tend to take place in a complete narrative world of their own e.g. *The Lord of the Rings* (J. R. R. Tolkien, 1954), *BtVS* very much belongs to the 'fantastic';

it is set in our world, albeit one where it is accepted that supernatural events take place. *BtVS* is also very akin to the science fiction theme of alternative history: it portrays our world with certain events slightly altered, or with certain rules no longer applying, i.e. supernatural elements are at work. Hence, *BtVS* combines various genres not only because of the way the show engages with the themes of the fantastic (vampires, witches, werewolves), but also in how it engages with science and technology – especially in seasons four and five, featuring mysterious military forces and the robot Adam created by the scientists from the Initiative.

As the show follows Buffy's life for seven years, *BtVS* is essentially about growing up in general and Buffy's development in particular. Thus, at 'a literal level' the series 'functions as a coming-of-age story about a girl with superpowers', while 'at the metaphorical level it deals with the fundamental themes of existence that haunt the post-modern condition' (Amy-Chinn and Williamson 2005: 280). Throughout the series, issues that are central to growing up are explored and Buffy's world is particularly special as:

> [the] problems teenagers face become literal monsters. Internet predators are demons; drink-doctoring frat-boys have sold their souls for success in the business world; a girl who has sex with even the nicest-seeming boy discovers that he afterwards becomes a monster. (Wilcox 1999: 16)

BtVS therefore deals with real life problems through the use of metaphors, from family break-ups ('Nightmares', 1.10) to domestic violence ('I Only Have Eyes For You', 2.19), drug addiction ('Wrecked', 6.10), homelessness ('Anne', 3.1) and even the death of a parent ('The Body', 5.16). For many scholars, these metaphors are the reason why the show has engaged and continues to engage viewers around the world. For instance, Tracy Little comments that such metaphors:

> have the capacity to help viewers put their own fears and emotions into perspective, deal with such fears and emotions in a more effective way, to provide a point of comparison with the reality of the viewer and that of the show, to recognise that the fears and the emotions played out by the show's characters may be similar to their own, and, finally, to legitimize the feelings of the viewer. The complex nature

of such metaphors also allows for multiple interpretations on the part of the viewer, providing the viewer with a means of agency for interacting with the show on a deeply personal level. (2003: 284)

In Buffy's world, then, 'facing one's demons' has both a literal and meta-phorical meaning (Bloustien 2002: 430) and 'the intertwining of social realism, motifs from neo-gothic fantasy and distancing humour and excess [...] gives the programme its particular tonal complexity and global visceral appeal' (ibid.). For these reasons, it seems that, thematically speaking, *BtVS* should be a straightforward show to translate for other cultures, since it is centred around experiences that all adolescents and young adults have gone or are going through. Indeed, the major success of *BtVS* worldwide does testify to its global appeal, and we shall see later on how certain specific elements of the show have survived in the French dubbed version.

5.3   *Buffy the Vampire Slayer* in America and the UK

BtVS is considered to be a niche show 'whose rich, intertextual narrative was designed to attract a large, literate and educated fandom' (Williamson 2005: 91). Specifically, one of the main elements for the 'intellectual fasci-nation with Buffy is its multilayered, esoteric, self-conscious referencing of classic texts as well as popular culture' (Bloustien 2002: 429). By creat-ing *BtVS*, Whedon has even gained the status of 'auteur', with Hills and Williams (2005) and Wilcox (2005: 162) noting that *BtVS* is 'generally seen as auteur television'. This status was confirmed when he created *BtVS*'s spin-off *Angel* (1999–2004) and *Firefly* (2002), both of which have received critical acclaim (Amy-Chinn and Williamson 2005: 273).[1] All of these elements make *BtVS* fit into the category of 'quality television' (McCabe and Akass 2007), defined by Robert Thompson in the following terms:

---

1   More recently, he has directed *The Avengers* (2012) and is a co-creator of the US TV
       series *Marvel's Agents of S.H.I.E.L.D* (2013).

[I]t is produced by experienced professionals or what are sometimes called television 'auteurs', it attracts a particular (educated, professional) audience, and it may initially be unappreciated or struggle for success. Formal identifiers include an ensemble cast allowing for multiple plot lines, a 'memory' enabling plot lines or characters to develop over time [...], a mixture of genres, a more literary style than other television shows, self-conscious references to culture and popular culture, incorporation of controversial subjects, and aspirations to realism. The final identifier is that all of the above result in achievement and critical appreciation. (1997: 13–16)

In America, *BtVS* was first broadcast on Warner Bros (premiere date: 10 March 1997), before moving to UPN (2001–3). In the UK, it was aired on Sky One and on the terrestrial channel BBC2, while at the time of writing it is still being shown on Syfy. *BtVS* was and still is a 'global phenomenon' (Wilcox 2005: 98), having enjoyed considerable success worldwide and still attracting a faithful fan base ten years after the airing of its final episode, as discussed in Jennifer Stuller's recent publication *Fan Phenomena: Buffy the Vampire Slayer* (2013), which testifies to the continuing dedication and admiration of fans for the show.

There is a proliferation of online fansites, blogs, chatrooms and forums such as http://allaboutspike.com and http://slayage.com in which Buffyphiles and 'cyber slayerettes' have been, and are still, discussing the show's developments and direction:

> *Buffy*'s fans construct web pages and engage in internet discussions about character and story arcs, they debate the politics of the show, and interpret subtexts. In this sense fan activity is not dissimilar to the academic activity surrounding *Buffy* (including of course this chapter). (Williamson 2005: 95)

When the show was in production, Whedon was aware of this fan base and is well-known for actively engaging with fandom on the internet (Hills and Williams 2005), even 'court[ing] fandom' by using 'inter-textual references', giving an 'invitation to bring your own subtext', and by interacting with 'fans on the internet' (ibid.). For instance, as we shall see in *5.5.1*, it was when Whedon realized how important Spike was to *BtVS* fans that he decided to keep the character around beyond season two.

Success or popularity can also be perceived through merchandising. As a matter of fact, *BtVS*:

continues to be a thriving source of licensing and merchandising revenue, with large numbers of websites selling everything from DVDs, video games, posters, photos, stickers, patches and jewelleries, to life-size cardboard stand-up figures of the show's stars, mobile phone ringtones, stationary sets, spin-off novels, guidebooks and fridge magnets. (Amy Chinn and Williamson 2005: 277)[2]

The show has also received a great deal of attention in various fields of academia, including Film Studies and Cultural Studies.[3] Turnbull (2004) notes that there are twelve serious academic books and one online journal devoted to *BtVS*, while Lavery (2004) makes reference to '390 scholar/ fans and fan/scholars' meeting at the Slayage conference in May 2004, which 'clearly identified itself as an academic conference' (Burr 2005: 376) but also attracted numerous fans and book stands presenting "fannish" publications, including copies of [a] *Buffy* magazine' and 'conference "merchandise": Slayage tote bags, T-shirts and posters' (2005: 377). There have also been seven international conferences on Buffy held in the UK, US and Australia. The sheer volume of work on *BtVS* testifies to its popularity and ongoing success.

BtVS has therefore become a cult TV series, successful at various levels and attracting a lot of attention from fans and academics alike, even if these fan/scholars have been criticized by Levine and Schneider (2003) for their failure to maintain critical distance in studying *BtVS* and their often 'unreflective' and 'narrow' scholarship (ibid.: 301), as well as for being pseudo-academic. *Buffy*

> has generated scores of academic articles, texts, anthology contributions and even a few academic websites. Joss Whedon won an Emmy award for the episode of *Buffy* entitled 'Hush' and a Saturn award for Best Genre Network Series. *Buffy* was ranked among the top ten shows by USA Today; it was ranked as number five by *TV Guide* and *Entertainment Weekly* called it 'the best drama on television'. *Buffy* was Warner Bros' second rated show and it's [sic.] most prestigious – the one that 'consistently lands on the critics' best lists (Poniewozik 2001: 1). These plaudits contribute to the

---

2   There are also comics and dolls.
3   See, for instance, Thomas (2006), Turnbull (2005), Bloustien (2002) and the special issue on Spike in *The European Journal of Cultural Studies 8.3.*

networks brand image as 'quality' and this (indirectly) helps viewer ratings among the desired demographics. (Jowett 2005: 91)[4]

Hence, the series' legacy and success are easily traceable through these paratexts, which offer a wealth of information that help one understand how audiences have experienced and continue to experience the show. Let us now consider the show's reception abroad.

5.4 Buffy's cross-cultural appeal

BtVS' worldwide success has been highlighted in many studies, including Geraldine Bloustien (2002), who presents results from work she conducted with fans of the series from the USA, Australia, UK, Israel and Spain 'through endless communications via global website fan bases and email' (2002: 428). Bloustien explains that, in 2002, there were '3705 global *Buffy* and *Angel* websites', in the USA, UK, Holland, Portugal, Spain, Italy, Sweden, Israel, Germany and Brazil. Amy-Chinn and Williamson also note that in 2005, two years after the show ended, there were still:

> 3973 sites dedicated to *Buffy* and *Angel*, including 1094 general *BtVS* sites, 627 sites featuring fan fiction from the two series and 612 sites focusing on the cast. (2005: 276)

They also comment that '[o]f these, 68 focus on Spike and/or James Marsters, with only Buffy and/or Sarah Michelle Gellar herself having more fan sites' (ibid.), another reason why Spike has been chosen for my own case studies.

Bloustien reports that the series has been screened in Argentina, Australia, Brazil, China, Denmark, Finland, Hungary, Israel, Japan, the

---

4   For more on this, see Williamson (2005), Nielsen in Amy-Chinn and Williamson (2005), Wilcox (2005), McCabe and Akass (2007) and Thompson (2003).

Netherlands, Norway, Poland, Portugal, Spain and Sweden (2002: 428),[5] while France, Canada, Switzerland and Belgium can all be added to her list. Bloustien's article focuses on fandom and essentially tries to understand why *BtVS* has been so popular by considering the experience of viewers and exploring their relationships with the show. According to Bloustien, *BtVS*'s success has been:

> possible since (televisual) speculative fictions such as *BtVS* can resonate with the adolescent experience – albeit nuanced by gender, ethnicity, race and class – even in social contexts far from their geographic origin. Indeed, as claimed previously, it is the power of fantasy and magic in these programmes that makes them so 'real' for many viewers and fans. (ibid. 428)

BtVS's cross-cultural appeal is undeniable. When Wilcox (2005: 97) consulted a fan site in 2003, she found that it 'listed contributions from fans from thirty-eight countries', and when David Lavery invited 'readers of *Slayage* to send in brief reports of their ways of "Discovering *Buffy*"', they 'received responses from viewers from all the regions of the USA, from England, Canada, Australia, Wales, New Zealand, Sweden, Ireland, Scotland, Israel, and Latvia; from people who have viewed *Buffy* in Germany, Malaysia, Japan, and the Czech Republic' (ibid.). As mentioned previously, the show's themes seem to have eased the way for its worldwide proliferation. However, it is still worth questioning what happens to the 'language' of the show in dubbed and subtitled versions since translation is not a transparent process.

One of the most praised aspects of *BtVS* is its use of creative language, called 'Buffyspeak' or 'Slayerspeak'. Buffyspeak is principally characterized by its use of humour, i.e. the 'ludic elements of Buffy's language', which include the use of neologisms (Wilcox 2005: 18) and slang (Adams 2003). For Wilcox, Buffyspeak is 'daring' (ibid.: 29) and gleeful, 'language [...] always [being] a matter of delight in *Buffy*' (Wilcox 2005: 18). Characters in the show are very much aware of their linguistic ability; Xander, for

---

5   Buffy reached Denmark and Norway in 1997, Germany in 1998, Spain, Hungary and Portugal in 1999 and Italy and Sweden in 2000.

instance, tells Willow that: 'I've always been amazed with how Buffy fights, but in a way I feel like we took her punning for granted' [Anne (3.1)]. This type of self-reflectivity is also an important element of the show's success.

When it comes to the language of the show, I am particularly interested in the opposition between British English and American English, since there are two British characters (Rupert Giles and Spike) whose characterization is primarily based on accent, vocabulary and cultural differences. When introducing the characters in *5.5*, I will therefore take this opposition into consideration and, where appropriate, mention other aspects of Buffyspeak such as humour and creative language (including slang).

In France, *Buffy contre les Vampires* ('Buffy against the vampires', my translation) first aired on 3 April 1998 on Série club (cable television); it also aired on M6 (terrestrial TV). At the time of writing, the series is still being aired on the cable channel TEVA. On terrestrial television, the programme was mostly on after 10.00pm, although for a short time it screened at 7.00pm. Even though France is traditionally seen as a 'dubbing country', there are two versions available: a dubbed one and a subtitled one. The subtitled version was shown on cable TV and the dubbed version on terrestrial and cable TV alike. Both versions are also available on the DVD destined to the French market.[6] The existence of these two translated versions provides interesting material for research into characterization and particularly into dubbing, since voices, accents and vocabulary will all undergo changes. As voices and accents remain the same in the case of subtitling, I am focusing mainly on the dubbed version given my interest in voice, although I may comment on the subtitled one for the purposes of comparison. It is important to note, however, that subtitling and dubbing have been undertaken by different companies. Differences between the two versions can therefore be linked to the distribution companies, the channel that broadcast the show and programming choices. The dubbing was

6   Region 1 DVD with Spanish, Dutch and French audio track; Region 2 with Danish, Finnish, Norwegian and Swedish audio track.

undertaken by PRODAC (seasons one to four)/LIBRA FILMS (seasons
five to seven) and the subtitling by Visiontext.[7]

There is no denying that the French versions of *BtVS* have been very
well received. This can be seen in the existence of many sites and blogs used
by French viewers to express their love for the show (e.g. M6 Forum). There
seems, however, to be a tendency among French fans to prefer the subtitled
version to the dubbed one. This may be because, as seen previously, *BtVS*
addresses a specific audience: fans of Whedon who are very sensitive to
his style. The musical episode ('Once More With Feeling', season six) is
a case in point; there are many comments from viewers expressing their
dislike for the dubbed version. I feel it is important to emphasize that the
work of all the agents contributing to the dubbing and subtitling process
is colossal and that without these professionals, foreign works would not
be able to travel and be seen by new audiences. It is thus not my goal to
criticize excessively the work of these professionals; rather, I wish to show
how challenging the translation of AV products is. This being said, when
comparing the original and dubbed version in terms of performance, I
will make a judgment if the choices take us too far away from the original
characters. First, however, I will introduce the characters used in my case
studies.

5.5 Characters

Buffy is surrounded by a group of friends who help her fight evil; this
group is collectively called the 'Scoobies' or Scooby Gang, a name that pays
homage to the US TV show *Scooby Doo*. At the centre of the Scoobies are

---

7   Sociétés: Prodac (saisons 1–4) – Libra Films (saisons 5–7). Direction: Philippe
     Peythieu, Sophie Arthuys, Emmanuelle Bondeville & Laurence Crouzet – Catherine
     Le Lann. Adaptation: Sophie Arthuys, Laurence Crouzet, Monique Nevers – Aziza
     Hellal, Franco Quaglia, Laurent Gourdon.

Willow Rosenberg and Xander Harris. When we meet both of them in season one, they are called 'losers' by their peers; however, Willow develops from being a geek to being a powerful witch ('Wicca'), and although Xander does not possess any 'superhero' power, he is a full-blown member of the team. The team also includes Rupert Giles (who is always simply called Giles), Buffy's Watcher. Giles has been appointed by the Council of Watchers, a British institution which oversees the job of the Slayer. As the series develops, other characters come and go from the gang: Cordelia Chase (a popular cheerleader, seasons one to three), Oz (Willow's werewolf boyfriend, seasons three to four), Riley Finn (Buffy's boyfriend, seasons four to five), Tara (Willow's girlfriend, seasons four to six), Anya/Anyanka (a fallen vengeance demon who becomes Xander's girlfriend, seasons three to seven). Beginning in season five, Buffy is 'given' a sister, Dawn. Buffy is also helped by two vampires who are at various times her enemies or lovers: Angel/Angelus/Liam (a vampire with a soul), who is her boyfriend and nemesis in seasons one to three, and Spike/William the Bloody, a distinctively English vampire who appears from season two and goes on to become Buffy's lover in season six. For my case studies, I have singled out three characters: Spike, whose use of British English is an important aspect of his personality and who will be examined first; Giles, the other Brit in the show, albeit with a different accent, and finally Buffy herself as the show's eponymous character.

5.5.1 Spike

The 'marvellously irritating' Spike (Wilcox 2005: 33) is a one-hundred-and-twenty year old British vampire played by American actor James Marsters. Whedon had first created Spike as an 'expendable' adversary or 'temporary villain' (Amy-Chinn and Williamson 2005: 278) who was slated to appear in one season (season two) and then was due to be 'killed off in the original scripts' (Havens 2003: 43). However, Whedon decided to keep him around when he found out how popular Spike was (ibid.). Spike first appears in 'School Hard' (2.3), arriving to Sunnydale with his vampire girlfriend Drusilla. Spike then leaves town, reappearing in only one episode of season three ('Lovers Walk', 3.8). When he returns again in season four, he is arrested by the Initiative, a group of military scientists who capture demons and neutralize them by planting 'chips' into their brain in order to render them harmless. Spike escapes but can no longer harm humans thanks to the chip. Towards the end of the season, Spike realizes that he can still harm demons and becomes part of the Scooby Gang. Spike then becomes the main vampire character from season four onwards, and in seasons six and seven he is a central character of *BtVS*.

Spike is particularly interesting to analyse from a translation point of view because of his English descent. For an American viewer, Spike is reminiscent of punk vampires as seen in *The Lost Boys* (Joel Schumacher 1987). However, the punk associations go even beyond that; Spike is a:

> peculiarly American interpretation of the 1980s English punk, and in fact pulls directly on the image of Billy Idol. He looks and dresses like Billy Idol, and affects the same self-conscious irony of camp. He even speaks like Billy Idol in a put-on mock cockney accent, or 'mockney'. That plays up to American preconceptions of the English bad-boy. (Williamson: 2005: 72)

Spike's otherness is therefore conveyed through a fascinating visual and linguistic performance of a stereotypical impression of English punk. *Mise-en-scène* is used to create Spike's different personas: 'costume and make-up are significant to Spike throughout the series in terms of consistency of style and look' (Abbott 2005: 336). He is 'generally depicted in a set costume: black leather coat, black jeans, boots, T-shirt, red shirt hanging loose and open, slicked back, bleached blond hair and black fingernail polish' (ibid.: 337). Spike is Sunnydale's bad boy; a 'cheerfully vicious black-leather-wearing punk with peroxide blond hair' (Wilcox 2005: 81).

As a human, Spike lived in Victorian times, was called William and belonged to an upper middle-class family. However, William loses his upper middle-class accent when he becomes a vampire, with Spike adopting a lower-class accent. The aristocratic English vampire is an important archetype that has been described at length in vampire studies (see, for instance, Gelder 1994). However, Spike does not conform to this archetype; he is cooler than that. Becoming working-class is an act of rebellion against what and who he was. As a vampire, then, Spike:

reinvents himself [...] adopting a working-class persona and becoming a fearsome killer. Over the course of more than 100 years he makes himself the scourge of Europe, and manages to kill two of Buffy's Slayer predecessors – one in 1900 during the Boxer Rebellion in China and another one in New York in 1977. (Amy-Chinn and Williamson 2005: 279)

Spike is also characterized by his use of humourous language in his vampire life. Williamson notes (2005: 73) that this links him more to the 'Scooby Gang' than it does to the vampire world: '[h]is sardonic one-liners and blasé posturing establish him as dangerously close to Buffy and her evil-fighters, the so-called Slayerettes or Scooby Gang' (Boyette 2001: online). He is an 'ironicist' (ibid.), wondering 'what's on TV' after he has killed a victim or calling the Master the 'Annoying One' instead of the 'Anointed One' ('School Hard', 2.3). Spike is 'irreverent towards outdated vampire lore' (Williamson 2005: 73) and mocks it on various occasions. Thus, humour plays an important part in the sympathy that Spike creates in the audience and viewers.

Within the Buffyverse and beyond it, Spike is a 'star' who has gained this status through his performance. After Buffy, he is the second most important character in terms of fandom: 'a great deal of the fandom for the series, including fan fiction, websites, convention attendances and so on, centres on the vampire Spike' (Williamson 2005: 72). There are many websites dedicated to Spike such as the Bloody Awful Poets' Society and Tabula Rasa (http://btvs-tabularasa.net/), which 'have been set up to champion the character and argue for his "redemption"' (Hills and Williams 2005: 345). Hills and Williams explain that his fame and 'fan adoration' is such that he received a 'full-page advert in the 24 March 2003 issue of *Variety* magazine, thanking the actor for his work on *BtVS* and his "unflagging generosity to his fans"' (2005: 346).

As a matter of fact, audiences know far more about Spike than they do about James Marsters, the actor playing him. Fiske (1991: 150) explains that 'television personalities merge into their characters or are submerged by them'. This is precisely what has happened to Marsters, Spike's 'earthly representative' (Williamson 2005a: 301). Thanks to *BtVS*, Marsters has become a cult TV celebrity (Hills and Williams 2005: 347), 'recognized and revered by many *BtVS* and *Angel* fans [...] [H]owever, he has little cultural currency outside those fandoms' (ibid.: 348). There is nevertheless a very important difference between the actor and his character: Marsters is American and does not have an English accent.

This type of fan identification raises the question of voice in translation, and more specifically that of what happens to the audience's engagement if a character speaks a different language and has a different voice. Will this engagement then be different? This seems a likely outcome, and Marsters' performance is certainly worth investigating further.

In her article 'Moments of Inspiration. Performing Spike', Turnbull (2005) describes the moment she first saw Spike on-screen and refers to her experience in terms of *ekphrasis*; that is, 'the verbal representation of visual representation' (Stern and Kouvaros (1999: 10). The first time Spike appears in the show, we see him spying on Buffy. Turnbull explains how:

> [h]e appears out of the darkness and the music stops. He circles the dancefloor, his eyes fixed only on her. But she is oblivious to his gaze, dancing and laughing to her own tune. He is hunting, he circles his prey, and I realise I am holding my breath. Something is happening and Spike is making it happen. (2005: 367)

The effect of Marsters/Spike's performance is powerful and transformative. For Turnbull, those moments when you hold your breath are:

> moments of suspension when we forget who and where we are just for a moment. Moments where we lose the rhythm of our own breath and breathe with and through the performance of actors [...] [A] moment which inspires and transforms us. (2005: 369)

Turnbull emphasizes that spectators engage with the '"embodied performance" of a character' and that this is 'the basis for fan engagement in the show' (ibid.: 367). Her account is interesting on three levels; firstly, because she emphasizes the powerful effect that Marsters' performance of Spike had on her, therefore emphasizing the importance of performance when understanding Spike's characterization and the impact he has (had) on viewers. Indeed, 'through his initial moment of performance Marsters breathed life into Spike, infusing the character with desires and agency which transcended the text' (ibid.: 372). Secondly, her comments remind us of the difficulty of turning feeling into words, highlighted in Chapters 1 and 2. In her own words, Turnbull is trying to capture what this experience felt like 'to make you feel the same way, [...] to recover and relive whatever it was that I experienced in the first place' (2005: 368). This highlights the double difficulty of describing film: recalling our experience and conveying it to others; a timely reminder before moving on to the analysis in Chapter 6. The final level concerns vocal release, as defined by Smith (2007) and as seen in Chapter 3. Marsters' performance of Spike conveys a powerful feeling through his voice, and it is worth wondering what happens in a dubbing context.

Therefore, '[o]ur understanding of Spike depends upon a number of extratextual factors: intertextual pop culture references, allusions to musical subcultures; and knowledge of the actor James Marsters, who plays him' (Amy-Chinn and Williamson 2005: 275). Marsters' linguistic and visual performance of Spike makes him an interesting character to analyse in translation.[8] Like Count Dracula, Spike is a '"cosmopolitan" or internationalized character who is excessive to national identities' (Gelder 1994: 23). He is also 'fiercely nationalistic' and has a 'strange intonation' (ibid.: 12). However, unlike Dracula, Spike does not want to blend in. He is British and wants to stay British. Throughout the show, he uses British English vocabulary and refers to England as his home. Spike is the English bad boy of American Sunnydale; he is irreverent, smokes, drinks and wears a signature black leather coat. He is both visually identifiable as a bad boy as well as through his speech. In translation, the visuals do not change; Spike still has his coat and his peroxide blond hair. However, important aspects do change; when dubbed, his voice and signature accent are different, as is the way he expresses himself. The question that must then be posed is how translation affects Spike's complex persona, one which is based on otherness?

8   For more on Spike, see – for instance – Wilcox (2002, 2005), Turnbull (2005), Amy-Chinn and Williamson (2005), Williamson (2005, 2005a), Jowett (2005), Boyette (2001), Wilcox (2002 and 2005), Abbott (2001 and 2005) and Fossey (2003).

5.5.2 Giles

The second character we will be taking into consideration is Rupert Giles, Buffy's Watcher, who is played by the British actor Anthony Stewart Head. Giles is a librarian in Buffy's high school and first appears in the pilot episode. When Buffy graduates and goes to college in the same city, Giles remains in his guiding position even after he is fired by the Council of Watchers. Giles is a 'reserved character' (Jowett 2005: 127) and the 'oldest [human] character in the team' (ibid.), although Angel and Spike, century-old vampires, are in fact older than him. Jowett comments that his age is 'highlighted by his traditional dress and speech (also related to his Britishness). Even in the early seasons, however, when he is at his most tweedy, Giles (and the show) is aware of this' (ibid.). Britishness is therefore an important aspect of Giles' characterization, although the connotations are different than Spike's. In Giles' case, Britishness mainly means being old fashioned and cultivated.

Relatively little has been written on Giles in comparison with Spike. Some studies, however, point out that Giles' most important role is to act as a father figure for Buffy. Giles is seen as a nurturer not only for Buffy but for the whole gang (e.g. Jowett 2005, Wilcox 2005), supporting the teenagers in moments of crisis. Indeed, in a show that presents a clear divide between adults' lives and teenagers, Giles is an 'integral part of the team and someone who understands what Buffy really is' (Jowett 2005: 183).

In terms of Britishness – my main concern when considering Giles – his posh accent and register are definitive parts of his character. Giles may be the father figure in the show and embody culture and stability, but he has had a tumultuous past that on some occasions comes back to haunt him. His alter ego in his 'past' life was called 'Ripper', about whom Jowett notes that:

> his language, like Giles', signals his difference, but it also signals a difference *from* Giles: the received pronunciation of the privileged and educated Brit in replaced in Ripper by a (rather exaggerated) generic southern English working-class 'accent'. (2005: 129)

Anthony Stewart Head, as opposed to James Marsters, is actually English and was used as a reference point by *BtVS*'s writers to pinpoint and establish Britishness in the dialogue. Stewart Head explains his role in an interview in *The Sunday Times*, in answer to the question: 'What do you think of Juliet Landau's Britpunk accent for Drusilla the vampire?':

> I think it's good. I spend a lot of time introducing British words into the script. I'm proud to have got 'pillock' in there. And I got 'bollocks' in as well, because Americans don't know what it means. James Marsters [...] said it in one episode – although they wrote it into the script as 'bollix', and that's how he pronounced it, so I had to correct them. Joss Whedon [...] is a real Anglophile. He lived in the UK, and he even did A-levels. He has started hosting Shakespeare readings every weekend where cast, crew and friends go over and do a whole play. (2001: 5)

Stewart Head had many roles on British television before landing the part of Giles and is also a talented singer. When listening to him in other roles or in interviews, one can hear that Stewart Head does not sound exactly like Giles; Giles' accent is actually an exaggerated performance of his own. In an interview with *Entertainment Weekly*, after the journalist Stephen Armstrong points out to Stewart Head that he does not have Giles' 'posh accent' (online), the actor comments:

> I'm kind of a long way from Giles in a lot of ways, which people realize when I walk in the door with my earring and my jeans and everything. But over the years, Giles has gotten a little closer to me, becoming a little hipper and a little funkier. (Armstrong 2000)

In terms of characterization, then, Spike' and Giles' marked vocabulary and British accents have a specific function and cast them into particular roles. However, both characters come from different social backgrounds, as is made evident by their accents and use of vocabulary. In my case studies, I will show what happens to Spike's and Giles' accents in the French translation, as well as what becomes of the marked vocabulary that they use. In order to identify the influence of the translators' choices on our perception of the characters, the focus will be on the translation of Britishness (and related British cultural elements), humour and interpersonal relationships in an excerpt from the episode 'Tabula Rasa' (6.8). The results will be interpreted by taking translation problems into consideration in terms of language as well as audiovisual constraints (lip sync, dialogue length/reading time). Let us now briefly introduce our heroine, Buffy.

5.5.3 Buffy

As mentioned previously, Buffy Summers at first glance appears to be a typical teenager but she is in fact the Chosen One, the Slayer. Buffy arrives in Sunnydale after being expelled from her previous school for setting the gym on fire. Because of the way she looks and her conversation style, popular girl Cordelia Chase initially singles her out to be part of her group of 'in girls'. However, Buffy does not follow Cordelia's advice to avoid well-known 'losers' Willow Rosenberg and Xander Harris, and by befriending them she also becomes a 'loser' – to all appearances, that is.

The main two adjectives used to describe Buffy by fans and academics alike are 'feminine' and 'powerful'. She is the 'action hero' of the show, joining 'femininity and feminism' (Jowett 2005: 21). *BtVS* is about Buffy's powerful and all-important role in the world, but also about the impression she gives. There is an obvious play on the character type that Buffy represents. Bellafante explains that '[t]he original idea for Buffy came to Whedon after years spent watching horror movies in which "bubblehead blonds wandered into dark alleys and got murdered by some creature" [...] [He said:] "I would love to see a movie in which a blond wanders into a dark alley, takes care of herself and deploys her powers"' (1997: 2). Indeed, Buffy is the stereotypical pretty blonde cast in American horror movies – a 'meek little girlie-girl', according to Willow in 'Phases' (2.15) – who is supposed to get killed at the beginning of traditional horror movies, whereas in 'reality' she is the one who can look after herself and everybody else.

There is also a tradition of vampire films in which the slayers are men, e.g. the famous Dr Van Helsing in *Dracula*. Buffy is an example of role reversal; she is the 'thing that monsters have nightmares about' ('Showtime', 7.11). Nevertheless, on many occasions Buffy plays up to the stereotype of the 'dumb blonde': her voice becomes very high pitched, her tone unsophisticated and she makes silly remarks about having to change into something more comfortable to fight demons or being able to recognize vampires simply because of their dress style. Buffy is well-known for her snappy comments and remarks. Bloustien comments that 'the "professional" trademark of Buffy, the petulant teenage slayer and eponymous heroine of the series, is known to be her witty repartee as she fights and just before she slays her demonic enemies' (2002: 436). This is alluded to on many occasions in the series, e.g. Xander's previously mentioned comment used or Anya's remark: 'Don't you have a clever retort for me? [...] Or is this like one of your little pop-culture references I don't get' ('Selfless', 7.05).

Buffy is played by the American actress Sarah Michelle Gellar. Before landing the role of Buffy, Gellar was not very well known, but *BtVS* was such a phenomenal success and Sarah Michelle Gellar's fan following so great that, according to Stephen Shaviro, Gellar 'will never escape her identification as *Buffy the Vampire Slayer*' (2010: 90). As a matter of fact, since being cast on *BtVS* Gellar has starred in a few horror films such as *I Know What you Did Last Summer* (Jim Gillespie 1997) and the American version of *The Grudge* (Takashi Shimizu 2004), while more recently she starred in the American TV series Ringer (CW, 2011–12). However, her major claim to fame remains *BtVS*, and it would indeed seem that she will always be remembered as the girl who breathed life into Joss Whedon's beloved character.

5.6 Conclusion

This chapter has introduced *BtVS*, emphasizing the show's global appeal and the characterization of Spike, Giles and Buffy in terms of nationalities, accents and stereotypes. Before moving on to the next section, I would like to emphasize my position as a French viewer of *BtVS*. In the same way as Jowett highlights that her 'position as a British viewer of *Buffy* also inevitably affects her viewing practice and her 'perception of the show' (2005: 8), I am aware that I am a French viewer who has been watching *BtVS* in the UK. I have discovered the show in its original version and as a viewer, as opposed to a researcher; I have only occasionally watched the dubbed version. I have therefore grown used to the original characters' voices and my encounter with the dubbed version has been, to say the least, uncanny. To my ears, the voices of French Spike and French Buffy do not really fit the original actors' bodies. For instance, Buffy sounds more sophisticated than her US counterpart and Spike's neutral French accent and vocabulary make him blend rather too smoothly into his new surroundings. In the next section, then, dubbed scenes from two episodes of the series, 'Once More With Feeling' and 'Tabula Rasa', will be scrutinized to see how dubbing really affects the actors' performances and their portrayal of the characters. This investigation of how Buffy and other characters come across in English and French will be realized through a multimodal analysis of verbal and non-verbal elements, including voice characteristics (e.g. vocabulary choices) and cinematography.

CHAPTER 6

Uncanny encounters: A multimodal analysis

6.1 Introduction

The aim of this chapter is to put into practice the multimodal model I have created for analysing audiovisual material, taking into consideration the acoustic and visual elements that comprise a filmic performance. This analytical model has been designed to help to identify aspects of characterization in audiovisual texts as well as in their translations to see if there are any shifts between the way characters are created and presented in the source and target audiovisual texts. Furthermore, one of my main goals is to bring more attention to the challenges involved in reading and translating original AV products.

The analysis considers pure dialogue as well as music-specific dialogue, as songs, like dialogue, can function as 'narrational device(s)' (Garwood, 2006: 93); that is, as narrative elements just like characters, objects, settings, shot composition and editing, and therefore contribute to characterization and plot development. I will be considering spoken and sung dialogue in the US television series *Buffy the Vampire Slayer* and its French dubbed version.

I have previously emphasized that performance is historically and culturally bound, the consequence being that audiences worldwide can be expected to interpret a performance according to their own specific historical and cultural backgrounds. Moreover, it is no secret that there is a common understanding among the general public that translations should be equivalent products to their original. Against this background, it is important to analyse translation to see what happens to what is assumed to be the same or a similar performance. In the context of this book, I therefore propose to uncover what happens to the characterization of Gellar/ Buffy, Marsters/Spike and Stewart Head/Giles in the French dubbed versions of the show, given that the actors have been given new voices in translation. The analysis sets out to show how dubbing has impacted on Buffy's, Giles' and Spike's characterization and how their performances can be read within a French context through a multimodal analysis of their performances.

Shots and scenes will be described meticulously and attentively from a visual and acoustic perspective, in line with Klevan's advice on how to sustain attention in a performance, as seen in Chapter 2. My study will focus on kinesics and paralinguistic information as they work together to create characters or actors' performances. The focus of the analysis will be on the interaction between the characters, the way they speak to and look at each other, their hand gestures, the tone of their voices and so on. As opposed to other AVT studies, which have placed more importance on linguistic information, I will include words in my analysis as they are part of the polysemiotic whole; that is, as they combine with images and with the paralinguistic information conveyed by voices. This analysis will also take into consideration dubbing constraints (e.g. lip-synchronization, dialogue length etc.) as well as the structural differences between English and French.

I will concentrate on the way characters come across by looking first at scenes from the original version, highlighting the characters' personas and then comparing these to the French dubbed version in order to identify the influence of the translators' choices on our perception of the characters. Ultimately, I am interested in seeing what happens to characters' distinctive features; i.e. Buffy's superhero/dumb blonde status as well as Giles's and Spike's otherness/Britishness. There are two case studies; one of a scene from *BtVS*'s musical episode 'Once More With Feeling' (season six, episode seven) and the other one from 'Tabula Rasa' (season six, episode eight).

6.2 Case Study One: '*Once More With Feeling*'

6.2.1 From 'Once More With Feeling' *to* 'Que le Spectacle Commence'

As mentioned earlier, Buffy dies at the end of season five, only to be resur-rected by her friends in season six. 'Once More With Feeling' is the seventh episode of this sixth season; Buffy has been alive again for a number of episodes, but all is not well. She is depressed, though her friends do not know exactly why – until this key episode. The audience has known the truth since episode six, when Buffy confided in Spike that, when she was dead, she felt at peace and thought she was in Heaven. 'Once More With Feeling' therefore marks a turning point in the season; this is where the truth comes out. However, the way it does so is peculiar; the characters do so through song, having fallen victim to a spell (cast by a demon called Sweet) that prompts them to sing involuntarily and voice their inner emo-tions. This is far from a 'happy' spell, however; those who have been bot-tling up their emotions for too long run the risk of combusting and dying.

Thus, 'Once More With Feeling' sees the characters burst into song, and as the narrative events are presented in the form of songs, singing becomes a 'mode of representation' (Banfield 1993: 6f, 270). In other words, a '*situation thus becomes labelled, denoted, represented or, if you wish, mod-elled by the song*, and at the same time, *articulated, dissected, and classified* by its respective parts' (Osolsobě, 1984: 1743, his emphasis, in Franzon 2005: 270). The episode is composed of diegetic songs, i.e. songs originating from within the world of the musical. The songs are logocentric since the lyrics are dominant over the music and function as narrational device. The phrase 'once more with feeling' is in fact a rehearsal instruction prompting actors to perform a scene again, albeit this time with greater involvement in the acting process. In French, the equivalent instruction is '*on la refait*' ('let's do it again'), although this was not chosen to be the title of the French version. The English title thus indicates that the episode will be about emotions, opening a window to the characters' inner selves and secret feelings. The diegetic songs, which introduce the narrative events, can thus be 'read' either as addressed monologues or as interior monologues (Albright 2005).

Hence, the fictional world of the episode is shaped around the musical performances and the songs represent the characters' subjectivity and emotional states. The lyrics of all of the songs as interpreted by the cast of *BtVS* are meaningful in terms of the fictional world of the series. The episode marks a turning point not just for Buffy, but also for the rest of the cast; it is the catalyst for Giles leaving for Britain, Tara breaking up with Willow after she realizes Willow has cast a memory-wipe spell on her, Anya and Xander acknowledging their fears about getting married and Spike re-asserting his love for Buffy. However, the most important plot development concerns the heroine: Buffy tells her friends the truth about where she was when she was dead, starts facing up to her feelings for Spike and also realizes that her sister, Dawn, has been stealing from the magic shop.

In terms of film aesthetics, the episode is shot in theatrical widescreen as a homage to Hollywood CinemaScope musicals. Scholars have praised the episode as a unit in its own right, as well as in terms of the series' structure and its production style, which echoed that of 'The Body' (the episode in which Buffy's mother dies), which contained no non-diegetic sound and music and diegetic non-musical sounds (5.16), and 'Hush', which is mostly silent (4.10). Moreover, fans of the series also embraced the idea of a musical episode, as can be seen by looking at the online reaction, for instance:

> wow! i am so looking forward to this! [referring to the forthcoming, season 6, musical episode of Buffy] and i hate musicals as a rule! But i have faith in joss and co. that it will be a very entertaining and funny hour. also, people keep saying 'we know amber can sing.' i'm aware that james marsters and anthony stewart are singers/guitarist but what is the info on amber benson? (kitty-k8, 2008) (in Bloustien 2002: 433)

Like the series as a whole, the episode has enjoyed and continues to enjoy worldwide success, and in the UK it even reached number thirteen in Channel Four's chart of the '100 greatest musicals', as voted for by the station's viewers.

In his DVD commentary (2004), Whedon explains that he drew on the specific talents of the cast when writing the episode. He thus gave important singing roles to Marsters, the lead singer of the American band 'Ghost of the Robot', and to Stewart Head, who is also a singer; as a matter of fact, Giles sings on a couple of other occasions throughout the series, such as in season four when he finds himself unemployed and sings at a Starbucks café in order to make ends meet. Whedon further comments that he gave a minor singing role to Alyson Hannigan (Willow) because of her 'inability' to sing (ibid.), and is very complimentary about the singing and overall performances of Emma Caulfield (who plays Anya) and Amber Benson, who plays Tara. As all of the cast were expected to sing, Gellar also had to perform both solo and group singing; however, she was experiencing difficulties with her singing, leading Whedon to suggest that she could have a voice double. Gellar refused, explaining:

> I basically started to cry and said, 'You mean someone else is going to do my big emotional turning point for the season?' In the end, it was an incredible experience and I'm glad I did it. And I never want to do it again. (Gellar in McCabe 2002: 6)

Gellar's statement is very interesting from a translation point of view. Indeed, in dubbing countries throughout the world, other 'people' have actually voiced Buffy's 'big emotional turning point', with the audience having to suspend disbelief as they listen to the dubbed versions. For them, the Buffy that they watch is seemingly the 'original' Buffy, the one that they see and not the one that they hear, even though they are not watching the series in its original language. In the French dubbed version, the same voice talents who usually work on the series performed the songs. In the particular case of song translation, it is therefore even more pertinent to wonder about the impact of translation on vocal performance. Indeed, how can we expect the French voice singing talents to be perfect matches to what Whedon set out to create and deliver the same performance?

When foreign musical films are released in cinemas in France, their dialogue is usually dubbed while the songs are kept in the original, albeit with subtitles; this was the case with both *Singin' in the Rain* (Gene Kelly, Stanley Donen 1952) and *The Sound of Music* (Robert Wise 1965). In certain instances, however, the whole soundtrack (speech, narration and song alike) is dubbed. This happens with, for instance, Walt Disney movies so that children, their main audience, are not excluded and can enjoy the whole of the performance. Although we are dealing with a TV series, it is somewhat surprising that the entirety of the episode was dubbed, as the technique used to translate adult drama is normally that mentioned previously for *Singin' in the Rain*, and so on.

Comments on Youtube[1] are particularly revealing when unveiling what viewers thought about the French dubbed version; some consider it to be a disaster, while others explain that it seems perfectly natural to have a dubbed version of the full episode, i.e. dialogue and songs alike, since French is the language of the country in which they live; others yet explain that they like the dubbed version but prefer the subtitled one. Buffy in French is dubbed by the actress Claire Guyot, who is also known for having given her voice to Walt Disney's *The Little Mermaid* (1989) and to Lois in *Lois and Clarke* (1993–7). Although there has been some criticism of the quality of French Buffy's singing voice, other viewers have praised it. One commentator in particular offers a very interesting insight: 'I laugh when I see that people love Claire Guyot when she sings in The little mermaid, and there, she sings.. jerk!' (charguigou, online).[2] The following comment contrasts starkly with those who did not like French Buffy's performance: 'Haha, the french dubber was a better singer than the actual Buffy. It goes to make the case for voice actors' (unabomberman, online).[3] This is a noteworthy comment which mirrors my own experience of French Buffy's performance in this episode, as will be shown later in the analysis.

The title of the episode in French is '*Que le Spectacle Commence*' ('Let the Show Begin'). The dubbed version was broadcast on French terrestrial television. My main goal in my analysis is to put into practice the model described in Chapter 4, thereby suggesting a new line of study and paving the way for future research at the intersection of Translation Studies and Film Studies. The ensuing analysis focuses on the penultimate number in the episode, 'Something to Sing About', translated as '*Donnez-moi ma vie*' ('Give me my life'), as this 'song-and-dance sequence' represents Buffy's specific moment of vocal release.

---

1   <http://www.youtube.com/watch?v=YnMrbPx4hNo>.
     <http://www.youtube.com/watch?v=yiiMxZwuYsk>.
2   <http://www.youtube.com/watch?v=k7qTPzJpmnA>.
3   <http://www.youtube.com/watch?v=iojgXgjIfoA>.

As seen in Chapter 4, songs in musicals have an expressive potential. This song, then, can be considered as an integrated number, since 'Something to Sing About':

> comes at a point in the musical narrative when the need for emotional expression has reached a particularly high point. Often this is an expression of feeling which can no longer be contained by the character(s), or an emotion which must be acknowledged and shared in order to progress the narrative (Laing 2000: 7).

In this song, Buffy finally reveals her feelings about having been brought back to life. Although she does not want to, she is compelled to tell the truth to her friends: they have not pulled her out of Hell as they assume, but from Heaven. It is therefore a crucial moment in the series' narrative. The episode then ends with a short duet between Buffy and Spike. From the perspective of traditional musicals, Buffy and Spike are the forming and lead couple; this short duet will thus be included in the analysis since they sing the concluding lines together.

My analysis focuses on the representation of Buffy and Spike by comparing scenes from the original English language version with its French dubbed version. As mentioned previously, the visuals remain the same in the dubbed version, but what does change is the relationship between what is seen (i.e. the camera work, the acting and the dancing) and what is heard: the voices and the singing. I will therefore look at cinematic parameters such as shot composition and paralinguistics (e.g. tone, intonation and pitch of voice), as well as linguistic choices, in order to examine characterization through performance in both versions.

6.2.2 'Something to Sing About'

The scene begins[4] as Buffy enters a room in which the demon Sweet is keeping her sister Dawn, whom he had kidnapped earlier. Buffy is first shot in medium close-up (MCU) as she breaks down the door. Sweet tells her:

---

4   Chapter 13, 38.20.

'I love a good entrance', to which she responds: 'How are you with death scenes?' As she walks in his direction, the MCU becomes a close-up (CU). After this short verbal exchange, she is shot mostly in MCU with the focus on her head and shoulders. She is ready to fight Sweet and has an offer for him: if she wins, he must leave them in peace, but if she fails to kill him, he can take her to his dimension, which she calls 'Hellsville'. Sweet asks her what would happen if he killed her. She tells him, in a deadpan tone: 'Trust me. Won't help.' In other words, there is no point worrying or thinking about this since it would not change anything; her friends would just resurrect her, as they did before. Sweet tells her how gloomy he finds her attitude and she responds: 'That's life.' He then adds: 'Isn't life a miraculous thing?' Buffy answers: 'I think you already know.' She is now shot in a medium shot (MS), so that we can see the whole of her upper body as she begins to sing.

As Buffy/Gellar utters these lines, her voice has a medium-to-high pitch and she uses the lower end of this pitch when trying to be assertive. Her voice is nasal, as though placed in her nose; in other words, it is a head voice as opposed to a chest voice. She sounds bored and disillusioned. Her nasality, most probably related to the fact that she is an untrained singer, may be linked to the sorrows that she feels as a reflection of the fact that she is restraining herself from telling her friends the truth, and has been doing so for many weeks. Her voice is also slightly grainy or raspy, particularly when she says: 'I think you already know' with the near fricative /r/ grating at the back of her throat. The words 'I think' are actually pronounced in a clearer way than the rest of the sentence, putting an emphasis on personal perception (modality). Her voice has a little roughness on some occasions, but is cleaner and slightly higher and more nasal when she is being sarcastic (e.g. in 'Trust me. Won't help') as there is more tension in her voice.

In the French version, Claire Guyot's voice has a lower pitch and is not nasal. Sarcasm can be heard in her voice when she says: '*Et ta sortie tu l'as sens comment?*' ([Back Translation (BT)]: And how do you feel about your exit? [Original Version (OV)]: How are you with death scenes?]; she sounds slightly aggressive and a little peremptory. She actually sounds quite sure of herself in this passage, as opposed to the 'I think' modality of the OV. Her voice is clear or bright, as if coming from the top of her cheeks. There is also no roughness in her voice. It is not grainy or raspy as Gellar's is; it is cleaner, conveying more assurance. For instance, when she says: *'J'crois que tu connais déjà la réponse'* [BT: I believe you already know the answer], there is almost a sense of enjoyment in saying the words, contrasting with the bored tone of the OV. One could say that the plosives /d/, /t/ and /k/ add to the clarity of the sentence. Moreover, the mixture of the voiced /j/ and near fricative /r/ in French does not lead to a rasping sound but a rather soft one. The succession of MCU and CU shots would have put pressure on the translators to find words to match the lip movements. Lip-synchronization seems to have been a high priority for the dubbed version [DV], and it is indeed achieved very well. In terms of performance and characterization, this short initial analysis shows that there are some differences in the way Buffy comes across in English and French; we shall soon see how this develops. My multimodal analysis will use the following symbols: () corresponds to information regarding the type of shot and angle, [] to specific visual information and {} to linguistic information:

Example 1

OV: Life's a show (MS) / And we all play our parts (MS) / And when the music starts (MS) [from 'and', the focus is on Sweet, then back on Buffy when she says 'starts'] / We open up our hearts (MS to LS) [she opens her jacket and drops it on the floor as she says 'hearts'].
It's all right (MS, low shot angle) [starts walking] / If some things come out wrong (MS) [low shot angle; when she says 'wrong', she is looking at the demons to her right] / We'll sing a happy song (MLS to LS, low shot angle to eye-level) / And you can sing along (BCU, eye-level).
DV: La vie {spoken off-screen} / C'est un show (MS) / Où chacun prend sa place (MS) / Et chante sa propre histoire (MS) [focus is on Sweet from 'Où', then back to Buffy on 'histoire'] Au reflet du miroir (MS – LS) [drops jacket on the floor after saying 'mirroir'].
BT: Life / It's a show / In which everyone takes their place / And sings their own story / In the mirror's reflection.
Tout va bien (MS) / Et si parfois tu pleures (MS, long shot angle; on 'pleures', she looks at the demons) / La chanson du bonheur (MLS to LS, low shot angle to eye-level) / Réchauffera ton cœur (BCU, eye-level).
BT: All is well / And if sometimes you cry / The song of happiness / Will warm up your heart.

Buffy/Gellar's first two stanzas constitute the opening lines of the song and remind the audience of the first song she sang in this episode, entitled 'Going Through The Motions', in which she explained that she has been feeling like a puppet going through life mechanically. Here, in 'Something to Sing About', the difference is that she now has to tell the truth to the rest of the world ('When the music starts / We open up our hearts'). The French DV, on the other hand, says that people take their place in life and sing their own story in the reflection of the mirror. Even though the translation retains the notion of role-play, there is no mention of telling the truth. The DV is therefore less informative; it does not reveal the real significance of the songs, i.e. that as a result of a spell, people have to 'open up their hearts'.

As for the visual elements, Buffy is first shot in MCU; then, when she says: 'We open up our hearts', this becomes a long shot (LS) in which we can see her fully. The visual and the verbal mirror one another as she opens her jacket and drops it on the floor. This 'undressing/opening' gesture draws a parallel between her actions and the words she is singing. However, there is no such parallel in the DV since this sentence is not translated literally. Buffy is static until she opens her coat, which would have had an impact on her breathing and the sound of her voice. Additionally, because of the type of shots, sizes and angles, Buffy's mouth movements are very much in focus. She is shot from a slightly low shot angle for the first lines, then at eye-level, while there are many medium shots (MS) and a big close-up (BCU). As mentioned previously, lip-synchronization seems to have been a priority in the dubbing of this episode, and the use of MS and particularly BCU would undoubtedly have led the translators to choose certain words over others in order to match lip movements. The lip-synchronization is flawless most notably on the BCU. Moreover, on top of the lip-sync, the translator's choices also reveal that they mostly focused on creating a 'singable' translation, one in which certain features, such as rhyme and rhythm, were given priority and the lyrics were made to fit with the music. Indeed, the original rhyming pattern (*parts/starts/hearts*) is partly maintained with '*histoire*' and '*miroir*'.

Let us now turn to the quality of the voices. Just as in the spoken dialogue, Buffy/Gellar has a head voice, but her voice is clearer when singing, as though it is coming from the top of her cheeks. Her pitch range is still restricted or restrained, but her pitch is higher. Drawing from Van Leeuwen, we could say that this narrow range conveys a feeling of misery and 'constrains the expression' of her feelings (1999: 160). The higher pitch also conveys the effort it takes to say how she feels, as well as some vulnerability. As there is more tension in her voice, it is consequently higher, sharper and brighter with higher overtones. The nasality heard in the spoken dialogue is still present, albeit less so, and the voice is not rough anymore; it is more polished. The volume of her voice is also higher, or louder, which conveys more power through the voice in singing than in speech. In terms of specific sound quality and consonants, one can hear that in the first line, the words 'life' and 'show' contain voiceless fricatives in the form of /f/ and /sh/ as well as the frictionless fricative /l/, all of which convey a sense of soft friction. Then, as Buffy/Gellar sings 'starts', she lowers her pitch and there is a little roughness in her voice, which again conveys some friction. Buffy/Gellar modulates her voice, particularly on 'parts' and 'starts'. As she says 'hearts' and opens her jacket, her mouth is open wide (BCU), the wide aperture of the vowels combining with the plosives to create an explosive sound visually and acoustically (or orally). Buffy/Gellar uses additional plosives in 'parts', again adding to the 'explosion'. Finally, there is extra friction as the unvoiced fricatives in 'show' and the voiced 'the' can also both be associated with this type of sound.

As in the OV, Buffy/Guyot's voice in the DV is higher in song than in it was in speech. Moreover, Buffy/Guyot's voice is higher than Buffy/Gellar's, with a slightly wider pitch range. Her voice is also more polished than in the OV; it is smoother. There is still some tension in her voice but less so than in the OV. The volume of her voice is high and conveys more power. Buffy/Guyot is venting her feelings in a more assured manner; for instance, she uses a controlled vibrato on *'histoire'*. As in the OV, Guyot lowers her pitch on *'histoire'* (used for 'starts'), but her voice is smoother. In the first line, *'C'est un show'*, the soft friction is replaced by slightly greater 'explosion' because of the plosive /t/. However, the unvoiced fricatives still convey some friction in *'show'*, *'chacun'* and *'chante'*. These are also combined with the plosives /t/ and /k/ and the voiceless plosive – or bilabial – /p/, as well as the near fricative /r/ in *'histoire'*, *'prend'*, *'place'*, *'propre'*, *'reflet'* and *'mirroir'*, all of which contribute to the 'explosive' nature of the song: the truth is about to be told. It is interesting to note, however, that the /s/ in '*place*' is not pronounced at all, leaving the word unfinished and the emphasis more on the plosive.

In the second stanza, Buffy/Gellar's high pitch voice is still tense; she sings loudly and is more nasal towards the end as she invites the audience to join her. She performs modulations, or short vibratos, on 'wrong' and 'song'. This stanza particularly highlights the importance of tone. The original is ironic: if songs could indeed make everything 'all right' then they would have worked for Buffy. Yet Buffy is only singing because the spell is making her do so, and what she ultimately voices is her unhappiness. This irony is conveyed mainly through Buffy's tone. Buffy/Guyot does not sound ironic. When she says '*tout va bien*', her voice is very well placed, and as she takes a breath on '*bien*', she sounds self-assured and in control. Furthermore, Buffy/Guyot is louder than in the previous verse, probably to cover some distance as she starts to move and walk. Her pitch is higher, cleaner than Buffy/Gellar and she is not nasal. Her voice is poised, more controlled and she gets louder as the verse progresses, sounding increasingly more assertive. The plosives in '*parfois*', '*pleures*' and '*cœur*' add to the firmness or confidence of her attitude. At the end of the stanza, Buffy/Gellar addresses the audience directly, saying: 'You can sing along'; a request to interact, with the interaction also being established through her gaze as she looks into the camera in BCU at eye-level. There is no such interaction in the DV; no invitation as she says '*la chanson du bonheur réchauffera ton cœur*'. Hence, the visual information is there, but the complementing verbal invitation is missing.

In the second verse, Buffy is shot in MS (during the first two lines), then in a MLS (third line) and finally in BCU (fourth line), just before she turns her head quickly to the right and begins to fight her enemies. In any type of CU shot, lip movements are very important in determining the vowel formants for the target version, as is apparent in this passage with the /o/ in 'song' and '*cœur*'. The BCU shot frames this one line of the text. In giving priority to lyrics which fit the music, rhymes and vowel formants, the translators may have felt that they had to ignore the verbal address or invitation in the original version. All in all, the DV presents a different picture by claiming that songs do in fact make you feel better by warming up your heart.

Hence, camera work, vocal quality, body gestures and facial expressions, as well as linguistic choices, combine to offer a complex picture of Buffy's character or persona. This attentive analysis of the first two stanzas in the OV and DV demonstrates that, even at this early stage, Buffy's performance – and therefore characterization – is a different experience in translation. The DV does not fully convey Buffy's high-pitched, almost childlike tone and her feelings of helplessness, as Buffy/Guyot has a more mature and assertive voice. The two versions 'sound' and 'feel' different because the combination of the various aspects of performance are altered in translation. We shall now see how this representation of Buffy progresses in the rest of the song.

In the next stanza, Buffy uses a series of clichés to describe her feelings towards life:

Example 2

OV: Where there's life, there's hope (MS/CU) / Every day's a gift (MS/MCU/MS) / Wishes can come true (MS/CU/MCU) / Whistle while you work (MS/MCU) / So hard all day (LS/MS)
DV: Oui l'espoir fait vivre (MS/CU/MS) / remercie le ciel (CU/MS)/ réalise tes rêves (MS/CU/MS) / supporteras, vaillant (MS/CU) / c'est dur d'être (LS)
BT: Yes, hope makes you live / Thank the heavens / Fulfill your dreams / (You) will accept, courageous / It's hard to be.

One can see that the OV has a thematic coherence between the clichés, all of which emphasize aspects of life in the form of short sentences. In the DV, however, '*supporteras, vaillant*' is not obviously coherent. What is clear is that '*vaillant*' was chosen to match Buffy/Gellar's mouth movement, since she is shot in CU at that point. Moreover, the DV establishes a clearer link between this verse and the next, as '*c'est dur d'être*' must be read or listened to in conjunction with '*comme toutes les autres filles*', which kicks off the next stanza.

The music accompanying this series of clichés has a faster rhythm than in the previous stanza and is mainly performed by electric guitars. At the visual level, Buffy can be seen fighting Sweet's minions through a series of kicks. The rhythm of the music and that of her singing is choppy and this is also reflected in the camera work, with the scene shot using a mixture of LS, MLS, MS/MCU and CU. The singing in this portion of the song is actually on the border between talking and shouting. Buffy/Gellar's voice is rougher than in the previous verses. In the first three lines, her pitch is lower, getting higher in the fourth one as more tension can be heard in her voice and she gets louder. Her voice conveys anger, though at the same time she sounds vulnerable. There is an accumulation of plosives, e.g. /d/, /g/, /k/ and /t/, as the words seem to explode from her mouth. The presence of the semi-vowels /w/ and /r/ adds some fluidity to her phrasing as the airflow is unrestricted. Moreover, /r/ can also be seen as a near fricative, adding to this feeling of anger and vulnerability.

Buffy/Guyot's voice is rougher and she shouts more than in the previous verses. If one listens attentively, it can be heard that her breath mixes with her voice as she moves and fights. As opposed to the OV, her tone and voice remains steady throughout the delivery and she does not sound vulnerable. There is an accumulation of the fricatives /z/ and /v/ and the near fricative /r/, e.g. in 'espoir', 'vivre', 'réalise' and 'rêves', which contributes to the roughness of her delivery. Furthermore, the absence of rounded sounds, apart from 'oui', may also be said to contribute to the absence of vulnerability in the dubbed version.

Buffy then goes on to explain what it is that she longs for:

Example 3

> OV: To be like other girls (MCU [she is static] / To fit in in this glittering world (LS) [camera on Giles and the others coming in, then back to Buffy; when she says 'glittering world' her arms are extended] / Don't give me songs (MLS) [on 'songs' we see Giles Anya, Tara, Willow and Xander] / Don't give me songs (said off-camera; we see Giles and others until 'songs' in MLS from the side) / Give me something to sing about (LS) [starts walking on 'about', shot from the side; Tara and Willow join her]/ I need something to sing about (MLS and LS) [shot from the front again, at eye-level].
>
> DV: Comme toutes les autres filles (MCU) / De faire partie du monde qui brille (camera back on Buffy in LS as she says 'du monde qui brille) / C'est pas pour moi (MLS) / des chansons j'en veux pas (off-camera, then back on her in MLS from the side on 'pas') / Je veux une vie qui chante pour moi (LS) [starts walking on 'moi', Tara and Willow join her] / Donne-moi une vie qui chante pour moi (MLS then LS) [shot from the front again, at eye-level].
>
> BT: [to be] like all the other girls / To belong to the world that shines / It's not for me. Songs, I don't want them / I need a life that sings for me / Give me a life that sings for me.)

Throughout the series, Buffy repeatedly says that she wishes to be like other girls and lead a normal life, but this is impossible as she is the Slayer and must perform her duties. This first line is therefore important in terms of character perception and development. From 'to be like other girls', Buffy is short in MCU, a shot that places the emphasis on her facial expressions and mouth movements. She looks upset and detached. When she starts uttering the second line, her friends come into the building (shot in MLS), and as she says 'glittering world', we can see her in a LS, alone, with her arms extended. These shots reinforce the information given in the lyrics. They visually represent Buffy's loneliness; she feels physically and emotionally alone even though her friends are physically close.

Buffy/Gellar's voice is softer than in the previous verse, probably as she is no longer fighting. She moves towards the camera and performs a very slow dance routine. Her voice is more nasal with a higher pitch, conveying tension and sadness. She modulates her voice on 'world'. When she sings the first: 'Don't give me songs', she sounds annoyed, and the use of the MLS means one can clearly see her eyebrows knitted in a frown and the movement of her mouth. Both the paralinguistic elements and her facial expressions convey her irritability as well as her desire not to be messed with. On her second utterance of 'songs', there is more softness in her voice, which could be seen as an expression of confidentiality: she is opening her heart and saying how she feels. The camera then moves from Buffy to her friends Tara and Anya, who come to dance with her when she says: 'Give me something to sing about'. This last shot, focused on the three women, reinforces Buffy's deep desire to be understood and supported by her friends. As she utters the last two lines, her voice grows louder; it is a demand: 'Give me'. She walks forwards and is shot from the side. Her voice is higher and carries more tension. The repetitive words and resulting recurrence of the plosives /d/ and /g/ and fricative /s/ in 'Don't give me songs' (repeated twice) and 'Give me something to sing about' / 'I need something to sing about' express this mixture of softness and explosiveness. In the last two lines, Buffy stresses her need for 'something to sing about', and finally positions herself as the subject through her use of 'I need'. Modality and transitivity mix together to show Buffy/

Gellar in a more active role, albeit not completely – she is, after all, still 'lacking'. This scene is shot in a series of LS and MLS, showing Buffy on the same level as her friends. These shots visually convey Buffy's yearning to be understood, fully present and part of the group.

Like Buffy/Gellar, Buffy/Guyot's voice is calmer in this sequence as the fighting has stopped. Unlike Buffy/Gellar, however, her pitch is high and she is not nasal. When she says '*filles*' and '*brilles*', she modulates her voice with a slight vibrato on the /i/, but this vibrato does not suggest frailty; it is assured and her voice conveys that she is in control. Her voice gets softer as she says: '*des chansons j'en veux pas*'. Moreover, unlike Buffy/Gellar, she does not get louder when she sings: '*Donne-moi une vie qui chante pour moi*'. There is, however, more tension in the voice, which is also higher. In terms of repetitions, one can see that 'Don't give me songs' has been translated by two different sentences in French: '*C'est pas pour moi, des chansons j'en veux pas*'. In the OV, 'Don't give me songs' is an address to the demon and also a direct mention to the spell that Buffy wants to break. This information is not actually conveyed in the DV: '*C'est pas pour moi*' ['It's not for me'] can be interpreted as a direct reference to the normal life that she craves but knows she cannot have. Buffy/Guyot only says that she does not want songs once, and so the emphasis is lost. Moreover, there are more fricatives in the French lines, with /s/, /sh/, /zh/ and the semi-vowel /r/ contributing to the softness of Buffy/Guyot's delivery. In the OV, Buffy does not want 'a life' to sing for her; she wants something to sing about herself. The modalities are different; she wants to 'feel'. Although in the lyrics Buffy/Gellar seems to be taking control over her singing – and, by extension, her life – she is unable to do so with her voice. Buffy/Guyot is less demanding in her tone and in what she says, and there is more depth and modulation in her voice, conveying additional feelings of control. These two Buffys seem to be in different emotional places and this arguably undercuts her characterization in French.

In the next two stanzas Buffy continues to express her feelings, as we get closer to her moment of vocal release:

Example 4

| OV: Life's a song (MCU) [low level, looking towards the demon] / You don't get to rehearse (MCU to MLS) [looking down directly at the camera on 'rehearse'] / And ev'ry single verse (MLS) [camera pans right, moving away from Buffy, Tara and Anya] / Can make it that much worse (MCU, low level) [looking at the demon] / |
| Still my friends (MLS with Giles and Willow in the background) [puts her hand and arm up, looks at her friends] / Don't know why I ignore (MCU) / The million things or more (MLS) [turning around] / I should be dancing for (MCU) [hands on her chest, which she then releases and places alongside her body]. |
| DV: La vie chante (MCU) / Un refrain sans retour (MCU to MLS) [on 'retour' looks down at the camera] / Dont les mots chaque jour (MLS) / T'apportent leur mal d'amour (MCU) / Mes amis (MLS) / N'savent pas pourquoi j'ignore (MCU) / Ces mille choses sans rapport (MLS) / Avec mon propre sort (MCU). |
| BT: Life sings / A refrain with no return / Of which words every day / Bring you their lack of love / My friends / Don't know why I ignore / These thousand things with no link / To my own fate. |

Buffy/Gellar returns to singing about the optimistic idea that 'life is a song', her voice lighter than in the previous stanza. Her pitch is higher in the first three lines, with some tension present. As she starts the fourth line, her voice gets lower and becomes more nasal as she gets more serious. This seriousness is also mixed with softness in her voice. There is more tension in her voice in the last three lines and her pitch becomes higher again. When she says 'don't know why I ignore', the modulation at the end of the word 'ignore' adds to this tension. When she sings 'I should be dancing for', her voice drops and becomes lower again. She puts her hands on her chest and opens her arms: she is visually, orally and linguistically opening up.

In terms of body posture, Buffy raises her left arm and extends her hand in a 'stop sign' before she utters 'still my friends'. This gesture can be interpreted as a request that her friends stop what they are doing and pay special attention to what she is going to say. She then starts spinning around, and we see her dancing with her arms extended as she sings 'million things or more'. From the word 'still', there is a sense that Buffy is about to reveal the truth; this approaching revelation is also hinted at by the irony in her voice while acknowledging her alleged lack of gratitude ('I should be dancing for'). In terms of linguistic information, this is when the truth begins to come out and, as the DV says, 'there will be no return'. Buffy/Gellar sings: 'Every single verse can make it that much worse' which is actually what is happening as she sings; she is telling a truth she wanted to keep as a secret because she did not want to hurt her friends. The combination of /s/, /z/ and /r/ as well as the voiced plosives /b/, /d/ and /g/ contribute to creating friction as well as a sense of unexpectedness over what is coming.

In the DV, Buffy/Guyot's pitch stays the same in the first four lines and, unlike Buffy/Gellar, does not drop lower; the French voice therefore has a narrower range on this occasion. From 'mes amis', her pitch is higher and there is more tension in the voice. There is a modulation and slight vibrato on 'ignore', 'rapport' and 'sort', but control can still be heard in her voice, which is smooth but not soft like Buffy/Gellar's. Buffy/Guyot's pitch is also lower than Buffy/Gellar's. Moreover, the French actress articulates more and does not shout as much as Buffy/Gellar, which could be interpreted as a sign of both being and staying in control.

Buffy is shot in MCU, then in MLS (when she utters 'rehearse') and back to MCU (on 'worse'). These types of shots, particularly the MCU, put lip-synchronization into focus and would explain the choice of 'amour' (rhyming with 'retour') in the DV. The French translation goes further, however, and focuses on a 'lack of love'. The English text indicates that life is unpredictable ('a song you don't get to rehearse') and that what you say can cause pain ('every single verse can make it that much worse'). The French text conveys additional emotions of helplessness ('a refrain with no return') and mentions an unavoidable lack of love in life ('words everyday bring you their lack of love'). Life seems even gloomier in the DV than in the OV. Moreover, Buffy/Gellar does not sing about a lack of love; this is not the root of her problems. These four lines once again suggest that the dubbing team has focused on creating a singable translation and that shot size has dictated vocabulary choices. The lip-sync is impeccable, and thus far the solutions to the problems created by the music, dubbing and visuals have been consistent and creative, even if they do lead to a different picture of what Buffy is talking about, i.e. plot outline, which will have consequences on performance and characterization.

Finally, as Buffy/Gellar sings 'dancing for' she places her crossed hands on her chest, bringing them back down to her side on 'for'. Visually, all of these gestures make this a dramatic performance, conveying Buffy's frustration and irritation. Her linguistic choices and tone also communicate these feelings; she is annoyed because her friends do not understand why she is unhappy despite having been brought back to life, and this annoyance can be heard in the tone of her voice. On the other hand, in the DV, Buffy/Guyot sings about 'these thousand things with no link to my fate'. This translation choice does not reveal anything about the fact that Buffy thinks that her friends expect her to feel differently; the sense of pressure on Buffy is thus eased. A rhyming pattern is maintained throughout in English and French: 'rehearse/verse/worse' and 'ignore/more/for' in English; *'retour/jour/amour'* and *'ignore/rapport/sort'* in French. Though different, both patterns focus on the consonant [r], which helps to maintain the rhythm of the passage and connotes feelings of pain and unease. Moreover, in both English and French, these vowels are open and rounded e.g. /e/, /o/ and /ou/ and the sequences of vowels in French flawlessly match lip movements. Through the use of the fricatives /s/, /z/ and /r/ and the plosives /b/, /d/ and /g/, a sense of friction and unexpectedness is also created in the translation. Therefore, the textures of the OV and DV are similar, although the words do not convey equivalent effects of pressure.

Next, Buffy starts criticizing her friends more explicitly for not letting her go:

Example 5

OV: All the joy life sends (LS-MLS) / Family and friends (MS) / All the twists and bends (MS – MLS on 'and bends') / Knowing that it ends (MCU) [shot from the side, raises first one arm, then the other, to the side] / Well that depends (MCU) [drops her arms at the same time, dramatically, and tilts her head back].
DV: Toutes les joies, les amis (LS, MLS) / la famille, ça finit (MS) / toutes les claques, coup du sort (MS – MLS on 'coup du sort')/ Lorsque frappe la mort (MCU) / Faut voir d'abord (MCU).
BT: All the joys, friends / Family, it ends / All the slaps, fate's strokes / When death strikes/ Needs to see first.

OV : On if they let you go (MCU) [from the side; we see Dawn's face on 'go'] / On
if they know enough to know (MLS) [Buffy is shot from behind and turns around
on 'enough', facing towards her sister; on 'to know', she starts going up the stairs] /
That when you've bowed (MLS) [back to the camera, going up stairs; then a shot of
Giles, Willow and Xander] / You leave the crowd (MLS-MS) [Buffy looks back at
the camera on 'crowd'] [low angle]

DV : Est-ce que tu sauves ta peau (MCU) [we see Dawn's face on 'peau'] / S'ils en
savent assez, s'ils en savent trop (MLS) [back to Buffy on 'savent trop'] / Mais quand
tu courbes le dos (MLS) / Ta vie prend l'eau (MLS-MS) [on 'eau'].

BT: Do you save your skin / If they know enough, if they know too much / But
when you bend your back / Your life takes water.

From 'all the joys' to 'depends', Buffy is dancing, and as she moves, she
also points at her friends, in rhythm. As she dances, her body gestures and
hair hide her face. When she goes up the stairs she is mainly shot from
behind, meaning that her mouth is only in focus on 'all the twists' and 'it
ends / Well, that depends'. Both the OV and DV have a rhyming pattern
and describe what happens in life, but one can see that the French translation is less coherent than the English one, as *faut voir d'abord* ('need to
see first') is not entirely self-explanatory. As Chaume explains, 'on-screen
dialogues have to match the dialogues uttered by on-screen characters'
mouths [...] whereas off-screen dialogues allow translators to produce
free, non-constrained solutions to the translation problems posed by the
source text' (2012: 109). Undoubtedly, the team has been constrained by
the MCU shots and their focus on a singable translation, at the expense
of the dialogue. Moreover, as we shall see in the DV, Buffy's criticism does
not come across as strongly as it did in the OV.

Buffy/Gellar's voice becomes rougher again, her singing bordering on
shouting; friction can therefore be heard in her voice. This verse is similar to
the previous stanza; it also features electric guitars playing in tandem with
Buffy's voice. Then, from 'on if they let you go', the music grows quieter
and Buffy/Gellar resumes a more conventional type of singing; her voice
is higher, with more modulations. When she says 'go', her pitch is higher,
her voice tenser, and one can hear the sorrow and pain in her voice. As she
says 'know', she looks around and sees her friends. On the last line, there is
more softness in her voice, she is slightly more nasal, conveying the pain

and tiredness she feels. After she says 'crowd', we see the demon gesturing towards her. It is his invitation for her to finish with what she has started. She looks at him in CU and is shot at a low angle from the perspective of the demon. The CU, with its clear focus on her facial expressions, shows us how sad Buffy/Gellar is. The combination of the nasals /m/ and /n/ and the semi-vowel /w/, as well as the many fricatives (such as /f/, /s/ and /v/) and the plosives /g/ and /b/ offer a complex mixture of sounds conveying anger, softness and sadness.

In the first stanza of the DV, one can say that Buffy/Guyot does not shout as much as Buffy/Gellar. From '*est-ce que tu sauves ta peau*', her voice is softer and there is a change in pitch as she gets lower. There is less difference in her voice between the lines '*faut voir d'abord*' and '*est-ce que tu sauves ta peau*' than there was in the OV. Hence, as noted previously, Buffy/Guyot's voice is more controlled. Moreover, there is more consistency in tone and pitch between the two portions of the text than there is in English. As a matter of fact, the presence of plosives /t/, /p/, and /b/ throughout the two verses may be said to contribute to this cohesion. Moreover, the alliteration of /r/ in '*sort*', '*Lorsque frappe la mort*' and '*voir d'abord*' add additional friction to the performance, thereby complementing the more unified tone of voice.

At this point, Buffy has walked up a few stairs and is on the same level as her sister and Sweet. After a CU of Buffy's brightly-lit face, the guitars stop, there is a pause, and soft piano music begins playing; this is the moment of vocal release the song has been building towards. Buffy reveals the cause of her suffering:

Example 6

> OV: There was no pain (CU) [she is looking down] / No fear, no doubt (CU) / 'Til they pulled me out (CU) [there is a shot of Sweet when she says 'pull'] / Of heaven (CU) [turns around and looks towards her friends] / So that's my refrain (MS) [facing her friends] / I live in hell (MCU of Willow) / 'Cause I've been expelled (MCU of Xander) / From heaven (MCU of Anya) / I think I was in heaven (CU) / So give me something to sing about (MCU) [watery eyes, trembling lips] / Please, give me something ... (CU) [on 'please', she turns to look at Sweet].

DV: Non pas de peine (CU)/ pas de pagaille (CU) / avant que j'm'en aille (CU)
[a shot of Sweet when she says 'j'm'en aille'] / loin du ciel (CU) / Voilà mon refrain
(MS)/ je vis en enfer (MCU of Willow) / mais que puis-je faire (MCU of Xander)
/ loin du ciel (MCU of Anya) / Ah j'étais bien là au ciel (CU) / Donne-moi une vie
qui chante pour moi (MCU) / Vite, donne-moi ma vie (CU) [on 'vite', she looks at
Sweet].

BT: No sorrow / No shambles / Before I left /Far from Heaven / Here is my refrain /
I live in Hell / But what can I do / Far from Heaven / Ah I was well in Heaven / Give
me a life that sings for me / Quick, give me my life]

Buffy is mostly shot in CU, although these shots are mixed with others of
her friends: we see Willow as Buffy says 'I live in hell ...', then Xander on
'... cause I've been expelled ...' and Anya on '... from heaven'. The editing and
shot composition in this verse are unquestionably governed by the particular rhythmic qualities of the song. Buffy/Gellar talks about pain, fear and
doubt, and reveals that she has been pulled out of Heaven. She sings with
a higher pitch than she had been previously, indicating more tension as she
reveals the truth. Her voice is soft, conveying intimacy and confidentiality.
It is also nasal, which may once again be related to the tension in her voice
and to what is happening in this moment of release. Pain and anguish can be
heard in her voice, particularly when she utters 'doubt' and 'out', which are
particularly nasal. She also modulates her voice slowly as she sings 'heaven'.
She then glides down as she utters 'refrain' and glides up on 'hell'. There is
also a slight roughness in her voice, conveying pain and anguish. Additionally,
Buffy/Gellar's voice has a certain softness to it, indicating she is confiding.

At the beginning of the verse, Buffy/Gellar's voice is soft and sad and
her pitch is at its highest. Through the use of the CUs, we see her looking
down while she utters the first three lines, the demon sitting and her standing. These CUs give the audience direct access to her facial expressions,
and on the last two lines we can see her eyes watering and her mouth trem-
bling. The choice of shot size and linguistic delivery therefore complement
one another, conveying additional poignancy. The energetic guitar music
returns for the last two lines as Buffy/Gellar sings loudly once again. There
is more strength in her voice as she demands a reason to live. She sounds
angry and her voice is full of frustration as she shouts 'give me something'.

When she utters 'please', there is a slight wavering in her voice; a vibrato. The combination of plosives, fricatives and nasals produce a complex soundscape: the 'h' in 'heaven' and 'hell' adds air and breath to her voice; 'pain', 'doubt' and 'pulled' sound like a series of shocks, while the /s/ and /th/ in 'something' and 'sing' contribute to the sound of sorrow.

In the DV, one can hear Buffy/Guyot's breath mixing with the tone of her voice more clearly. There is also softness, communicating intimacy. The word *'peine'* is a false friend as it does not mean 'pain' but rather 'sorrows'; however, in terms of lip-synchronization, it fits perfectly. When Buffy/Guyot utters this word, her voice is breathy, conveying vulnerability and fear. Her pitch is also higher in this verse than it was previously, which can be interpreted as a sign of tension. However, there is less than in the OV as Buffy/Guyot's voice is not nasal. When she says 'ah', her breath mixes with the open vowel, before her voice changes significantly as it grows louder on *'Donne-moi une vie qui chante pour moi'*. Though loud, Buffy/Guyot is not as loud as Buffy/Gellar; she does not shout like her, nor does she sound frustrated like Buffy/Gellar – her voice conveys more sadness. Just as in the OV, there is a combination of nasals, fricatives and plosives which, though placed at different moments, convey Buffy's vulnerability and sadness, e.g. the /r/ in *'enfer'*, *'refrain'* and *'faire'*, as well as anger with the plosives /t/ and /d/ in *'donne'* and *'vite'*. The accumulation of /l/ sounds in *'aille'*, *'ciel'*, *'loin'*, *'pagaille'* and *'voilà'* could, however, be said to bring a sense of fluidity that is at odds with her feelings of depression and sadness.

Finally, in terms of paralinguistic information, Buffy/Gellar has a childlike tone that permeates the lyrics, brought about by her nasality and high pitch. Her voice does not convey a wide range of emotions, which is actually in line with her feelings of being depressed and frustrated. She only sounds angry when she sings: 'So give me something to sing about.' The quality of Buffy/Guyot's voice is much deeper, warmer and more emotionally coloured, heightening the pathos of the moment in this passage.

Analysing the OV linguistically tells us more about Buffy/Gellar's frustration and helplessness. Indeed, the passive mode in 'I've been expelled from heaven' indicates that Buffy has been acted upon. In this verse, the vocabulary is loaded with modality with positive shading (e.g. 'pain' and 'doubt').[5] In French, however, 'pain, fear and doubt' become 'sorrow and shambles', which do not fully convey Buffy's intense suffering but do have fricative consonants, therefore still expressing some friction. Buffy/Guyot is also turned into an active agent: she *left* Heaven (*'avant que j'm'en aille loin du ciel'*) as opposed to being taken out of it. The strong sense of passivity and helplessness in the original is not prominent in the DV, apart from the line '*mais que puis-je faire loin du ciel*' ('but what can I do far from Heaven'). Just after revealing that she was in Heaven, Buffy looks at Giles and Xander, who both appear shocked. When Buffy/Gellar utters 'refrain', the camera is once again back on her in MS. Starting with 'I live in hell', there is a succession of MCUs of Willow, Xander and Anya. The camera is back on Buffy/Gellar as she sings 'I think I was in Heaven' in CU while looking down. This CU of the actress' face adds visual strength to her vocal release, as we can see very clearly her depressed facial expression juxtaposed with her friends' surprise in MCU. Another interesting linguistic twist is that, in the OV, Buffy says that she *thinks* she was in Heaven, whereas in the DV she *knows* she was. The shift in modality is obvious; Buffy/Guyot is clearer about what happened to her and can be perceived as more confident.

Buffy then looks at her friends and angrily sings: 'Give me something to sing about'. As she utters 'please', she turns back to Sweet, who shakes his head. In the OV, she begs to have something to sing about, whereas in the DV she demands a life that sings for her. The mode of experience is different. She sounds more desperate and helpless in the OV as she wants to be in charge of her life, but cannot. In the DV, she seems to already be in control. The camera then cuts back to Buffy in CU: she looks upset, jumps down in a back flip and starts an 'out of control' dance routine. This is actually one of the effects of the spell: when people vocalize deep pain, they also dance, and in most cases end up dancing faster and faster until

---

5   Positive modality is characterized by the use of *verba sentiendi* (Uspensky's 1973), i.e. words denoting thoughts, feelings and perceptions, thereby signaling a subjective point of view as well as evaluative adjectives and adverbs. For more on this, see Bosseaux (2007: 39–44).

they die by combustion. Buffy has reached the end of her 'performance' and she should die, i.e. be consumed by her pain. Buffy continues to spin, but Spike stops her by grabbing her arms. He then starts to sing:

Example 7

OV: Life's not a song (MCU) [frowns and shakes his head in a comforting manner] / Life isn't bliss (MCU) [back of his head; we see Buffy's face] / Life is just this (MCU) / It's living (MCU) [he looks into her eyes] / You'll get along (CU) [we see Buffy; he touches her hair, gently] / The pain that you feel (MS) [shot of Dawn] / You only can heal (MCU)/ By living (CU) [Buffy's face]/ You have to go on living (CU) / So one of us is living (CU-MS) [smiles slightly, both shot from the side].
DV: La vie n'chante pas (MCU) / la vie n'est pas bonne (MCU) / elle ne te donne (MCU) / que la vie (MCU) / Avance tout droit (CU) / tes larmes, ta douleur (MS) / changeront de couleur (MCU) / dans la vie (CU) / Il faut que tu restes en vie (CU)/ que l'un de nous reste en vie (CU-MS).
BT : Life doesn't sing /Life isn't good / It only gives you / Life / Walk straight / Your tears, your pain / Will change colour / In life / You have to stay alive / That one of us stays alive.

Spike and Buffy are both shot in MCUs and CUs. The camera goes back and forth between them as he sings his lines and they look into each other's eyes. The camera zooms in gradually from MCUs to CUs. As it does, the shots get bigger so that Buffy's and Spike's facial expressions are very much under scrutiny. As Spike sings 'you'll get along', he touches Buffy's hair. After he has finished his lines, the camera pans left to Buffy's sister Dawn, who says: 'The hardest thing in this world is to live in it.'[6] The camera pans back to Buffy, who looks at her sister sadly. Spike turns his head to the side and then turns back to look at Buffy. They are shot from the side in MCU at eye-level as they look at each other intensely. The same shot size and angle is reproduced at the end in their short duet (which will be discussed presently), showing visual continuity between the scenes. These specific shots frame the dialogue and emphasize the emotional and

---

6   These were the final words that Buffy said to her sister before dying in season five.

physical intensity present between Buffy and Spike. As such, they also reinforce their lines and performance style.

Spike/Marsters' voice has a rough and hoarse quality to it. It is soft and slightly breathy, as his breath can be heard mixing with his voice. His pitch is low and his pitch range restricted. His voice is placed in the throat and there is no tension. The voice is lax, relaxed and mellow. There is softness in his voice, communicating intimacy and confidentiality. The voice resonates in his mouth and throat. He is comforting her as he looks into her eyes and places his hand on her hair, smiling gently. His physical gestures and his voice are comforting. When he utters 'by living', his voice is even lower, conveying an even greater sense of comfort and hope. There is a slight vibrato in the voice and it is grainy. These two attributes convey emotion and the vibrato is slight enough that it does not express a loss of control. There is tenderness in his eyes and tone. When we see his face, he is shot from a lower angle, representing Buffy's point of view. The camera zooms in slowly to focus on Spike and Buffy's expressions as Spike sings. We therefore go from MCU to CU as the camera pans from left to right, from Spike to Buffy. There is an accumulation of the frictionless fricative /l/ in 'life', 'living', 'along', 'feel', and 'heal', which adds fluidity and effortlessness to Spike's delivery style. The unvoiced fricatives /s/ and /f/ also contribute to this. There are a few plosives in 'pain' and 'get' and voiced fricatives /zh/ and /z/ in 'just this', for instance, but their presence is limited and the overall impression is one of softness and reassurance. Spike/Marsters delivers his lines smoothly with a sustained tone, i.e. the tone of his voice is regular and even, and as such, more soothing, stable and inclined to assuage her pain.

The French actor who dubs Spike is called Serge Faliu; he has also lent his voice to the character of Al Boulet in *ER* (NBC, 1994–2009). In the DV, the texture of Spike/Faliu's voice is likewise grainy, but not breathy. His voice is placed in the throat, as it was with Spike/Marsters, but it is also nasal, particularly when he says '*vie*'. There is less control in his voice, with slightly more modulations as it varies from higher to lower notes. His delivery is less effortless than Spike/Marsters and consequently it may be described as less soothing. Spike/Faliu's voice is also cleaner. Overall, Spike/Marsters' voice is softer and deeper then Spike/Faliu; he has more control over his voice and can whisper effortlessly. There is an accumulation of plosives in the DV with /b/, /d/, /t/ and /k/ adding more rhythm or tempo to the lines. The alliteration in /l/ is reproduced throughout the verse, somehow counterbalancing the effect of the plosives. However, the overall effect is not one of prevailing effortlessness as it is in the OV.

Linguistically speaking, there is also a greater sense of purpose and direction in the DV through the use of '*marche tout droit*' ('walk straight') as opposed to 'You'll get along'. Spike does not promise anything straightforward in the original; on the contrary, he talks about feelings and healing because he understands her pain. Feelings and their expressions are crucial in this episode, as indicated in the title ('Once More With Feeling'), though neither the French title nor lyrics reflect this. In English, the emphasis is on the experience of living, not on life. The emphasis on experience is also reinforced by the choice of lexical items on which the rhyme falls (heal/feel/living). Spike/Faliu talks about life in general and the emphasis on experience is missing in the DV. Indeed, the use of a noun (life) as opposed to a verb in the continuous form (living) changes the mode of experience. In terms of modality, 'have to' in English implies external obligation, while 'must' is directly imposed by the self or another.[7] The DV uses '*il faut que*', exhibiting another type of modality. Although encoding external imposition, the impersonal construction 'il faut que'[8] is weaker than 'you have to'. The modality of obligation is thus slightly less strong in the DV.

Spike and Buffy's duet ends here, marking the end of the spell, which Spike has helped to break. The group starts singing the next song, 'Where Do We Go From Here?', together, wondering how they will manage to go on after what has happened. Spike begins singing along with them until he realizes that, now that the spell is broken, he has a choice; he decides to leave. In the final scene, Spike leaves the room and Buffy follows him

---

7   For example, 'I must see you tomorrow' implies that the speaker demands or requires it, i.e. the obligation comes from the speaker. On the other hand, 'I have to see you tomorrow' implies that the speaker cannot do anything about it, i.e. the constraint/ obligation is external.

8   '*Il faut*' stems from the verb '*falloir*', an impersonal verb only used in the third-person singular in the indicative and subjunctive modes.

outside. As she starts singing, they gradually begin to walk towards each other, looking into each other's eyes. There is a brief exchange of dialogue in which he tells her to go back inside. She responds that she does not want to, to which he responds that when she knows 'what you do want, there'll probably be a parade. Seventy-six bloody trombones'. She tries to interrupt him and he replies: 'Look, you don't have to say anything'. She then starts singing and he joins her:
    // indicates they are singing at the same time:

Example 8

OV: *Buffy*: I touch the fire and it freezes me (MCU) [she walks towards him] / *Spike*: I died … (MCU) [he walks towards her] / *Buffy*: I look into it and it's black // *Spike*: So many years ago. (MCU) [after 'into it', the camera pans to Spike] / *Buffy*: This isn't real (MCU) / *Buffy*: But I just want to feel // *Spike*: But you can make me feel (MCU) [shot from the side – she kisses him]
DV: *Buffy*: Je touche le feu et c'est un feu de glace (MCU) / *Spike*: j'suis mort … (MCU)/ *Buffy*: il est aussi noir que la mort (MCU)// *Spike*: depuis tellement longtemps (MCU) / *Buffy*: C'est illusoire (MCU)/ / *Buffy*: pourtant je veux y croire// *Spike*: mais toi tu me fais croire [shot sideways – she kisses him]
BT: *Buffy*: I touch the fire and it is a frozen fire / *Spike*: I died … / *Buffy*: It is as black as death / This is illusory / But I want to believe / *Spike*: So many years ago / But you make me believe.

The camera pans from left to right, showing us Spike and Buffy facing each other in MCU. Then, as they start walking towards each other, they are shot from the side. When Buffy says 'this isn't real', they are again shot from the side, looking into each other's eyes, getting closer. When they say 'feel', they kiss. Buffy/Gellar's voice is nasal, full of tension, and her pitch is high, clear and smooth. This is in complete contrast with Spike/Marsters' voice, which is softer, rough and low pitched. Their voices mix together as they sing their lines, almost overlapping. They say 'feel' at the same time and then kiss, shot from the side in MCU. These shot movements (panning) and sizes (MCUs) are typical of the end of a (musical) film, where the hero and heroine kiss and the end credits start rolling. Spike and Buffy's vocal 'coming together' is thus reinforced visually by evoking a specific film tradition.

In terms of the linguistics of the DV, the replacement of 'feel' with *'croire'* ('believe') adds to the indication of two opposed modes of experience. The DV focuses more on beliefs and hopes than experiencing and feeling. In terms of vocal textures, Buffy/Guyot's voice is not nasal; on the contrary, it is clear, and her pitch modulates between medium and high. Spike/Faliu's voice is soft and lower than Buffy's, as though he were more submissive, which does indeed reflect their emotional situation. Spike/Faliu's voice is also slightly nasal and higher than Spike/Marsters', which in a way contribute to an impression of submissiveness, as these considerations are gender stereotypes. In terms of texture, Spike/Faliu's voice has neither the grain nor the roughness of Spike/Marsters' voice. Spike/Faliu's voice seems to exacerbate the softness that is already present in Spike/Marsters'. However, because this softness is more apparent and the voice is more high-pitched, Spike's tameness and passivity is accentuated. This is not out of character, as Spike is quite passive or submissive in his relationship with Buffy and in this scene it is indeed Buffy who comes after him and kisses him. However, this dimension of the characters is overplayed in the DV and Spike can be said to lose some of his complexity in French.

6.2.3 *The dubbing effect: Buffy and Spike*

This case study has demonstrated that translating songs that are part of a film's or TV series' narrative is not a straightforward endeavour. Indeed, there are many modalities for translators and voice artists to take into consideration: internal rhymes, the way words are sung, pauses, elongating sounds, how feelings are expressed through songs and how phrasing ties in with the acting, particularly in song-and-dance sequences.

The vocal and audiovisual analysis of 'Something to Sing About' has revealed shifts in the way we perceive Buffy and Spike in the French version. Buffy/Gellar has a nasal voice, somewhat flat with very few modulations, i.e. limited rise and fall in the voice pitch. Her speech pattern is characterized by a very fast pace with hardly any variations. Her voice has a childlike tone to it, whereas Buffy/Guyot has a more mature voice with more depth and variation. Overall, one can say that Buffy's French voice does not always fit Gellar's body nor the images and stereotypes she represents and is, as such, uncanny. Indeed, as seen in Chapter 5, Buffy is the stereotypical blonde cast in American horror movies who should, by rights, get killed at the beginning of the film. Her nasal, fast-paced voice, Californian accent and childlike tone correspond to or reinforce this representation. Her singing voice often saturates; in other words, it reaches its limits as Buffy/Gellar's *tessitura*, or vocal range, is rather limited. This saturation, however, is in line with the character's feelings of frustration and depression. As the song unfolds, Buffy/Gellar expresses stronger and stronger feelings, while paradoxically maintaining a 'bored' tone. At one point, she is on the brink of combustion because of the spell, yet she still maintains the same tone. Buffy/Guyot's singing voice, on the other hand, sounds more trained, with a wider tonal range. As a matter of fact, the actress has also provided the voice of Ariel in the French version of the cartoon musical Walt Disney's *The Little Mermaid* (Ron Clements 1989). Guyot does not need to use the full power of her voice all of the time and has more control over her vocal delivery. When she sings the rhymes, she lingers on the diphthongs and shows more vocal mastery. In some ways, this can be said to play against Buffy's characterization since this vocal mastery does not quite reflect Buffy's situation. Buffy/Guyot's vocal delivery thus makes her appear to be more sophisticated and in control of the situation.

This first case study has highlighted how important it is not to rely solely on linguistic analysis when investigating audiovisual material. A detailed analysis of actors' performance through the visual and acoustic channels has helped to show how challenging it is to read audiovisual products in their entirety. There are two further important considerations to be made. Firstly, there are definitive limitations when describing the scenes; ideally, the visuals should be made available to readers/viewers so that they can see, hear and savour the performance. Due to copyright restrictions, however, it has not been possible to include the scenes. This first study therefore confirms how challenging it is to talk and write about films, as well as how important it is to do so in order to understand how audiovisual materials convey meaning and what is at stake in translation. I therefore hope that readers will have appreciated the depth of my analysis and will be inspired to carry out their own. Secondly, it must be noted that in this sequence shot sizes have clearly put pressure on the translation team in their attempt to create a singable translation with impeccable lip-synchronization. The rhyming patterns in combination with the shot sizes have dictated certain vocabulary choices, which has led to a somewhat different picture of Spike and Buffy in the French version. In terms of dealing with dubbing constraints, then, the dubbing team has done impressive work. However, the same cannot be said for the choice of vocabulary and voices, which do not fully fit the original actors' bodies or convey Buffy's and Spike's personalities. Let us now turn to the second case study in order to test further the framework that I have elaborated for examining performance and characterization by means of a multimodal analysis.

6.3　Case Study Two: '*Tabula Rasa*'

*6.3.1　From '*Tabula Rasa*' to '*Tabula Rasa*'*

Planchenault (2008: 182) explains that the cultural identity of a particular social group is perceived through vocabulary choices and phonological variations, and that this perception can be modelled by the linguistic stereotypes of these groups. Similarly, Claire Kramsch writes that '[g]roup identity is not a cultural fact, but a cultural perception [...] What we perceive about a person's culture and language is what we have been conditioned by our culture to see' (1998: 67). Those views can easily be applied to Spike and Giles and the way they speak in *BtVS*. Indeed, when spectators watch the OV and hear Spike's and Giles' British accents in contrast to Buffy's American accent, for instance, they will most probably think about the stereotypes associated with these two different cultures. The following case study on 'Tabula Rasa' (season six, episode eight) will show some of these stereotypes at work in the OV and French DV of the episode.

In 'Tabula Rasa', Willow casts a spell so that Buffy and Tara forget about their painful experiences. As we have seen in the previous case study, Buffy has been resurrected by her friends and now feels depressed, while

Tara is disappointed that Willow, her girlfriend, relies so much on magic. The spell goes wrong, however, and everyone – not just Buffy and Tara – forgets who they are after falling into a deep sleep. As the episode unfolds, the characters slowly recover their identities, with Giles and Spike coming to realize that they are both British. The analysis focuses on how these two British protagonists come across in the OV and how their otherness is conveyed in the DV. The scene under analysis takes place at the beginning of the episode as the characters attempt to recover their identity. Within the context of performance, my ultimate goal is to reveal the impact of the translator's choices on character portrayal.

6.3.2 Britishness as otherness

In this scene Giles, Anya, Spike, Willow, Buffy, Dawn and Xander are all gathered in the magic shop, which is owned by Giles. Anya works there alongside Giles and it is where the group meets socially and also to do research on the creatures that they have to fight. Having all lost their memories, they are trying to understand what they are doing in this location. After Willow and Tara conclude that they are in a magic shop, Giles comments:[9]

Example 9a

> OV: Magic? (Giles – MCU, eye-level) / Magic's all balderdash and chicanery (Willow, MCU, Spike, MS) / I'm afraid we don't know a bloody thing (Giles then Anya, MCU) / Except I seem to be British, don't I? (Giles and Buffy, MCU) / And a man, with glasses (Giles, MCU) [takes glasses off as he says 'glasses'] / Oh, that narrows it down considerably (Buffy and Dawn, MS) / We'll get our memory back and it'll all be right as rain (Buffy and Dawn MS, Giles MCU).

In terms of *mise-en-scène*, Giles, who is shot in MCU, is the main focus of the scene. As for the angle, Giles is shot at eye-level, meaning the audience is placed on the same level as he is. This is the horizontal level referred to

9   Chapter 6, Giles starts speaking at 00: 17: 23.

by Vanoye (1985) and Pérez-González (2007), and the way the audience engages with Giles in this scene is very straightforward: the eye-level shot gives us direct access to Giles' facial expressions. Using a high or a low angle shot would have put the audience or the other characters in different positions, e.g. a superior or inferior one. By using this eye-level angle, information is conveyed directly and is (seemingly) not distorted. This is also reflected at the linguistic level: Giles is speaking candidly. As a matter of fact, since the whole of the exchange is shot at eye-level with no change, it puts all of the participants in a similar position as that of the audience and there is a sense of equality in the exchange. This part of the dialogue is thus characterized by plain-speaking, equality and honesty.

Visually, as Giles is shot in MCU, the focus is specifically on his face and facial expressions: the way he moves his head around and blinks his eyes. On an acoustic and linguistic level, the focus is on the way he pronounces the words and his tone, which convey distrust in magic through mockery. Throughout the verbal exchange, the camera cuts from him to the other participants, and although most of them remain quiet during the exchange, their body postures and facial expressions all convey confusion and surprise at what is happening. The shots keep changing: we first switch from Giles to Willow in MCU as Giles utters 'balderdash and chicanery', while Spike is also visible in MS in the background. Willow looks surprised and slightly upset as she looks down. The camera then returns to Giles, with a shot change to Anya in MCU as he says 'bloody thing': she is staring at him and her facial expressions convey confusion and questioning. We again return to Giles up until he says 'don't I', at which point we see Buffy in MCU raising her eyebrows, looking confused and clueless.

We then return to Giles, who seems to be rediscovering everything about himself – even the fact that he wears glasses, which he glances at as they rest on his nose. He then takes them off on saying 'glasses'. Finally, as he says 'narrows it down considerably', the camera cuts back to Buffy and her sister Dawn, shot in MS. They look at each other and Buffy appears confused. Due to the use of the MS, we see her arms crossed in front of her chest, adding some more physical information to her already 'closed' position. Dawn is shot from the side and tells Buffy that she does not like the situation. Buffy responds: 'It's OK, don't worry. We'll take care of each other'. They are shot in MCU as Buffy strokes Dawn's hair, at which she brightens up. When Giles states 'We'll get our memory back', the camera shows Buffy touching a scared Dawn's hair with an affectionate protective gesture. The camera then cuts back to Giles in MCU on 'It'll all be right as rain'; at this point, he has taken off his glasses and is looking down at them.

In terms of vocal sound, Giles' pitch is high to medium and his range is moderate to high as he varies between the medium and higher scales of his voice. This pitch range conveys the surprise that he is communicating verbally. His pitch is higher at the beginning of his lines and drops when he says 'I'm afraid'. Giles does not speak very loudly and his voice is relatively soft, adding a sense of intimacy to the scene; an intimacy which is also reflected visually, as they are all in the same room. There is no tension in his voice; on the contrary, it has roughness and grain as though it were coming from the throat. Moreover, when he speaks in a lower tone, his voice seems to originate more from the chest, such as when he says: 'Well, that narrows it down considerably.' His tone and vocabulary also express some humour. Giles utters this sentence as though he were slightly amused by the situation, or as though nothing bad were happening. Additionally, his breath mixes with the tone of his voice in this sentence, once again adding softness and intimacy. The roughness in his voice is communicated through friction sounds, particularly in the words containing fricatives at the beginning of his speech, e.g. 'magic', 'balderdash' and 'chicanery', featuring a /g/ and unvoiced /s/ sound. In fact, when he says the word 'magic' he lets out a little laugh, almost a snigger, and so sounds slightly condescending. His sentences are rhythmical with an accumulation of voiced consonants like /l/ and the nasals /m/ and /n/, all of which contribute to the non-committal tone of the passage. There is quite a melodic aspect to his phrasing and more rhythm is added via his breath. Indeed, Giles' sentences are punctuated by breathing; he inhales more loudly after 'chicanery' and before 'that narrows' and 'and 'it'll all be right as rain'.

The end of the passage is slightly more assertive with the use of the plosives /k/ and /d/, the intervocalic /t/ and the voiced /g/ in 'get', as well as /b/ in 'British', which is articulated frontally and sounds like a small explosion. However, there is still softness in the form of the unvoiced /s/ in 'seem' and 'except' and the near fricatives in 'right' and 'rain'. There is also positivity in his voice, and he almost laughs as he says 'considerably'. All in all, his voice, with its rhythm and changes in tone, responds or corresponds to the shot changes. Indeed, the camera keeps cutting from him to the rest of the characters throughout his lines. We first see Willow, then Anya and finally Buffy and Dawn in MS. These changes of perspective show each of the characters looking confused or surprised as Giles comes to realize that he is British. His voice, in particular, corresponds well with the other characters' body gestures. For instance, we hear Giles' soft and intimate tone as Buffy comforts her scared sister by stroking her hair. Let us see what happens to the richness of this scene in translation. In the DV, Giles says:

Example 9b

DV: Magie! (Giles – MCU, eye-level) / ah! la magie n'est que billevesée et crétineries (Willow, MCU, Spike, MS)/ Nous n'en savons guère plus je le crains (shot of Giles, then Anya, MCU) / Si ce n'est que j'ai le flegme britannique, hé, hé (Giles and Buffy, MCU) / Donc je suis anglais, je suis un homme qui porte des lunettes (Giles, MCU) [takes glasses off as he says 'glasses'] / Voilà qui réduit notre champ d'investigation (Buffy and Dawn, MS) / Nous retrouverons notre mémoire et le brouillard se dissipera (Buffy and Dawn MS, Giles MCU).

BT: Magic, ah! magic is all stupidity and nonsense / We hardly know more I'm afraid / Except that I've got British composure eh, eh / So I'm English, I'm a man who wears glasses / Well this reduces our field of investigation / We'll get our memory back and the fog will dissipate.

Giles' voice in French is that of Nicolas Marié, who is also known for dubbing Jarod from the US series *The Pretender* (NBC, 1996–2000). Giles/Marié's voice is higher in French than it is in English. This is actually in line with the rest of the dubbed voices, as most of the characters in *BtVS*, female and male alike, have a higher pitch in the dubbed version; this is particularly true of Anya, who has a very high pitch voice in French. It is also striking that Giles/Marié sounds much younger than Giles/Stewart Head. In terms of tone, when he says '*la magie*', Giles/Marié's voice is more condescending than Giles/Stewart Head and there is no doubt that he thinks that the whole idea of magic is ludicrous. Moreover, there is more laughter in Giles/Marié's voice, adding to the mockery. Giles/Marié's voice still has a little grain, but the combination of grain and laughter takes away the comforting element present in Giles/Stewart Head's voice. In a nutshell, Giles/Marié sounds more condescending, jokey and light-hearted. Giles is actually more cheerful and more positive in the DV; he has a faster pace and sounds more defensive than calm.

In terms of accents, there is no trace of Giles' Britishness in the DV. Giles/Marié's accent in French is rather neutral and he sounds well educated because of the vocabulary he uses. Giles' 'higher' status as a Brit is conveyed through register as he uses flowery vocabulary and words with Latin roots (e.g. 'field of investigation' and 'the fog will dissipate'). In the DV, Britishness is associated with composure and weather, two very stereotypical images of Britishness in France. The weather reference was also present in the original, whereas the other was not.

In terms of vocals, Giles/Marié sounds assertive throughout, conveyed by an accumulation of plosives, e.g. /k/, the intervocalic /t/ and the voiced /g/ in 'flegme' or 'guère'. There are also many /b/ sounds, as in 'britannique', 'billevesées' and 'brouillard', which are articulated frontally and therefore sound like small explosions every time the words are pronounced. There are also fricatives, e.g. /r/, which are mixed with plosives in, for instance, 'crains', 'crétineries', 'britannique' and 'retrouverons'. These sounds convey some friction, though there is also some fluidity due to the voiced consonants like /l/ in 'la', 'le', 'billevesée', 'lunettes' and 'flegme', /m/ in 'homme' and 'mémoire' as well as /n/ in 'britannique' and 'crétineries'. Although there is some melody in the French phrasing, it is not as rhythmical as the OV. The sentences are also slightly breathier than Giles/Stewart Head, as we can hear Giles/Marié taking a breath after 'ah', 'crétineries' and 'crains'. There is also softness conveyed with the unvoiced /s/ in 'plus', 'suis' and 'dissipera'. Finally, at the end of the passage, Giles/Marié sounds particularly amused ('investigation') and slightly pedantic when he says 'le brouillard se dissipera'. There are also many nasals (/m/ and /n/), contributing to the feeling of uncertainty. All in all, there is more homogeneity in his delivery than there was in the OV.

In terms of visual information and how it combines with the linguistic and vocal information, one can see that the words have been carefully chosen to match shot changes, as when Giles/Marié holds up his glasses and looks at them as he says '*lunettes*'. However, as the British-English vocabulary is not reproduced in the French version, there is a discrepancy between the British words and the characters' visual responses to them, i.e. the way they look at one another or at Giles. For example, Anya looks confused when she glances at Giles as he utters the words 'bloody thing'. This is because the word 'bloody' is typically British and therefore foreign to her American ears. In the DV, this strangeness is neutralized, with 'bloody thing' translated as: 'We hardly know more, I'm afraid'. Therefore, when the camera grants us access to Anya's emotions, her gaze still conveys confusion but the reason for this confusion is different. In the OV, it is because he is speaking strangely; in the DV, it is probably because she does not understand what is happening. Although the visual information has not changed in translation, Anya is seen to react to another piece of information and one could say that her reaction does not entirely make sense. Indeed, all of the characters are looking at Giles in the OV because he sounds strange and uses foreign vocabulary, whereas in the French version, Giles speaks standard French and sounds well-educated or upper-class. The surprise or confusion in the DV emanates from different, if related, reasons. In the OV, they can hear that he is English; in the French version, they cannot, and the surprise and confusion are only linked to the words 'I'm English', not to the specific British English vocabulary.

Returning to the OV, Giles/Stewart Head is then interrupted by Spike saying:

Example 10a

OV: Oh, listen to Mary Poppins (MCU of Giles) / He's got his crust all stiff and upper (Spike, MS) / with that Nancy-boy accent. You Englishmen are always (Buffy and Dawn, MS) / so … (Spike, MS).

Spike then realizes that he is also English and adds: Bloody hell (Spike, MS). Sodding (MCU of Giles), blimey, shagging, knickers, bollocks. Oh God. I'm English.' (Spike, MS).

When Spike starts speaking, the camera is still on Giles who is looking at his glasses in MCU. We see Giles looking surprised as Spike utters the words 'Mary Poppins' and the camera then cuts to Spike, who is shot in MS behind the counter as he says 'he's got his crust'. As with Giles' monologue, there is then a series of reaction shots, i.e. we see the camera cut from one character to the next to show their reactions. The shot changes go hand in hand with Spike's utterances, and so for each sentence there is a different shot. The verbal and the visual mix at a quick pace: we see Buffy and Dawn as Spike says 'Nancy-boy accent', shot in MS and looking confused. Buffy is facing the camera and Dawn is shot from the side. Dawn glances first at Buffy, appearing confused, and then they both look in Spike's direction as he says 'you Englishmen'. The expression on Buffy's face is different than before; she does not look as concerned and there is a slight indication of amusement on her face. We then cut back to Spike in MS as he says 'always so', with Willow looking at him in the background from where she stands in the lower right corner. We do not see any of their faces, but the shot allows us to see that everybody is looking in Spike's direction. When Spike says 'bloody hell', the camera cuts back to Giles in MCU. Giles looks very surprised and intrigued. Then, when Spike utters 'blimey', we cut back on Spike for the rest of his line. We can see him in MS using his fingers to enumerate the British words he knows. He is looking downwards and when he says 'Oh God, I'm English', he simultaneously lowers his arm in a defeated gesture and looks in Giles' direction, Giles being the only other Brit in the room.

Spike/Marsters' pitch range is more monotonous than that of Giles/ Stewart Head. Although his voice does go from a medium to a low pitch, there is hardly any variation; it is a restricted range. There is also some roughness in his voice, but it is more nasal than rough. Spike does not speak particularly loud, but he is louder than Giles and his voice is clear. Spike's pitch is especially low in the long line 'Oh, listen to Mary Poppins. He's got his crust all stiff and upper, with that Nancy-boy accent', all of which is uttered in one go. After finishing the line, Spike takes a deep breath, almost as though he were out of breath. His verbal complaint goes hand in hand with the nasality in his voice, which conveys exasperation. There is a mixture of voiced and voiceless plosives: the voiced /g/ in 'got' and /b/ in 'boy' and numerous voiceless consonants in 'Poppins' and 'upper', with its frontally articulated /p/; the intervocalic /t/, articulated in the middle, and /k/ from the back of the throat in 'crust' and 'got'. There are also fricatives, both unvoiced (/s/ and /sh/) and voiced (/z/ in 'listen',

'Poppins', 'he's', 'his', 'crust, 'stiff', 'with that', 'accent' and 'always so'). This mixture of fricatives and plosives, combining sounds of friction and explosion, contributes acoustically to the snappiness of the dialogue.

Furthermore, when Spike enumerates the British-English words, his voice is clear with a little tension to it. 'Bloody hell' is uttered with a slight grain and is pronounced lower and more softly than the rest of the sentence. His voice is clearer or brighter when he enumerates the British-English words relating to sex ('sodding', 'shagging'), anatomy ('bollocks') and items of clothing ('knickers'), while there is also an interjection ('bloody hell'). The adjective 'bloody' is one of the series' recurrent words, used mainly by Spike and occasionally – though significantly less often – by Giles. These plosives, along with the voiced /b/ in 'bloody', 'blimey' and 'bollocks', /g/ in 'God' and the unvoiced /k/ in 'knickers' and 'bollocks', add to the sudden element of self-discovery. The fricatives, voiced /s/ and /sh/ in 'sodding', 'shagging', and 'bollocks' and the unvoiced /z/ in 'knickers' complement the rasping effect, as can hear friction when the air is coming out of Spike's mouth. This mixture is particularly apparent in the word 'English', which contains both. Moreover, the close proximity of the word 'God' with the two plosives foregrounds the explosive quality or snappiness of the dialogue; Spike's dialogue is unexpected, as one can see from the other characters' faces. Visually, this passage, along with the previous one, is quite homogenous in terms of shot types. Indeed, characters are shot mostly in MCU and MS, which added some pressure in terms of lip-synchronization, even though many of the words are uttered off-screen. The verbal and the visual combine to produce a rhythmically fast-paced exchange.

Giles' retort to Spike's speech is:

Example 11a

OV: 'Welcome to the Nancy tribe'.

He is shot in MLS, standing next to Anya, who looks very unsure about what is happening. We then see Giles put his glasses back on. His tone in this line of dialogue is different from before; he now sounds slightly annoyed, yet still retains his good humour. His hand gesture nicely accompanies the sharpness of the line: he is putting an end to this conversation. His voice is grainy and soft and contrasts clearly with that of Spike. The /r/ in 'tribe', combined with the intervocalic /t/, a voiceless plosive formed at the back of the mouth, adds to the rasping sound in his voice. The main contrast between the two men's voices is that Giles/Stewart Head is keeping his cool and sense of humour and has some grain in his voice, whereas Spike/Marsters' voice is tenser and clearer, more nasal and a little grainy. Through the use of the MLS, we can see the setting, the background behind Giles', and we return to our initial view. The shot conveys information about the characters' physical and emotional position; it is concluding in nature, just like his line. The language of the image and the linguistics combine to convey a sense of closure. Let us now see what happens in the DV.

As Spike/Faliu interrupts Giles, he says:

Example 10b

DV: Ecoutez-le le rosbif (MCU of Giles) / A l'entendre on croirait qu'il annonce la météo à la télévision (Spike, MS)/ Vous les Anglais, vous êtes (Buffy and Dawn, MS) / tellement ... Bon sang (MCU of Giles), Reine Elizabeth, Big Ben, Tour de Londres, Tamise, Buckingham / Oh non. Je suis britannique (Spike, MS)

BT: Listen to the 'roast beef'. Hearing him, you could think he's announcing the weather forecast on TV / You Englishmen are so/ Damned, Queen Elizabeth, Big Ben, the Tower of London, the Thames, Buckingham / Oh no. I'm British.

To which Giles/Marié responds:

Example 11b

DV: Bienvenue au club des rosbifs (Giles and Anya MLS).

BT: Welcome to the roast beef club.

As one can see, the DV plays on different stereotypes to the OV, in which Spike referred to *Mary Poppins*, a Walt Disney musical film directed by the British director Robert Stevenson (1964). In this film, the main character, Mary Poppins, played by British actress Julie Andrews, is a magic-using but otherwise quintessential English nanny. The musical has often been ridiculed for its Cockney stereotypes, especially the chimney sweep played by American actor Dick Van Dyke, and this ties in nicely with other references to Britishness in *BtVS* in general and this episode in particular. Mary Poppins' name therefore carries connotations of gentleness and kindness, and Giles is similarly looking after everyone; he is calming people, trying to make sense of the situation whilst keeping his composure. Spike's choice is witty and informed. Moreover, with 'Nancy boy', which is slang for a gay man, the OV also plays on the stereotyped view that English people, as opposed to Americans, have an effeminate accent. The DV picks up on the vocabulary used in English about rain and follows a well-known English stereotype – that English people are obsessed with the weather and talk about it all the time. For Spike, Giles talks as though he were announcing the weather on television, i.e. very properly. Some reference is thus made to Englishness in the DV, but the reference to Mary Poppins is dropped and the term '*rosbif*' ('roast beef') is used to refer to Giles. '*Rosbif*' is a pejorative term used to allude to the way British people traditionally cook beef. When he realizes that he himself is English, Spike/Faliu first says '*bon sang*' – used in place of the very British 'bloody hell' – which can be translated literally as 'good blood', but is commonly used as a swearword and usually translated as 'damned'. It is therefore an equivalent translation, albeit dated in French. In the DV, Spike/Faliu then begins to list English landmarks, as though establishing that he is British because he can enumerate these various sites that are famous in England. In the DV, Britishness is therefore identified through iconic monuments, dated vocabulary, food and allusions to the weather. All sexual connotations are erased and the slang is neutralized, or to use Peter Fawcett words, 'expunged' or 'weakened' (2003 and 1996).

In terms of voice, Spike/Faliu speaks lower than Giles/Marié, as in the OV, although the difference is not as marked. Spike/Faliu sounds more exasperated in the DV than the character was in the OV. Additionally, Spike/Faliu speaks slower and takes more time to utter his lines, and so does not sound out of breath; he therefore does not take a loud breath after his first line. When he says '*bon sang*', there is some surprise in his voice as well as a degree of anxiety. Spike/Faliu does not sound as shocked or surprised as Spike/Marsters was; he also sounds more high-class, more educated and slightly more reserved than in the OV, with a higher pitch. There is less

roughness and depth in the French version than there was in Spike/Marsters'
original voice; his voice is cleaner, smoother and not grainy. Interestingly,
Spike/Faliu sounds older than Giles/Marié, which is not in line with the
actor's age. Moreover, Spike/Faliu does not really sound cheeky; he is more
pessimistic. In terms of accent, there is no apparent trace of Britishness and
his French accent is neutral. In the OV, his English accent is used to convey
a 'bad boy' attitude and cheekiness, but these attributes are not obvious in
the DV. The DV effaces layers of Spike's identity, with Spike vocally blend-
ing in more than he does in the OV owing to his standard French accent.
In a way, it is easier to convey Giles' 'posh' character in French than it is to
convey the connotations of Spike's accent, although this can be compensated through register on other occasions. As there are many issues related
to translating accents, this is a subject I shall return to in the next section.

In terms of sound, there is an accumulation of fricatives such as /l/ in
the various uses of '*le*', '*les*', '*la*', '*l*' and '*ll*', as well as '*tellement*' and '*télévision*';
/th/ in '*télévision*', the liaison '*vous êtes*' and '*Tamise*', and the /s/ sound in
'*rosbif*'. The plosives /b/ and /t/ in '*rosbif*', '*télévision*', '*Big Ben*', '*Buckingham*',
'*bon sang*' and '*tellement*' convey a sense of explosion. Spike/Faliu's lines
are therefore rhythmical, as was the case in the OV. However, his lines are
much more nasal, with an accumulation of /n/ and /m/ sounds in '*on*',
'*annonce*', '*météo*', '*Londres*', '*Tamise*', '*no*' and '*britannique*'. This nasality
in vocal sound is actually in line with Spike/Marsters' voice, even if it is
exaggerated in the DV.

The way the visual, linguistic and vocal information combines in this
exchange works nicely, with the shot changes and chosen words matching
on all occasions. This is particularly noticeable as there has been an effort
to select words in French that relate to Britain rather than America, even
if the connotations of the French words are different than the original
ones. The shot changes and verbal cues of Britishness match visually, but
what makes Spike British does not operate on the same level in the DV.
Indeed, Buffy and Dawn's looks and facial expressions still convey that
what Spike says, or the way he says it, is a source of strangeness, but what
changes is the reason for this strangeness: words have different connotations and values and the characters' surprise emanates from different factors.
Moreover, the DV presents or reinforces a different way of characterizing

or stereotyping Britishness: British people are identified through iconic monuments, stereotypes connected to the weather, composure, food and conservative or out-dated vocabulary. One could even say that Spike in the DV sounds more educated because of this 'cultural' knowledge, as well as more reserved because of the vocabulary he uses (i.e. there are no allusions to sex). Consequently, his 'bad boy' attitude may be less apparent in the DV.

The process of recovering their identity then continues, and as Spike and Giles are both English, they begin to think that they may be related. Spike thus asks:

Example 12a

OV: You don't suppose you and I? (Spike in MS) [Pause: shot change to Anya and Giles, MLS] We're not related are we? (Spike MS, arm movement).

Spike is shot in MS, meaning we can see him clearly raising his right hand and arm to point at Giles after he says 'you and I', at which point the camera directs our attention to Giles (and Anya) in MLS. Then we cut back to Spike as he utters 'we're not related are we?' in MS. When saying this last sentence, Spike/Marsters' voice becomes much lower and grainier, as though coming from the back of his throat. This grain is conveyed principally through the accumulation of the near fricative /r/ in 'we're not related, are we'. This sentence is pronounced in a much lower pitch than the previous one, which as a question was pronounced in a higher pitch. Moreover, the plosives /d/ and /p/ also express an element of questioning, i.e. Spike is wondering what his relationship to Giles might be and the plosives convey this inquiring element. There is one shot change in between Spike's sentences. The use of the MS places the focus on Spike/Marsters' mouth movements, which would have put pressure on the dubbing team. In French, Spike/Faliu says:

Example 12b

DV : 'Vous ne pensez pas que nous sommes (Spike in MS) [Pause: shot change to Anya and Giles, MLS] de la même famille vous et moi' (Spike MS, arm movement)

BT: You don't think that we are from the same family, you and I?

Linguistically or grammatically speaking, it can be seen that this is one sentence in French as opposed to two interrogative sentences in English, meaning that there is less opportunity for questioning in the French than there was in the original: two rises (or glide-ups) in English as opposed to one in French. There is therefore not as much variation in the voice as there was in the OV. Spike/Faliu delivers this sentence with a clear voice that has no grain, as though it were coming from the cheeks or nose. The line does not sound as explosive as the original one. On the other hand, there is more friction and a degree of complaint with the voiced fricatives /v/ in 'vous' and the liaison 'vous et moi', which in French transcribes as /z/, as well as the accumulation of nasals /n/ and /m/. The MS allows us to see Marsters' mouth distinctly; his lip movements are perfectly synchronized, showing once again that, as in the first case study, lip-synchronization was a priority when dubbing *BtVS*.

To this, Anya (in MCU) responds that '[t]here is a ruggedly handsome resemblance' between Spike and Giles. The camera cuts to Giles, shot in MS, who looks very pleased at her comment. He then takes a breath and adds:

Example 13a

> OV: (inhaling sound) (Giles in MCU)/ And you do inspire a, um, (Giles and Anya, MLS) a particular feeling of (shot change to Spike, MS, walking towards Giles) familiarity and ... (Giles, MCU) disappointment (shot change to Spike, MCU). Older brother?' (Giles, MCU).

Giles (and Anya) are shot in MLS as he begins this sentence. When he says 'inspire', the camera cuts to Spike, whom we see walking towards Giles in MS. Spike looks at Giles from top to toe, scrutinizing him intensely. Therefore, from 'inspire' to 'familiarity', Giles is speaking off-camera. When Giles/Stewart Head utters 'familiarity', we see his face in MCU, and this shot type allows us to see his facial expressions clearly, which convey unhappiness and discontentment about the nature of his feelings for Spike; his eyebrows are knitted in a frown and his lips are tight. When he says 'disappointment', he looks towards Spike, and the camera follows his gaze to show us Spike in MCU looking less than pleased. We then cut back to Giles/

Stewart Head as he says 'older brother', looking less irritated and actually a little proud. As he utters these words, he puts his left hand on his chest, and the rhythm of his voice is much slower than it previously was; there is hesitation in his voice, as though he is trying to find the right words. His voice is low until he says 'older brother', which as a question is higher in pitch, i.e. it is a glide-up. The word 'disappointment', with the plosives /d/, /p/ and /t/, sounds like a verbal stabbing and the intonation is falling; it is a glide-down used to place emphasis on the important word. The MS and MCU allows us to see Giles' feelings as well as Spike's reaction to the words, and in this short space of time, his facial expressions convey elements of questioning, confusion, pride and a feeling of disappointment towards Spike.

In the French version, Giles/Marié says:

Example 13b

> DV: heu, ah, (inhales, Giles in MCU)/ quand à vous vous m'inspirez heu (shot changes to Spike, MS, walking towards Giles) / un sentiment particulier de familiarité et de ... (Giles, MCU) déception je serais (shot changes to Spike, MCU)/ votre grand frère? (Giles, MCU).
>
> BT: Hum, as to you, you inspire a particular feeling of familiarity and ... disappointment, I would be your older brother?

Giles/Marié's voice is much higher than previously and most definitely a head voice. The facial expressions are still conveying unhappiness, but as Giles/Marié's voice is high in pitch, the combination of facial expressions and vocal sounds convey more an element of questioning than disappointment. The line is richer in fricatives, both voiced and unvoiced (/v/, /f/), and nasals (/m/, /n/). In terms of sounds, the French word '*déception*', a direct equivalent for 'disappointment', is softer than the original since / pt/ transcribes as the fricative /s/. The dubbing team has used the last few seconds of the shot of Spike to introduce '*je serais*'. The full grammatical sentence '*je serais votre grand-frère?*', which re-establishes the subject and verb, conveys a different type of modality: Giles/Marié sounds less sure of the situation than his English counterpart. All in all, Giles/Stewart Head sounds more incisive and sure of himself in the OV than he does in the DV.

Spike/Marsters then responds:

Example 14a

> OV: 'Father (Spike, MCU). Oh (MCU of Giles, back of Spike's head in foreground) God, how I must hate you.' (Spike, MCU).

Spike/Marsters' voice is at the lowest and grainiest it has been so far, in line with his obvious resentment. He snorts before saying 'father', sounding very certain that Giles is his father. As he utters this word, he is shot in MCU and one can see his mouth articulating slowly the unvoiced fricative /th/, almost like a diphthong. His facial expression is unquestionably one of repugnance. There is a counter shot of Giles looking outraged and mouthing the beginning of the word 'father' with his hand on his chest. This gesture adds more drama to the words: Giles looks and sounds extremely shocked. The camera then cuts back to Spike just as he finishes saying 'oh God'. At the beginning of the shot, we can see the back of Spike's head in the foreground; he is shaking his head as though saying 'no'. The word 'God', with its two voiced plosives (/g/ and /d/), adds to his irritated tone, and at this point his voice is extremely grainy and low; his tone has fallen to its lowest in a glide-down to emphasize the word and emotions associated with it.

In French, Spike/Faliu responds:

Example 14b

> DV: 'Mon père ouais (Spike, MCU). Ah Seigneur (MCU of Giles, back of Spike's head in foreground) à quel point je dois vous haïr' (Spike, MCU).
> BT: My father, yep. Ah Lord, how much I must hate you.

Spike/Faliu's voice is lower than it previously was, in line with Spike/Marsters' performance. To keep the isochrony between the OV and the DV, the interjection 'ouais' has been added. Lip-synchronization is therefore achieved particularly well, as we see the French words perfectly matching Marsters' lips. The interjection 'ouais' adds more disrespect or irreverence to Spike's line and tone, which is in line with his situation as the defiant son. Moreover, the nasals (/n/, /m/ and /ng/) and plosives (/p/, /k/ and /d/) add to his disdain and sense of complaint. When he says '*hair*', Spike/Faliu's voice is very low and throaty, and even though it is not as low as Spike/Marsters', there is still a glide-down and Faliu's raspy voice does emphasize Spike's hatred for his newly-found father.

Giles and Spike's conversation is interrupted by the other characters, who are now in the process of trying to remember their names. When it comes Giles' and Spike's turn, Giles asks Spike: 'What did I call you?' As Giles utters these words, we can see Spike laughing in a silly and smug manner in the background. Spike is shot in MCU as he looks in his suit jacket to find some form of identification, only to come up empty-handed. He then sees a label inside his suit jacket and reads aloud:

Example 15a

> OV: (smacks his lips) Hum (smacks lips) *Made with care for Randy*. Randy Giles?
> (shot change to Giles and Anya MCU) Why not just call me 'Horny' Giles or
> 'Desperate for a shag' Giles. I knew there was a reason I hated you. (Spike MCU).

After Spike/Marsters says 'hum', he sighs gently and searches his pockets in an attempt to find his name. He finds a label, smacks his lips and takes a breath as he starts reading. His voice is nasal, grainy and extremely focused as he is reading attentively. He is shot from the side as he reads, but on his second utterance of 'Randy' he turns his head to look towards Giles. Spike looks very offended by this choice of name. The shot changes to Giles looking amused in MS, with Anya in the background appearing quite oblivious to what is being said as she does not seem to understand British-English vocabulary. Indeed, in British-English, the adjective 'randy' means to feel great sexual desire; an expression synonymous with feeling 'horny', which Spike also uses. Spike's Britishness is once again expressed in the OV through his accent as well as British-English vocabulary. The camera cuts back to him when he says 'why not', and we see him looking offended and upset. He lowers his hand and is no longer holding his jacket. His voice is louder and tenser and rises when he asks the question 'why not', before growing deeper as he utters 'Giles'. His tone is full of reproach and the glide-down contributes to conveying his emotions explicitly. Spike/ Marsters repeats 'Giles' three times, and each time his voice gets lower and grainier in comparison with the other words, i.e. with glide-downs to mark emphasis. The actor fidgets slightly but predominantly remains in the same spot as he utters the last sentence: 'I knew there was a reason I hated you', which is pronounced more monotonously and with more grain than the beginning of the lines. His body language, i.e. stillness and slight fidgeting, as well as his facial expressions (he frowns from 'why not') further convey his deep anger. To this, an amused Giles responds: 'Randy is a family name, undoubtedly.' He is shot first in MCU, with Anya also visible, then in MLS. In the DV, Spike/Faliu says:

Example 15b

DV: euh (takes an in-breath, slight lip smack), *Manufacturé pour Candide* (smacks lips slightly) / Candide Giles? (shot change to Giles and Anya MCU) Autant m'appeler 'innocent' Giles ou bien 'simplet' Giles tant qu'on y est! / J'étais sûr d'avoir une bonne raison de vous détester (Spike MCU).

BT: Manufactured for 'Candid'? / Why not call me 'innocent' Giles or 'simple' Giles while you're at it / I was sure there was a good reason why I hated you.

When Spike/Faliu says 'euh', he looks into his pockets to find his name. He smacks his lips and takes a gentle breath as he starts reading. As in the OV, Spike/Faliu's voice is focused and attentive. When he says '*Candide*', there is a sense of achievement in the voice. He then smacks his lips as realizes what that means and repeats '*Candide*'. At the beginning of the passage, Spike/Faliu's voice does not modulate as Spike/Marsters' did; he sounds angry, but not as much as Spike/Marsters. When he says '*Candide*', he looks offended and looks towards Giles. It is now Giles' turn to be amused, but for different reasons than in the OV. Moreover, Anya's lack of reaction as she fiddles with her shirt goes unnoticed. Spike/Faliu's voice is smoother and there is no particular emphasis on the word 'Giles'. There is modulation on the last sentence as his voice goes higher on saying *j'étais sûr d'avoir* and then lower on *une bonne raison de vous détester*. Giles then responds: '*Il y avait sans doute des Candides dans notre famille*' (BT: 'There must have been "*Candides*" in our family').

In terms of vocabulary choices, 'Randy' has been translated with *'Candide'*. *'Candide'* is the title of a tale by the eighteenth-century French author Voltaire, in which the main character, Candide, is characterized by his naivety and credulity, as indicated by his name. There is therefore no connection between the connotations of the OV and those of the DV, meaning the two operate on two very different levels: the DV refers to innocence and naivety, whereas the OV plays with sexual connotations. The word *'Candide'* does, however, work nicely in terms of lip-synchronization and vocal sounds, as the word detonates due to the two plosives /d/ and /k/.

The other linguistic dimension worth mentioning is related to inter-personal politeness, through the translation of the personal pronoun 'you'. In French, there is a distinction between the two forms – *'tu'* / *'vous'* – which no longer exists in English. At the beginning of their conversation, Spike/ Faliu and Giles/Mariés use *'vous'* when they talk to one another. Then, once they start to argue, Giles switches to *'tu'* whereas Spike carries on using *'vous'*. There are different dimensions to be taken into consideration when choosing between *'tu/vous'*: 'age, generation, sex, kinship status, group membership, jural and political authority as well as emotional solidarity' (Anderman 1993: 65), and switching from one pronoun to the other can convey various feelings such as anger, contempt, intimacy, remoteness or respect (Mailhac 2000: 145). When Giles/Marié switches to *'tu'*, he sounds angry at Spike/Faliu because Spike has insulted his presumed girlfriend. Moreover, in this scene, Giles is thought to be Spike's father and is older, so this switching could merely be seen as following the norm. That being said, Spike's use of *'vous'* is still significant since it is only in very specific social contexts that children would address their parents using *'vous'*, e.g. in high-class society or conservative families. When making choices in a filmic text, '[v]isual, narrative and linguistic clues' (Chaume 2012: 144) all need to be taken into consideration, and as efforts have been made thus far to emphasize the snobbery and conservatism of British people, particularly of Giles, it could be said that Spike's use of *'vous'* over *'tu'* is an informed choice made by the dubbing team. Furthermore, the combination of *'vous'* and *'détester'* is interesting in this context because it adds even more scorn to Spike's statement. Indeed, saying to someone that you 'hate' them usually implies some level of intimacy and the corresponding use of '*tu*'. Therefore, in the OV, irreverence was conveyed mainly through a contemptuous tone, something the DV makes more explicit. The use of '*tu*' would be expected in a son-father relationship, but in terms of characterization, it is more creative to have '*vous*' in the DV. Therefore, one could also say that, though Spike/Faliu's voice is not as scornful as Spike/Marsters', this particular choice may compensate for a lack of tone.

In terms of visual information, the facial expressions and body gestures indicating anger and upset are still present, although Spike/Faliu does not sound as upset as he was in the OV. This is probably because there are fewer reasons to be upset if one is called 'simple' as opposed to 'randy'. Moreover, the OV uses the adjective 'horny' and then the verb 'shag' to further insist on Britishness. Spike is shot in MCU in this scene, meaning the focus is on himself, with one quick shot of Giles smiling and laughing as Spike gets annoyed at being called 'Randy'. As previously mentioned, shots do not change in translation: the MCU gives us direct visual access to Spike's annoyance as he frowns and raises his eyebrows repeatedly in both the OV and DV. What does change, however, is how the facial expressions and words combine and work together to convey meaning. The consequence here is that the degrees of humour, irony and annoyance in the two versions do not work on the same level. Finally, it is important to re-emphasize the difficulty of translating accents, which stand at the intersection of voice and vocabulary.

6.3.3 *Translating accents*

Giles' and Spike's characterization is based on their English accents, and transferring this to French, or any other language, is undeniably a challenging task. Geographical dialects, also known as diatopic variations, temporal dialects, non-standard dialects, social dialects, jargons or idiolects, are a well-known problem for translators. Difficulties in translation can even arise between different types of a same language, e.g. the use of Scottish-English in *Trainspotting* (Danny Boyle 1996) made the film so difficult to understand that it had to be dubbed for the US market. Under social dialects or idiolects, one can also mention the difficulty for translators in conveying teenager speak (such as Buffyspeak), which is characterized by taboo words, colloquialism and disrupted syntax.

When it comes to accent, Chaume comments that, in the past, 'dialectal equivalents between languages were more commonly found in dubbed films'. For instance, in *Gone with the Wind* (Victor Fleming 1939):

> Mammy, the house servant, speaks Black Vernacular English (African American Vernacular English), an ethnolect and sociolect spoken by many African Americans and many non-African Americans in the United States. In the Spanish translation, Manny was dubbed with a Cuban accent, an accent reminiscent of the last Spanish colony in America at the time. (Chaume 2012: 141)

Although Chaume identifies this as an older practice, Mailhac (2000), who investigates the dubbed and subtitled versions of the French film *Gazon Maudit* (Josiane Balasko 1994), identifies a similar treatment of accents in this more recent film. In the OV, one of the characters, Antoine, played by French actor Ticky Holgado, has a very thick Mediterranean accent. In the American DV, Antoine becomes Antonio and gains an Italian accent. Mailhac explains that, in the context of this film, swapping one accent for another works in as far as it shows the 'Mediterranean flavour' of the character. Furthermore, in the OV, the Spanish actress Victoria Abril, who speaks fluent French, resorts to Spanish on numerous occasions. Her words – or even whole sentences – are retained in the DV but not in the subtitled version, and Mailhac concludes that, 'as far as accents are concerned [...] the dubbed version does greater justice to characterization by avoiding the neutralisation inherent in subtitling' (2000: 136). This is an interesting statement which is not really applicable to the DV of *BtVS*, since by replacing the British accent with a French one, the Britishness has been neutralized in translation.

Mingant (2010), when comparing the French DV of Tarantino's *Inglourious Basterds* (2009) and its OV, also stresses the complexity of rendering voices and accents. Indeed, the film:

> raises the traditional issue of conveying the varieties of the English language in French. Besides the fact that many more varieties seem to exist in English than in French, there is no equivalence between, for example, a Southern American and French accent. (2010: 721)

For instance, Brad Pitt plays Aldo with a strong 'Tennessee drawl', while there is also an opposition between 'American and English intonations' (ibid.), all of which would have caused great difficulties for the French dubbing team. In French, the actor dubbing Brad Pitt, Jean-Pierre Michaël, has no accent; Aldo's geographical provenance is therefore neutralized. Mingant discusses French accents and explains that giving Aldo a southern accent with its 'singing intonation' might have given a 'different persona' to the character, making him more 'warm, sympathetic, and potentially comical' (ibid.). Another option could have been to give him a 'strong farmer's accent', which would not have worked either as it may 'lead the audience to dismiss Aldo's character as backward and irrelevant' (ibid.). The 'most logical choice was then to simply do away with the accent altogether' (ibid.), as 'trying to find an equivalent would probably' have been 'detrimental to Aldo's character, divert[ing] the audience's attention and get[ting] in the way of the story' (ibid.). In this case, neutralization seems to have been the less problematic option, although Mingant concedes that 'suppressing the character's accent means suppressing part of their background, presumably lost on a French audience' (ibid.: 722). Nevertheless, Mingant adds that the loss of accents is compensated with 'another technique, more meaningful to a French audience: the play on register with the use of swearwords and idiomatic expressions, incorrect grammatical forms and phatic forms that are "low register"' (ibid.). This technique is also noted by Chaume (2012: 142), who argues that register 'seems to offer a much better solution than dialect' when there is a mixture of both dialects and accents.

The use of accents in the French DV of *BtVS* is actually quite different from Mingant's corpus, since the English accents in this series are used to further characterize Spike as a stereotypical English 'bad boy' and Giles as an old-fashioned librarian. In the OV, Giles has a very stereotypical upper-class English accent. Although his tempo varies, Giles does not, in general, speak fast; he is composed and collected. On the whole, the rhythm of his speech is rather constant, without much change in speed. He sounds formal and a little snobbish but at the same time very positive, with a relaxed and soothing voice. He is calm and in control. His voice is smooth and his pitch is higher than Spike's. Spike's English accent is more working-class than Giles'; it is 'mockney'. As we have seen, the difference between the two accents has not been reproduced in French. When trans-lating Spike and Giles into French, it would have been a very marked choice if these two characters had been given French accents or, more extremely, had spoken with English accents in French in an attempt to convey their Englishness. Instead, vocabulary choices and register are used to convey their foreignness, as they were in the OV. This means that Britishness only works on one level in the DV as opposed to two in the OV.

Neutralizing accent therefore seems to be a 'norm' in French dubbing (Mingant 2010), and Spike and Giles do not escape this treatment, lead-ing to a homogenization of their speech, a natural result when accents are neutralized. For instance, Bouzet (1981) explains that the Italian film *La Pelle* (Liliana Cavani 1981), which features Italian and English dialogue, was fully dubbed into French. When interviewing the dubbing director, Natacha Nahon, Bouzet reports that Nahon explained to her that, in Italian, regional accents were used to differentiate between characters, but this range of accents is unfortunately not available in French; consequently, 'it is a much more artificial and delicate matter' to render the range of accents in the dubbed French version (Nahon in Bouzet 1981, my translation) and highly localized features of the original were neutralized. Nahon explains that they were 'lucky to have Marcello Mastroianni dubbing himself as it could give an authentic "colour" to the character of Malaparte' (ibid.). However, when dubbing other characters, they had to find compensation strategies and 'play on diction and social characterisation' (ibid.). Nahon's and Mingant's comments on accents and register mirror my own conclu-sions on Giles and Spike's characterization. That being said, all the studies referred to in this section also highlight the importance of finding creative compensation techniques, and there are indeed many creative solutions in the French version of *BtVS*'s 'Tabula Rasa'.

6.3.4 The dubbing effect: Giles and Spike

This case study has shown that translating Britishness in *BtVS* was not an easy task, as the sequence is loaded with cultural elements that are used to create a cultural and linguistic gap between American and British people.

It has also highlighted that there seems to be a tradition of neutralizing accents in French dubbing and that lexis and grammar as part of register may be used to compensate for a loss in characterization. However, dubbing in my corpus has brought to light the fact that such compensation strategies sometimes 'burst at the seams, revealing their artificiality to an attentive ear' (Mingant 2010: 723) since the characters are expressing their Britishness in French.

The vocal and audiovisual analysis of this sequence of 'Tabula Rasa' has shown some changes in the characterization of Spike and Giles in French. Within the Scooby Gang, Spike is an outsider; he is the vampiric other, and his Britishness further reinforces this otherness or sense of not belonging. Giles is also an outsider, being the older man in the group, the father figure. Spike and Giles are recognizably different on various levels, and it is fair to say that Whedon's intention when creating these characters as British was to emphasize their otherness. Spike's and Giles' characterization, mainly based on their otherness in the OV, has to be conveyed in French through other means than accent and vocabulary choices identified as inherently British. Giles, for reasons explained previously, is consistently identified as a Brit throughout the series, whereas Spike's association with Britain is subtler. Both characters are neutralized in the DV, with Spike being toned down even further.

Danan has famously explained that 'dubbing is an attempt to hide the foreign nature of a film by creating the illusion that actors are speaking the viewer's language' (1991: 612). Consequently, dubbed versions give the illusion that we are watching the originals using strategies of neutralization and assimilation. Mingant concludes that, 'collectively', the 'accumulated loss of references to the English language' brought about by the many transformations identified in her corpus 'contributes to a shift from the American to the French cultural point of view' (2010: 728). Similarly, Planchenault (2008: 182) claims that it is through dubbing that the distributors of foreign films try to facilitate the spectators' 'retrouvailles' ('coming together', my translation) with themselves. Both of these statements apply to the French DV of *BtVS*, as there is assimilation and neutralization of Giles and particularly Spike and we end up with a product that can be said to speak more to French audiences. However, the situation is not merely black and white, and some of the translation strategies can be said to have successfully managed to maintain elements of otherness and cultural identity. Despite having lost their signature English accents in the French DV, Giles remains a Brit and Spike is still recognizably British on specific occasions.

There may be multiple reasons behind the changes made in the DV. It is often the case that an adaptation (or DV) is conceived in order to facilitate the introduction and diffusion of a television series in the target country, with possible consequences for the perception of the characters' and the original's identity. In France, dubbing is usually made for broadcast whereas subtitling is done for DVDs. TV schedules, air time and ratings are also important; when it aired on the terrestrial channel M6, *Buffy* had a PG 12 certificate and was screened alternately at 10pm and 7pm. This means that there are two different audiences for a translated audiovisual product and, in France, the audience for dubbed versions is a larger one. Michel Sarthou explains that the larger the audience, the more the language will be neutralized. Therefore, because of audience requirements, highly localized features would inevitably be lost in any translation (2006). In my case, this could explain why there is some 'blandness' in the DV, although it is still successful in conveying a certain amount of Britishness.

In terms of voices, I noted that the characters' respective pitch and tone were higher for both Spike and Giles in the OV than they were in the DV. Speaking about *Inglourious Basterds*, Mingant (2010) also highlights that the voice of French Aldo, Jean-Pierre Michaël, and that of the French actor, Christian Gonon,[10] who lends his voice to the British officer Hicox, are more similar in French than they are in the original. In the OV, Hicox's voice is 'more high-pitched than Aldo's in the OV [and] the two voices are much more similar in French' (ibid.: 722). This may be something that dubbing directors wish to take into consideration when searching for voice talents in order to ensure that there is more cohesion between voices within dubbed films and that voices better fit actors' bodies, thereby limiting the uncanny effect of dubbing.

---

10 Gonon also voices Colin Firth's character in *Bridget Jones's Diary* (Sharon Maguire 2001).

By carrying out a multimodal analysis relying on a study of voice, visuals and linguistics, this second case study has shown how all elements combine to generate meaning and that when analysing audiovisual products, we should not forget that we are confronted with different modalities. Once again, the fact that it was not possible to provide my readers with the episode proved challenging to my analysis, although describing scenes in such a context did remind me of the challenges faced by audio-describers who have to try and put images into words for the benefit of blind and partially blind audiences. However, as with the first case study, I do not think this is a paralyzing limitation, as by carefully describing the sounds and the images as they unfold together it is still possible for viewers to appreciate a transcribed audiovisual experience. Finally, it must be noted once again that the lip-synchronisation in this episode is done beautifully, even though there are some issues with voices and overall characterization.

Where do we go from here?

Dubbing as a practice has a long history and is very much ingrained in the psyche of the audiences that have grown used to it, even though the situation is changing with the advent of DVDs and the internet. As a consequence, audiences from countries commonly referred to as 'dubbing countries', such as France, Spain or Thailand, are accustomed to watching dubbed versions. The main role of dubbing can be summarized as allowing spectators to have access to the works of directors, necessitating a process of 'localisation' or 'naturalisation' (Mingant 2010: 730) in which not only dialogue is translated but also 'cultural allusions', 'adapting to local dubbing conventions [and] finding convincing voices' (ibid.). Strategies used in dubbed versions will therefore correspond to what a local audience 'expects' from this dubbed version, with audiences accepting that American or German actors speak French or Thai; this is the suspension of disbelief that permeates the dubbing experience. However, as some of the online comments by fans of *BtVS* have shown, dubbing is not accepted blindly by all audiences.

This monograph was written with three main goals in mind: to emphasize the complexity of reading audiovisual products, to examine the effect that dubbing has on performance and characterization and finally to show the importance of multimodal analysis, thereby suggesting a new line of research that bridges the gap between analyses in Translation and Film Studies. I therefore started with a reflection on the various elements of *mise-en-scène*, with an emphasis on performance and voice, in order to then describe the status of research into dubbing. As such, it is hoped that my work will contribute to drawing even more attention to the fact that audiovisual products are semiotically complex and that dubbing is an extremely complex practice with many factors to take into consideration. I have also claimed that voice is an integral part of a character's identity and presented a multimodal method for studying characters in audiovisual products. As early as 1936, Jean Fayard, editor of the well-known French journal *Pour Vous*, commented:

> Then, all over the world, people will know that it is only possible to appreciate Wallace Beery, Katharine Hepburn or Clark Gable if they hear their original voice; their gestures, without the intonations that go with them, lose all their significance. (1936, my translation)

What Fayard points out is that, if audiences cannot hear the voices of actors, there will be a mismatch between what is seen and what is heard and the whole of the performance will cease making sense. The method that I have proposed in this book addresses Fayard's concerns and makes it possible to analyse the various elements of performance and see how dubbing impacts on performance and characterization. That is not to say that voice actors should mimic the intonation of the original, a practice that Chaves (2000) identifies in the Spanish context as '*la curva*' and which was used with the first dubbed American films. As Mompeán puts it, they should instead 'bear in mind the intended purpose and try to reproduce the same effect by making use of their own patterns, which could indeed coincide in both languages' (2012: 95).

Fayard's comment can also be read in the context of the dubbing vs. subtitling debate. He is in favour of the latter and also claims that, since German, English or American actors have 'enriched us', if we were to 'renounce' the possibility of hearing original versions we would 'abandon the pleasure that they have given us, what they have taught us'. We would only be watching 'ghosts' with 'borrowed and derisory voices', conveying 'weakly' the original actors' passions (1936, my translation). My work is not concerned with the 'subtitling vs. dubbing' debate, but Fayard's mention of pleasure fits nicely with my argument that we should not forget that watching films and television series is a pleasurable activity and that pleasure can also be a legitimate criterion for film analysis. The fact that film watching is a subjective experience does not invalidate research findings, as many film scholars have demonstrated in their analyses. Moreover, Fayard's use of the word 'ghost' echoes my claim that the effect of dubbing is uncanny, a point to which I will presently return.

My work, like those of many AVT scholars before me, emphasizes that reading audiovisual products is a complex task. The visual and acoustic elements combine to generate meaning and there are many modalities to consider. I have also emphasized that meaning is not fixed and can – and often will – vary from one audience to the next. The primary focus for my analysis was on actors as they embody characters through their performance. I have emphasized repeatedly that actors and their bodies are central to performance:

> As Merleau-Ponty so rightly said, if the body is the minimal medium for our feelings and actions, if it is what cannot be detached from us, not our property but nevertheless something which is our own, then, conversely, it is the body that gives substance, for us, to outside objects, through contact, apprehension, the senses. It is always the starting point for something to occur. (Hennion 2007: 7)

Actors and celebrities such as Sarah Michelle Gellar are known almost universally and also within a given culture; they have a 'high recognition index' (Bonner 2003: 83). However, as Shaviro points out when discussing Graces Jones' performance in the video of 'Corporate Cannibal' (2008) and the possible perpetuation of (racist) mythology, 'no performance is entirely able to control its own reception and interpretation' (2010: 23). Indeed, when (audiovisual) products travel in translation it is hard to know how they will be received or perceived and it would be unrealistic to expect the same effect to take place with a different audience. In Mingant's words, a DV is a 'balanced negotiation between strict fidelity to the original and careful interpretation' (2010: 728).

I have also claimed that the effect of dubbing is uncanny since we are hearing a voice that does not belong to the body of the actor whom we see performing. Borrowing Chion's term (1982), I wish to add the claim that the dubbed voice is 'acousmatic'. Chion developed the concept of the 'acousmatic voice' in cinema to talk about a voice whose source cannot be seen, i.e. an off-camera (or off-screen) voice, such as a non-diegetic voice over. Examples of acousmatic voice can be found in religious texts (for instance, God appearing as an acousmatic voice), popular culture, e.g. the wizard in *The Wizard of Oz* or the voice of the mother in *Psycho* (Alfred Hitchcock 1960), as well as in everyday life, such as when we use the telephone or listen to the radio. Because these voices are heard without being seen, Chion describes them as sensory phantoms; like the wind, they can be heard but never seen. It is therefore easy to establish a link with the magical powers that the uncanny is said to have, just like the magic first associated with new technologies as explained in Gunning (2003). Although Chion did not have dubbing in mind when he advanced this concept, the acousmatic seems very applicable to dubbing, particularly if one considers Dolar's description of the acousmatic voice as a 'voice in search of an origin, in search of a body, but even when it finds its body, it turns out that this doesn't quite work, the voice doesn't stick to the body, it is an excrescence which doesn't match the body' (2006: 61). Of course, the effect of dubbing is different as we do see a source for the new voice; the body of the foreign actor. However, this voice is not this body's original voice and the source of the voice is a body which we do not see. The dubbed voice can therefore be seen as a ghost haunting another actor's body; there is a 'gap between its [the voice's] source and its auditory result, which can never be quite bridged' (Dolar 2006: 67). Furthermore, dubbing can be seen as a form of ventriloquism, a practice by which voice comes from an individual's stomach without them moving their lips, therefore truly coming from the body. Dolar explains that there is:

> always something totally incongruous in the relationship between appearance, the aspect of a person and his or her voice, before we adapt to it. It is absurd, this voice cannot possibly come from this body, it doesn't sound like this person at all, or this person doesn't look at all like his or her voice. Every emission of the voice by its very essence is *ventriloquism*. (2006: 70, his emphasis)

Via a process akin to ventriloquism, the original actor becomes a 'dummy' or a ghost brought to life by the acousmatic voice of an other. By assigning Spike, Buffy and Giles new voices, their performance and characterization are altered. And when we truly understand that these actors in fact have different voices than what we are used to, this realization can be said to be uncanny.

My second related goal was to suggest a multimodal model that could be used to analyse audiovisual material, taking into consideration the acoustic and visual elements that comprise a performance – whether dealing with pure dialogue or singing parts. This analytical model was created in order to help identify aspects of performance in original audiovisual texts and then in their dubbed versions and then see how dubbing may affect characterization. Through a careful analysis of visual (e.g. body movements, facial expressions), oral (vocal) and linguistic elements, I have demonstrated how dubbing has an impact on performance. The impact, I have claimed, is neither negative nor positive *per se*; rather, it just is. Indeed, how could we expect full equivalence in translation if we are translating into another language, another system, another culture? Yet we can perhaps start thinking more seriously about how to limit the impact on characterization, a process that – as I shall argue shortly – involves working more closely with practitioners.

My final primary aim was to bridge a gap between Film Studies and Translation Studies, since these two disciplines are not currently communicating extensively on the impact translation has on audiovisual material, be it films or television series. There are some exceptions in AVT, such as Chaume (2004 & 2012), who advocates for more convergences between the two fields, as well as a few pioneering pieces of research on film dialogue, scriptwriting, screenwriting and screenplays, e.g. Aline Remael (2000, 2004 and 2008), Cattrysse and Gambier (2008) and, more recently, Martínez-Sierra (2012). However, as we have seen, Film Studies and film scholars do not usually pay attention to translation in the film process, with the notable exception of Egoyan and Balfour (2004). As such, I see this monograph as a first step towards establishing better communication between our fields. Moreover, my research has also implications in terms of practice, as will be discussed next.

Practical considerations

According to Lambourne (2012), only 0.1 per cent–1 per cent of a film's production budget is devoted to AV translation (including accessibility). This is a very minimal amount, particularly if we are to consider the revenue of blockbusters worldwide. Romero-Fresco has compiled such information and explains that:

> over half (60.5% and 57%, respectively) of the revenue obtained by the leading top-grossing and Best Picture Oscar-winning Hollywood films made between 2001 and 2011 came from foreign markets. Of this, more than three-quarters (80.4% and

76.3%, respectively) was from foreign countries where these films are subtitled or dubbed. The remaining revenue came from territories where the films are shown in English but where some viewers are likely to watch them with AD and especially SDH. (2013: online)

A paradox thus emerges: if translation provides so much of the revenue of a film, why is it so often left as an 'afterthought rather than a natural component of the film' (Sinha 2004: 174)? This is not only true of subtitling, Sinha's focus, but also dubbing, with dubbed versions also 'suffer[ing] from a lack of means at postproduction stage' (Lebtahi 2004: 409, my translation). Romero-Fresco (2013: online) explains that in order to make films which are more accessible, filmmakers need to be aware of the impact translation has on a finished product. He therefore argues that, instead of relegating translation at the post-production stage, it needs to be taken into consideration at the pre-production and production stages. Romero-Fresco therefore calls for Accessible Filmmaking (AFM):

> the consideration during the filmmaking process (and through collaboration between the translator and the creative team of the film) of some of the aspects that are required to make a film accessible to viewers in other languages and viewers with hearing or visual loss. (2013)

Throughout this book, dubbing has been shown to have an impact on performance and characterization. Therefore, like Romero-Fresco (2013), I would like to argue that dubbing should not be confined to the distribution process, but instead form at least part of the post-production process, with directors engaging in conversations with translators.

It is promising to see that some changes are already happening in the film industry in the form of 'part-subtitling' (O'Sullivan 2008) in multilingual films, e.g. in blockbusters like *Slumdog Millionaire* (Danny Boyle 2008) and *Inglourious Basterds* (2009), in which 'subtitles take up as much as 70 per cent of the dialogue' (Romero-Fresco 2013), and also creative subtitling (McClarty 2012), e.g. in the Russian film *Night Watch* (Timur Bekmambetov 2004). Moreover, what Romero-Fresco advocates can be done at a practical level (such as training) as well as a theoretical level (i.e. research) in order to create:

an exchange between film(making) studies and AVT, where film scholars and film
students learn about the aspects of AVT and accessibility that may have an effect
on the realisation and reception of (their) films, while AVT scholars and translation
students explore the elements from filmmaking and film studies that can contribute
to the theory and practice of translation and accessibility. (2013)

AFM, Romero-Fresco emphasizes, 'does not necessarily involve a dramatic
change in standard filmmaking practice' (ibid.). Instead it requires the
consideration of 'various issues, which often go unnoticed' during the pre-
production, production and post-production stages. These include 'the
provision of metadata for translators', 'collaboration between the subtitler
and the creative team in pre-production if subtitles are to be used as part of
the original film (part-subtitling)', 'attention to framing if subtitles are to
be used' for translation or accessibility purposes and 'collaboration between
the translator and the post-production team' (ibid.).

My work therefore aims to raise awareness of the impact of dubbing
on performance and characterization at a theoretical level, though it also
has practical implications. If, as we have seen, character creation is based
on extensive work by actors on their voices – e.g. Daniel Day Lewis in
Lincoln (Steven Spielberg 2012) or Woody Harrelson in *Natural Born
Killers* (Oliver Stone 1994) – that a dubbing crew and particular voice
actor only have a few days to reproduce, are we not then going to lose
part of what the director intended to portray? Quentin Tarantino, speaking about *Inglourious Basterds* (2009) when it premiered at the Cannes
Film Festival, is purported to have said that 'it does not make sense to
dub this film' (quoted in Mingant 2010: 713). Different characters speak
English, German, French and Italian throughout this film and scholars
have commented that Tarantino was very much concerned with its fluency
(O'Sullivan 2010, Mingant, 2010, Sanz Ortega forthcoming, 2015). The
use of languages and issues of fluency were therefore part of Tarantino's
'artistic endeavour' (Mingant 2010: 723); nevertheless, his film has been
dubbed into French, Italian and Spanish. This is what an Italian reviewer
had to say about the Italian dub:

When a film like this is impossible to dub, it is unavoidable that dubbing, no matter
how good, is done bad [sic.], so the evaluation is affected by it. I give a 0 to the film

distribution company that maybe in a rather Freudian way, did not think it was important to include an explanation in the Italian DVD version.[1]

This comment shows that the dubbed version may have had a better reception if there had been an effort at contextualising what has been done in the dubbed film, e.g. explaining where the characters come from or what their accents are. This is something worth considering since films have to be dubbed or subtitled in order for them to travel the world. Paying more attention to how they are dubbed would therefore represent the first step towards making them more 'accessible', to use Romero-Fresco's term.

Future research

This monograph has addressed an under-researched topic in order to suggest a new line of enquiry in Audiovisual Translation using multimodal analysis to consider the many communicative/semiotic layers of audiovisual translation and foregrounding the way visual, oral and lexical dimensions interplay. My work is therefore presented as a starting point for the systematic investigation of characterization in audiovisual products (both the original and translated versions), and it is my hope that it will pave the way for future research at the intersection of Translation Studies, Film Studies and Television Studies. My emphasis was on developing a multimodal method, wherein *Buffy the Vampire Slayer* was used as a case study to demonstrate the model's validity. I therefore hope that researchers working with other materials and language combinations will find it useful too.

I have chosen to illustrate my method with material from a television series rather than films. These are two separated media and so characterization will be constructed differently. In the same way as the serial form allows a 'potentially progressive narrative form' (Jane Feuer 1984: 128),

1   <http://www.asinc.it/eng/ase_rwn_09.html>.

characters in a television series have the opportunity to develop over time, e.g. *Buffy the Vampire Slayer* comprises seven seasons, leaving ample space and time for the actors to develop their performances. In films, however, characters are introduced and developed over the course of two or three hours. However, as Bosseaux (2012) demonstrates, it is also possible to apply this method to a film.

I have also refrained from speculating about the reasons behind any changes made, although future research could investigate further the reasons behind the changes that occur in dubbing *Buffy the Vampire Slayer* for a French audience. Was there, for instance, a deliberate attempt to alter the viewer's perception of characters? Analysing dubbing in terms of manipulation, censorship and 'self-imposed' censorship (Scandura 2004: 133) could also be rewarding. Another direction would be to consider Buffy's genre in (French) translation. I have mentioned repeatedly that the way we read performance signs is culturally and historically bound. The genre to which *Buffy* belongs, namely fantasy fiction, is typically American, and there is no indigenous equivalent in the French system. To my knowledge, this has never been commented on in the literature, but it seems reasonable to suggest that when Buffy performs her 'saving' role and uses a vocabulary heavily loaded with references to good and evil, displaying a Manichean vision of the world, she sounds more artificial, pedantic and patronizing in the French version; French has no tradition similar to the American one upon which to draw. Moreover, the vocabulary of French-speaking Buffy in the subtitled (Bosseaux 2008) and dubbed versions is often selected from a higher register and can come across as more affected, pompous and archaic. This may be worth examining in future studies.

Ultimately, this monograph has given me the opportunity to reflect on the translation process at a deeper level; on what translation is and what it does. It seems to me that translation can be conceptualized as a liminal state. In his work dedicated to rituals and rites of passages, Victor Turner defines a liminal space as 'a realm of pure possibility whence novel configurations of ideas and relations may arise' (1967: 97); a space where 'new meanings [...] can be introduced' (1981: 161). Consequently, the liminal state is characterized by ambiguity, openness and indeterminacy, as one's sense of identity to some extent dissolves, bringing about disorientation.

Liminality is a period of transition, during which our normal limits with regard to thought, self-understanding and behaviour are relaxed, paving the way for something new. Drawing from Turner, I would like to argue that translation is a liminal, in-between space where the transition of meaning occurs, as well as a rite of passage for meaning to exist fully. To me, there is no point in only discussing translations in terms of 'right' and 'wrong' or, like Virginia Woolf, of being overly scared about loss in translation:

> When you have changed every word in a sentence from Russian to English, have thereby altered the sense a little, the sound, weight, and accent of the words in relation to each other completely, nothing remains except a crude and coarsened version of the sense. Thus treated, the great Russian writers are like men deprived by an earthquake or a railway accident not only of all their clothes, but also of something subtler and more important – their manners, the idiosyncrasies of their characters. (1925: 182)

Spike may have lost his signature accent in translation, but he still has his emblematic black coat. And maybe this is where the main difference between monosemiotic texts (such as books) and polysemiotic texts (like films) lies; the visuals will always be there in a dubbed film to remind us that we are watching a translated product and also help us make sense of the whole of the performance. After all, even if equivalence is what we want to achieve when translating characters into another language, full equivalence can never be reached. And this should not be a problem; I feel that if we conceptualize translation as space between the possible and the impossible, we are able to think about it more creatively. Translation, to me, is a new version of someone's work, and in the case of case of dubbing, I find it much more rewarding to refer to a dubbed version as another version of a film, a new version which could be called a 'dubber's cut', akin to the well-known concept of a 'director's cut' (Mingant 2010: 730). Translation calls attention to the liminality of meaning since it is in translation that meaning *becomes*. Ultimately, if Spike, Buffy or Giles are to exist globally, we have no choice but to translate them, and even if we may disagree with what has happened to them in dubbed versions, translation allows them to exist again, and again, and again. And that is something that I, for one, am very happy about.

Bibliography

Primary sources

'Once More With Feeling', written and directed by Joss Whedon, *Buffy the Vampire Slayer* (6.7).
'Tabula Rasa', written by Rebecca Rand Kirshner and directed by David Grossman, *Buffy the Vampire Slayer* (6.8).

Secondary sources

Abbott, S. (2001). 'A Little Less Ritual and a Little More Fun: the Modern Vampire', *Slayage. The Online Journal of Buffy Studies* 1.3 [3] (June) <http://slayageonline. com/essays/slayage3/sabbott.htm> (last accessed on 26 March 2015).
Abbott, S. (2005). 'From Madman in the Basement to Self-Sacrificing Champion. The Multiple Faces of Spike', *European Journal of Cultural Studies* 8(3): 329–44.
Abecassis, M. (2008). 'Langue et cinéma: Aux origines du sons', *Glottopol* 12: 6–16.
Adams, M. (2003). *Slayer Slang. A Buffy the Vampire Slayer Lexicon.* Oxford University Press.
Affron, C. (1997). *Star Acting, Gish, Garbo and Davis.* New York: E. P. Dutton.
Agost, R. (1999). *Traducción y Doblaje: Palabras, Voces e Imágenes.* Barcelona: Ariel Practicum.
Albright, R. S. (2005). 'Breakaway Pop Hit or ... Book Number? "Once More with Feeling" and Genre', *Slayage. The International Online Journal of Buffy Studies* 5(1) <http://www.slayageonline.com/essays/slayage17/Albright.htm> (last accessed on 10 February 2015).
Alburger, James. R (2011) *The Art of Voice Acting: The Craft and Business of Performing Voiceover*, fourth edition, Focal Press.
Amy-Chinn, D. (2005). 'Queering the Bitch. Spike, Transgression and Erotic Empowerment', *European Journal of Cultural Studies* 8(3): 313–28.

Amy-Chinn D. and Williamson, M. (2005). 'Introduction' in *The Vampire Spike in Text and Fandom: Unsettling Oppositions in* Buffy the Vampire Slayer, special issue of *European Journal of Cultural Studies* 8(3): 275–88.

Anderman, G. (1993). 'Untranslatability: the Case of Pronouns of Address in Literature', *Perspectives: Studies in Translatology*: 57–67.

Angelou, M. (1969). *I Know Why the Caged Birds Sing*. New York: Random House.

Apter, R. (1985). 'A Peculiar Burden: Some Technical Problems of Translating Opera for Performance in English', *Meta* 30(4): 309–19.

Armstrong, N. (2004). 'Voicing "The Simpsons" from English into French: A Story of Variable Success', *The Journal of Specialised Translation* 2: 97–109.

Armstrong, N. and Federici, F. M. (eds) (2006). *Translating Voices, Translating Regions*. Rome: Aracne.

Armstrong, S. (2000). 'An Englishman Abroad: Buffy's Rupert Giles' [Interview], *Sunday Times*, 10 December <http://www.betsyda.com/ash/items/ahtimes. html> (last accessed on 26 March 2015).

Assis, R. A. (2001). 'Features of Oral and Written Communication in Subtitling', in Gambier, Y. (ed.), *(Multi)Media Translation. Concepts, Practices and Research*, pp. 213–21. Philadelphia and New York: John Benjamins.

Baker, M. (2011). *In Other Words, a Coursebook on Translation*. London: Routledge.

Bakhtin, M. M. (1984). *Problems of Dostoevsky's Poetics*, ed. and trans. by Emerson, C. Minneapolis: University of Michigan Press.

Baldry, A. and Taylor, C. (2004). 'Multimodal Concordancing and Subtitles with MCA', in Partington, A., Morley, J. and Haarman, L. (eds), *Corpora and Discourse*, pp. 57–70. Berlin: Peter Lang.

Baldry, A. and Thibault, P. J. (2006). *Multimodal Transcription and Text Analysis*. London and Oakville, CA: Equinox.

Ballard, M. (ed.) (2001). *Oralité et Traduction*. Arras: APU, Collection: Traductologie.

Baños-Piñero, R. (2006). 'Estudio descriptivo-contrastivo del español oral en una serie de TV de producción propia y en una serie de TV de producción ajena. El caso de Siete Vidas y Friends', unpublished Master's thesis, Universidad de Granada.

Baños-Piñero, R. and Chaume, F. (2009). 'Prefabricated Orality: A Challenge in Audiovisual Translation', *Intralinea*, online translation, Journal 6 <http://www. intralinea.org/specials/article/Prefabricated_Orality> (last accessed on 26 March 2015).

Barthes, R. (1977). 'The Grain of Voice', in *Image-Music-Text*, essays selected and trans. by Heath, S., pp. 179–89. London: Fontana Press.

Bellafante, G. (1997). 'Bewitching Teen Heroines', *Time*, 5 May, 82–5 <http://www. time.com/time/magazine/article/0,9171,986288,00.html> (last accessed on 26 March 2015).

Biagini, M. (2010). 'Les sous-titres en intéraction: le cas des marqueurs discursifs dans des dialogues filmiques sous-titrés', *Glottopol* 15: 18–33.

Birdwhistell, R. L. (1970). *Kinesics and Context*. Philadelphia: Pennsylvania: University of Pennsylvania Press.

Bloustien, G. (2002). 'Fans with a Lot at Stake: Serious Play and Mimetic Excess in "Buffy the Vampire Slayer"', *European Journal of Cultural Studies* 5(4): 427–49.

Bonner, F. (2003). *Ordinary Television*. London: Sage.

Bordwell, D. and Thompson, K. (1997/2007). *Film Art: An Introduction*. New York: McGraw-Hill.

Bosseaux, C. (2007). *How Does it Feel? Point of View in Translation*. Amsterdam and New York: Rodopi.

Bosseaux, C. (2008). '"Buffy the Vampire Slayer". Characterization in the Musical Episode of the TV Series', special issue of *The Translator: Studies in Intercultural Communication* 14(2): 343–72.

Bosseaux, C. (2012). 'Some Like it Dubbed. Translating Marilyn Monroe', in Minors, H. J. (ed.), *Music, Text and Translation*, pp. 81–92. London: Continuum Books.

Bouzet, A.-D. (1981). 'Natacha Nahon et la tour de Babel' <http://www.ataa.fr/blog/comment-doubler-un-film-multilingue/> (last accessed on 26 March 2015).

Boyette, M. (2001). 'The Comic Anti-Hero in "Buffy the Vampire Slayer", or Silly Villain: Spike is for Kicks', *Slayage. The Online Journal of Buffy Studies* 4 (December). <http://slayageonline.com/PDF/boyette.pdf> (last accessed 11 February 2015).

Branigan, E. R. (1984). *Point of View in the Cinema: A Theory of Narration and Subjectivity in Classical Films*. The Hague: Mouton.

Brooker, W. and Jermyn, D. (eds) (2003). *The Audience Studies Reader*. London and New York: Routledge.

Brooks, P. (1976/1995). *The Melodramatic Imagination: Balzac, Henry James, Melodrama and the Mode of Excess*. New York: Yale University Press.

Brown, R. S. (1994). *Overtones and Undertones: Reading Film Music*. Berkeley: University of California Press.

Burr, V. (2005). 'Scholar/'shippers and Spikeaholics: Academic and Fan Identities at the Slayage Conference on "Buffy the Vampire Slayer"', *European Journal of Cultural Studies* 8(3): 375–83.

Caillé, P.-F. (1960). 'Cinéma et traduction: le traducteur devant l'écran', *Babel* 6(3): 103–9.

Campanella, S. and Belin, P. (2007). 'Integrating Face and Voice in Person Perception', *Trends in Cognitive Sciences*, 11(12): 535–43.

Cattrysse, P. and Gambier, Y. (2008) 'Screenwriting and Translating Screenplays', in Díaz-Cintas, J. (ed.), *The Didactics of Audiovisual Translation*, pp. 39–55. Amsterdam: John Benjamins.

Cavell, S. (1996). *Contesting Tears: The Hollywood Melodrama of the Unknown Woman.* Chicago: University of Chicago Press.

Chandler, D. (©1994–2015). 'The Grammar of Television and Film' <http://visual-memory.co.uk/daniel/Documents/short/gramtv.html> (last accessed on 26 March 2015).

Chaume, F. (1997). 'Translating Non-verbal Information in Dubbing', in Poyatos, F. (ed.), *New Perspectives and Challenges in Literature, Interpretation and the Media,* pp. 315–25. Amsterdam: John Benjamins.

Chaume, F. (2004a). *Cine y traducción.* Madrid: Cátedra.

Chaume, F. (2004b). 'Film Studies and Translation Studies: Two Disciplines at Stake in Audiovisual Translation', *Meta* XLIX (1): 12–24.

Chaume, F. (2004c). 'Synchronization in Dubbing: a Translational Approach', in Orero, P. (ed.), *Topics in Audiovisual Translation,* pp. 35–52. Amsterdam: John Benjamins.

Chaume, F. (2004d). 'Discourse Markers in Audiovisual Translation', *Meta* XLIX (4): 833–55.

Chaume, F. (2012). *Audiovisual Translation: Dubbing.* Manchester: St Jerome Publishing.

Chaume Varela, F. (1998). 'Textual Constraints on the Translator's Creativity in Dubbing', in Beylard-Ozeroff, A., Kralova, J. and Moser-Mercer, B. (eds), *Translators' Strategies and Creativity.* Amsterdam: John Benjamins.

Chaume Varela, F. (2007). 'Dubbing Practices in Europe: Localisation Beats Globalisation', *Linguistica Antverpiensia* 6, special Issue, A Tool for Social Integration? Audiovisual Translation from Different Angles: 203–17.

Chaves, M. J. (2000). *La Traducción Cinematográfica: El Doblaje.* Huelva, España: Universidad de Huelva Publicaciones.

Chiaro, D. (2006). 'Verbally Expressed Humour on Screen: Reflections on Translation and Reception', *JoSTrans* (06) <http://www.jostrans.org/issue06/art_chiaro.php> (last accessed on 26 March 2015).

Chion, M. (1985/1994). *Le son au cinéma.* Paris: Editions de l'Etoile.

Chion, M. (1988). *La parole au cinéma. La toile trouée.* Paris, Cahiers du Cinéma.

Chion, M. (1994). *Audio-Vision: Sound on Screen,* trans. C. Gorbman. New York: Columbia University Press.

Chion, M. (1999). *The Voice in Cinema,* ed. and trans. C. Gorbman. New York: Columbia University Press (translation of *La Voix au cinéma,* Paris: Cahiers du cinéma, 1982).

Chuang, Y.-T. (2006). 'Studying Subtitle Translation from a Multi-modal Approach, *Babel* 52(4), 372–83.

Corrius, M. (2008). 'Translating Multilingual Audiovisual Texts. Priorities, Restrictions, Theoretical Implications', PhD thesis, Universitat Autònoma de Barcelona.

Crystal, D. (1991). *A Dictionary of Linguistics and Phonetics*, 3rd edn. Oxford: Blackwell.

Danan, M. (1991). 'Dubbing as an Expression of Nationalism', *Meta* 36(4): 606–14 <http://www.erudit.org/revue/meta/1991/v36/n4/002446ar.pdf> (last accessed on 26 March 2015).

Dechert, H., Möhle, D. and Raupach, M. (eds) (1984). *Second Language Productions*. Tübingen: Narr.

De Higes A. et al. (2013). 'Subtitling Language Diversity in Spanish Immigration Films', *Meta* 58(1), 134–45.

De Linde, Z. and Kay, N (1999). *The Semiotics of Subtitling*. Manchester: St Jerome.

Desilla, L. (2009). 'Towards a Methodology for the Study of Implicatures in Subtitled Films: Multimodal Construal and Reception of Pragmatic Meaning Across Cultures', unpublished PhD thesis, Manchester University.

Díaz Cintas, J. (1998). 'The Dubbing and Subtitling into Spanish of Woody Allen's "Manhattan Murder Mystery", *Linguistica Antverpiensia* 32, 55–71.

Díaz Cintas, J. (2001). *La traducción audiovisual: El subtitulado*. Salamanca: Almar.

Díaz Cintas, J. (2003). 'Audiovisual Translation in the Third Millennium', in Anderman, G. and Rogers, M. (eds). *Translation Today. Trends and Perspectives*, pp. 192–204. Clevedon, Buffalo, Toronto, Sydney: Multilingual Matters.

Díaz Cintas, J. (2004a). 'Dubbing or Subtitling: the Eternal Dilemma', *Perspectives*: 31–40.

Díaz Cintas, J. (2004b). 'Subtitling: the Long Journey to Academic Acknowledgement', *JoSTrans* (1), 50–68 <http://www.jostrans.org/issue01/art_diaz_cintas.php> (last accessed on 26 March 2015).

Díaz-Cintas, J. (ed.) (2008). *The Didactics of Audiovisual Translation*. Amsterdam John Benjamins.

Díaz Cintas, J. (2011). 'Dealing with Multilingual Films in Audiovisual Translation', in Pöckl, W. et al. (eds), *Translation, Sprachvariation, Mehrsprachichkeit*, pp. 215–33. Frankfurt a/M.: Peter Lang.

Díaz Cintas, J. and Remael, A. (2007). *Audiovisual Translation Subtitling*. Manchester: St Jerome.

DiBattista, M. (2001). *Fast Talking Dames*. New Haven and London: Yale University Press.

Dix, A. (2008). *Beginning Film Studies*. Manchester and New York: Manchester University Press.

Dolar, M. (2006). *A Voice and Nothing More*. Cambridge, MA: MIT press.

Dore, M. (2009). 'Target Language Influence over Source Texts: A Novel Dubbing Approach in "The Simpsons", First Series', in Federici, F. (ed.), *Translating Voices for Audiovisual*, pp. 134–56. Rome: Aracne.

Driscoll, M. (2002). 'From Kino-eye to Anime-eye/ai: the Filmed and the Animated, in Imamura Taihei's Media Theory', *Japan Forum* 14(2): 269–96.

Dyer, R. (1979/1998). *Stars*. London: British Film Institute.

Dyer, R. (1993). 'Dracula and Desire', *Sight and Sound*, January, 8–15.

Egoyan, A. and Balfour, I. (2004) (eds). *Subtitles: on the Foreignness of Film*. Cambridge, MA: MIT Press.

Fawcett, P. (1996). 'Translating Film', in Harris. G. T. (ed.) *On Translating French Literature and Film*, pp. 65–88. Amsterdam: Rodopi.

Fawcett, P. (2003). 'The Manipulation of Language and Culture in Film Translation', in Calzada-Pérez, M. (ed.), *Apropos Ideology*, pp. 145–63. Manchester: St Jerome.

Fayard, J. (1936). 'Doublage … or Not Doublage', *Pour Vous* n° 372, 2 janvier 1936 <http://www.ataa.fr/blog/doublage-or-not-doublage/> (last accessed on 26 March 2015).

Federici, F. (2009) (ed.). *Translating Voices for Audiovisual*. Rome: Aracne. (See pages 134–56.)

Fiske, J. (1987/1991). *Television Culture*. London: Routledge.

Fodor, I. (1976). *Film Dubbing: Phonetic, Semiotic, Esthetic and Psychological Aspects*. Hamburg: Helmut Buske.

Fonagy, I. and Magdics, K. (1972). 'Emotional Patterns in Intonation and Music', in Bolinger, D. L. (ed.), *Intonation*, pp. 286–312. Hardmondsworth: Penguin.

Fossey, C. (2003). '"Never Hurt the Feelings of a Brutal Killer": Spike and the Underground Man', *Slayage. The Online Journal of Buffy Studies* 2.4 [8] (March) <http://slayageonline.com/essays/slayage8/Fossey.htm> (last accessed on 26 March 2015).

Franzon, J. (2005). 'Musical Comedy Translation: Fidelity and Format in the Scandinavian "My Fair Lady"', in Gorlée, D. L. (ed.), *Song and Significance. Virtues and Vices of Vocal Translation*, pp. 263–98. Amsterdam and New York: Rodopi.

Franzelli, V. (2008). 'Traduire la parole émotionnelle en sous-titrage: colère et identités', *Etudes de linguistique appliquée* 150: 221–44.

Freddi, M. and Pavesi, M. (eds) (2009). A*nalysing Audiovisual Dialogue. Linguistic and Translational Insights*. Bologna: Clueb.

Freud, S. (1919). *Essay on the Uncanny*. Harmondsworth: Penguin.

Garwood, I. (2006). 'The Pop Song in Film', in Gibbs, J. and Pye, D. (eds), *Close-Up 01*, pp. 89–166. London and New York: Wallflower Press.

Gelder, K. (1994). 'Vampires in Greece: Byron and Polidori', in Gelder, K. (ed.), *Reading the Vampire*, pp. 24–41. London and New York: Routledge.

Gibbs, J. (2002). *Mise-en-scène: film style and interpretation* (Short Cuts). London: Wallflower Press.

Gibbs, J. and Pye, D. (eds) (2005). *Style and Meaning. Studies in the Detailed Analysis of Film*. Manchester and New York: Manchester University Press.

Gibbs, J. and Pye, D. (eds) (2006). *Close-Up 01*. London and New York: Wallflower Press.

Gibbs, J. and Pye, D. (eds) (2007). *Close-Up 02*. London and New York: Wallflower Press.

Gorbman, C. (1987). *Unheard Melodies: Narrative Film Music*. London: BFI.

Goris, O. (1993). 'The Question of French Dubbing: Towards a Frame for Systematic Investigation', *Target* 5(2), 169–90.

Gorlée, L. D. (ed.) (2005). *Song and Significance. Virtues and Vices of Vocal Translation*. Amsterdam and New York: Rodopi.

Gottlieb, H. (1994). 'Subtitling: Diagonal Translation', *Perspectives: Studies in Translatology* 2(1): 101–21.

Gottlieb, H. (1997). '"You Got the Picture?" On the Polysemiotics of Subtitling Wordplay', in Delabastita, D. (ed.), *Traductio. Essays on Punning and Translation*. Namur: St. Jerome Publishing and Presses Universitaires de Namur.

Gottlieb, H. (2005). 'Multidimensional Translation: Semantics Turned Semiotics', MuTra 2005conference proceedings <http://www.euroconferences.info/proceedings/2005_Proceedings/2005_Gottlieb_Henrik.pdf> (last accessed on 26 March 2015).

Graver, D. (1997). 'The Actor's Bodies', *Text and Performance Quarterly*, 17(3): 221–35.

Gregory, M. and Carroll, S. (1978). *Language and Situation: Language Varieties and Their Social Contexts*. London: Routledge and Kegan Paul.

Gunning, T. (2003). 'Renewing Old Technologies: Astonishment, Second Nature, and the Uncanny in Technology from the Previous Turn-of-the-Century', in Thorburn, D. and Jenkins, H. (eds), *Rethinking Media Change: The Aesthetics of Transition*, pp. 39–60. Cambridge and London: MIT Press.

Gwenllian-Jones, S. (2003). 'Histories, Fictions and Xena', in Brooker, W. and Jermyn, D. (eds), *The Audience Studies Reader*, pp. 185–91. London: Routledge.

Halliday, M. A. K. (1994). *An Introduction to Functional Grammar*, 2nd edn. London, Melbourne and Auckland: Arnold.

Hatim, B. and Mason, I. (1990). *Discourse and the Translator*. New York: Longman.

Hatim B. and Mason, I. (1997). *The Translator as Communicator*. London and New York: Routledge.

Hatim, B. and Mason, I. (2000). 'Politeness in Screen Translating' in Venuti, L. (ed.) *The Translation Studies Reader*, pp. 430–45. London and New York: Routledge.

Havens, C. (2003). *Joss Whedon: The Genius Behind Buffy*. London: Titan Books.

Hennion, A. (2005). 'Pour une pragmatique du goût'. Centre de Sociologie de l'Innovation (CSI): *CSI Working Papers Series* 1, 1–14.

Hennion, A. (2007). 'Pragmatics of Taste', in Jacobs, M. D. and Hanrahan, N. W. (eds), *The Blackwell Companion to the Sociology of Culture*. Oxford: Blackwell.

Hermans, T. (1999). *Translation in Systems. Descriptive and Systemic Approaches Explained*. Manchester: St Jerome.

Hewitt, E. (2000). 'A Study of Pop-Song Translation', *Perspectives: Studies in Trans-latology* 8(3): 187–96.

Hills, M. and Williams, R. (2005). '"It's All my Interpretation". Reading Spike Through the Subcultural Celebrity of James Marsters', *European Journal of Cultural Studies* 8(3): 345–65.

Hollander, R. (2001). 'Doublage et sous-titrage. Etude de cas: "Natural Born Killers" (Tueurs nés)', *Revue Française d'Etudes Américaines* 88: 79–88.

Howell, P. (2006). 'Character Voice in Anime Subtitles', *Perspectives: Studies in Trans-latology* 14(4): 292–305.

Hsu, W. F. Y. (2004). 'Misreading the Random: A Translational Reading of the Japanese Anime Cowboy Bebop', unpublished MA thesis, University of Virginia.

Ivarsson, J. (1992). *Subtitling for the Media. A Handbook of an Art.* Stockholm: Transedit.

Ivarsson, J. (2002). 'Subtitling Through the Ages. A Technical History of Subtitles in Europe', *Language International* (April 2002): 6–10.

Izard, N. (1992). *La Traducció Cinematogràfica.* Barcelona: Publicacions de la Generalitat de Catalunya.

Jackson, R. (1981). *Fantasy: The Literature of Subversion.* London and New York: Methuen.

Jakobson, R. (1959). 'On Linguistic Aspects of Translation', in Brower, R. A. (ed.), *On Translation*, pp. 232–9. Cambridge, MA: Harvard University Press.

Jowett, L. (2005). *Sex and the Slayer. A Gender Studies Primer for the Buffy Fan.* Middleton: Wesleyan University Press.

Kaindl, K. (2004). 'Translating Multiple Texts: Popular Song Translation as Mediation'. Unpublished paper presented at the 4th International EST Congress, 'Translation Studies: Doubts and Directions', University of Lisbon, 26–9 September 2004.

Kaindl, K. (2005). 'The Plurisemiotics of Pop Song Translation: Words, Music, Voice and Image', in Gorlée, L. D. (ed.), *Song and Significance. Virtues and Vices of Vocal Translation*, pp. 235–62. Amsterdam and New York: Rodopi.

Kalinak, K. M. (1992). *Settling the Score: Music and the Classical Hollywood Film.* Wisconsin: University of Wisconsin Press.

Karamitroglou, F. (2000). *Towards a Methodology for the Investigation of Norms in Audiovisual Translation.* Amsterdam and Atlanta: Rodopi.

Katz, S. D. (1991). *Film Directing Shot by Shot: Visualizing from Concept to Screen.* Studio City, CA: Michaël Wiese Productions in conjunction with Focal Press.

Klevan, A. (2005). *Film Performance.* London & New York: Wallflower Press.

Kozloff, S. (2000). *Overhearing Film Dialogue.* Oakland, CA: University of California Press.

Kramsch, C. (1998). *Language and Culture.* Oxford: Oxford University Press.

Kress, G. and van Leeuwen, T. (1996). *Reading Images: The Grammar of Visual Design*. London: Routledge.

Kress, G. and van Leeuwen, T. (2001). *Multimodal Discourse: The Modes and Media of Contemporary Communication*. London: Arnold.

Laing, H. (2000). 'Emotions by Numbers: Music, Song and the Musical', in Marshall, B. and Stilwell, R. (eds), *Musicals: Hollywood and Beyond*. Exeter: Intellect.

Lak, R. (1997). *Twenty Four Frames Under*. London: Quartet Books.

Lambourne, A. (2012). 'Climbing the Production Chain', paper presented at the 2012 Languages & The Media conference, Berlin, 21–3 November 2012.

Lavery, D. (2004). 'I Wrote my Thesis on You: Buffy Studies as an Academic Cult', *Slayage. The International Online Journal of Buffy Studies*, 13–14 <http://www.slayageonline.com/essays/slayage13_14/Lavery.htm> (last accessed on 26 March 2015).

Lebtahi, Y. (2004). 'Télévision: Les artefacts de la traduction-adaptation', *Meta* 49(2): 401–9.

Lemke, J. L. (1985). 'Ideology, Intertextuality, and the Notion of Register', in Benson, J. D. and Greaves, W. S. (eds), *Systemic Perspectives on Discourse, Volume 1: Selected Theoretical Papers from the Ninth International Systemic Workshop*, pp. 275–94. Norwood: Ablex.

Leeuwen, T. van (1999). *Speech, Music, Sound*. Basingstoke: Macmillan.

Lefevere, A. (1998). 'Acculturating Bertold Brecht', in Bassnett, S. and Lefevere, A, (eds) *Constructing Cultures, Essays in Literary Translation*. Bristol: Multilingual Matters.

Levine, M. P. and Schneider, S. J. (2003). 'Feeling for Buffy: the Girl Next Door', in South, J. (ed.) *Buffy the Vampire Slayer and Philosophy*, pp. 294–308. Chicago: Open Court.

Levi-Strauss, C. (1966). *The Savage Mind*. Chicago: University of Chicago Press.

Little, T. (2003). 'High School is Hell: Metaphor Made Literal in "Buffy the Vampire Slayer"', in South, J. (ed.), *Buffy the Vampire Slayer and Philosophy*, pp. 282–93. Chicago: Open Court.

Lomax, A. (1968). *Folk song Style and Culture*. New Brunswick, NJ: Transaction Books.

Low, P. (2005). 'The Pentathlon Approach to Translation', in Gorlée, L. D. (ed.), *Song and Significance. Virtues and Vices of Vocal Translation*, pp. 185–212. Amsterdam and New York: Rodopi.

Luyken, G. et al. (1991). *Overcoming Language Barriers in Television. Dubbing and Subtitling for the European Audience*. Manchester: The European Institute for the Media.

Machin, D. (2010). *Analysing Popular Music: Image, Sound and Text*. London: Sage.

Mailhac, J.-P. (2000). 'Subtitling and Dubbing, for Better or Worse? The English Video Versions of Gazon Maudit', in Salama-Carr, M. (ed.), *On Translating French Literature and Film II*, pp. 129–54. Amsterdam: Brill.

Martin, J. (2000a). 'Factoring out Exchange', in Coulthard, M., Cotterill, J. and Rock, F. (eds), *Working with Dialogue*, pp. 19–40. Tübingen: Max Niemeyer Verlag.

Martin, J. (2000b). 'Beyond Exchange: Appraisal Systems in English', in Hunston, S. and Thompson, G. (eds), *Evaluation in Text: Authorial Stance in the Construction of Discourse*, pp. 143–75. Oxford: Oxford University Press.

Martínez-Sierra, J. J. (2008): *Humour y traducción. Los Simpson cruzan la frontera*, Universitat Jaume I, Castellón.

Martínez-Sierra, J. J. et al. (2010). 'Linguistic Diversity in Spanish Immigration Films. A Translational Approach', in Berger, V. and Komori, M. (eds), *Polyglot cinema: Migration and Transcultural Narration in France, Italy, Portugal and Spain*, pp. 15–31. Vienna: LIT.

Martínez-Sierra, J. J. (2012). 'On the Relevance of Script Writing Basics in Audiovisual Translation Practice and Training', *Cadernos de Tradução* 29(1): 145–63.

Marzà, A. and Chaume, F. (2009). 'The Language of Dubbing: Present Facts and Future Perspectives', in Freddi, M. and Pavesi, M. (eds), *Analysing Audiovisual Dialogue. Linguistic and Translational Insights*, pp. 31–40. Bologna: Clueb.

Mason, I. (1989). 'Speaker Meaning and Reader Meaning: Preserving Coherence in Screen Translating', in Kölmel, R. and Payne, J. (eds), *Babel: The Cultural and Linguistic Barriers Between Nations*, pp. 13–24. Aberdeen: Aberdeen University Press.

Mason, I. (2001). 'Coherence in Subtitling: the Negotiation of Face', in Chaume, F. and Agost, R. (eds), *La Traducción en los Medios Audiovisuales*, pp. 19–33. Castello de la Plana: Universitat Jaume I.

Mayoral, R., Kelly, D. and Gallardo, N. (1988). 'Concept of Constrained Translation. Non-linguistic Perspectives of Translation', *Meta* 33: 356–67.

McCabe, J. and Akass, K. (eds) (2007). *Quality TV: Contemporary American Television and Beyond*. London and New York: I.B. Tauris.

McCabe, K. (2002). 'Buffy Hits a High Note', *Sunday Mail* (Queensland, Australia) (14 April), 6.

McClarty, R. (2012). 'Towards a Multidisciplinary Approach in Creative Subtitling', in Agost, R., Orero, P. and di Giovanni, E. (eds), *Monographs in Translating and Interpreting* (MonTI) 4: 133–55.

Melvin, A. (2011). 'Sonic Motifs, Structure and Identity in Steve McQueen's "Hunger"', *The Soundtrack* 4(1): 23–32.

Merino, R. et al. (eds) (2005). *Trasvases culturales: Literatura, cine, traduccion 4*. Vitoria: Universidad del Pais Vasco.

Mével, P.-A. (2008). 'Traduire La Haine: banlieues et sous-titrage', *Glottoppol* 12: 161–81.

Meyer-Dinkgräfe, D. (2007). 'Thoughts on Dubbing Practice in Germany: Procedures, Aesthetic Implications and Ways Forward', *Scope. An Online Journal of Film Studies* 8 <http://filmsound.org/theory/DMD-Synchron.htm> (last accessed on 26 March 2015).

Mingant, N. (2010). 'Tarantino's "Inglourious Basterds": a Blueprint for Dubbing Translators?', *Meta* 55 (4), 712–31.

Minors, H. J. (ed.) (2012). *Music, Text and Translation*. London: Continuum Books.

Mulvey, L. (1977/8). 'Notes on Sirk and Melodrama', in *Movie* 25: 53–6.

Mulvey, L. (2006). *Death 24x A Second*. London: Reaktion Books.

Munday, J. (2006). 'Style in Audiovisual Translation', in Armstrong, N. and Federici, F. M. (eds), *Translating Voices, Translating Regions*, pp. 21–36. Rome: Aracne.

Nedergaard-Larsen B. (1993). 'Culture-bound Problems in Subtitling', *Perspectives: Studies in Translatology* 1(2): 207–41.

Oever, A. van den (2010). *Ostrannenie. On 'Strangeness' and the Moving Image: The History, Reception, and Relevance of a Concept*. Amsterdam: Amsterdam University Press.

Orero, P. (ed.) (2004). *Topics in Audiovisual Translation*. Amsterdam: John Benjamins.

O'Sullivan, C. (2008). 'Multilingualism at the Multiplex: a New Audience for Screen Translation?', *Linguistica Antverspiensia*, LANS6: 81–97.

O'Sullivan, C. (2010). 'Tarantino on Language and Translation', *MA Translation Studies News*, 21February <http://matsnews.blogspot.co.uk/2010/02/tarantino-on-language-and-translation.html> (last accessed on 26 March 2015).

Palencia Villa, R. M. (2002). 'La influencia del doblaje audiovisual en la percepción de los personajes', unpublished PhD thesis, Universitat Autónoma de Barcelona <http://www.tesisenred.net/TDX-1118102–182436/> (last accessed on 26 March 2015).

Parini, I. (2009). 'The Transposition of Italian American in Italian Dubbing', in Federici, F. (ed.), *Translating Regionalised Voices in Audiovisuals*, pp. 157–78. Rome: Aracne.

Perego, E. and Taylor, J. (2009). 'An Analysis of the Language of Original and Translated Film: Dubbing into English', in Freddi, M. and Pavesi. M. (eds), A*nalysing Audiovisual Dialogue. Linguistic and Translational Insights*, pp. 57–74. Bologna: Clueb.

Pérez-González, L. (2007). 'Appraising Dubbed Conversation. Systemic Functional Insights into the Construal of Naturalness in Translated Film Dialogue', *The Translator* 13(1): 1–38.

Pérez-González, L. (2014). *Audiovisual Translation: Theories, Methods and Issues*. London: Routledge.

Perkins, V. F. (1999). *The Magnificent Ambersons*. London: British Film Institute.

Phillips, P. (2000). *Understanding Film Text: Meaning and Experience*. London: British Film Institute.

Planchenault, G. (2008). '"C'est ta live!" Doublage en français du film américain Rize ou l'amalgame du langage urbain des jeunes de deux cultures', *Glottoppol* 12: 182–99.

Powrie, P. (2008). 'The Haptic Moment: Sparring with Paolo Conte in Ozon's "5x2"', *Paragraph*, 31(2): 206–22.

Pye, D. (2000). 'Movies and Point of View', *Movie* 36: 2–34.

Pye, D. (2007). 'Movies and Tones', in Gibbs, J. and Pye, D. (eds), *Close-Up 02*, pp. 1–80. London and New York: Wallflower Press.

Ramière, N. (2004). 'Comment le sous-titrage et le doublage peuvent modifier la perception d'un film. Analyse contrastive des versions sous-titrée et doublée en français du film d'Eli Kazan, A Streetcar Named Desire (1951)', *Meta* XLIX (1): 102–14.

Ranzato, I. (2011), 'Translating Woody Allen into Italian: Creativity in Dubbing', *Journal of Specialized Translation*, 15: 121–41.

Ranzato, I. (2012). 'Gayspeak and Gay Subjects in Audiovisual Translation: Strategies in Italian Dubbing', *Meta* 57(2): 369–84.

Reay, P. (2004). *Music in Film. Soundtracks and Synergy*. London and New York: Wallflower Press.

Remael, A. (2000). 'A Polysystem Approach to British New Wave Film Adaptation, Screen Writing and Dialogue', PhD thesis. Leuven: Katholieke Universiteit Leuven.

Remael, A. (2003). 'Mainstream Narrative Film Dialogue and Subtitling', in Gambier, Y. (ed.), *Screen Translation*, special issue of *The Translator* 9(2): 225–45.

Remael, A. (2004). 'A Place for Film Dialogue Analysis in Subtitling Courses', in Orero, P. (ed.), *Topics in Audiovisual Translation*, pp. 103–26. Amsterdam: John Benjamins.

Remael, A. (2008). 'Screenwriting, Scripted and Unscripted Language. What do Subtitlers Need to Know?', in Díaz-Cintas, J. (ed.), *The Didactics of Audiovisual Translation*, pp. 57–67. Amsterdam: John Benjamins.

Richart Marset, M. (2012). *Ideología y traducción. Por un análisis genético del doblaje*. Madrid: Biblioteca Nueva.

Robinson, T. (2001). 'The Onion / A.V. Club Interview with Joss Whedon', *The Onion*, 37, (31) 5 September <http://www.avclub.com/articles/joss-whedon,13730/> (last accessed on 26 March 2015).

Sánchez Mompeán, S. (2012). 'The Intonation of Dubbed Dialogue: a Corpus-based Study on the Naturalness of Tonal Patterns in the Spanish Version of "How I

Met Your Mother"', unpublished MA dissertation, University of Roehampton (London).

Santamaria, L. (2001). 'Subtitulació i referents culturals. La traducció com a mitjà d'adquisició de representacions socials', unpublished PhD thesis, Barcelona: Universitat Autònoma.

Sanz Ortega, E. (forthcoming, 2015) 'Beyond Monolingualism: a Descriptive and Multimodal Methodology for the Dubbing of Polyglot Films', unpublished PhD thesis, University of Edinburgh.

Sarthou, J.-L. (2006). 'Plus la traduction est destinée à un vaste public, plus on demande au traducteur de banaliser, d'aseptiser, son langage', in Armstrong, N. and Federici, F. M. (eds), *Translating Voices*, pp. 216–29. London: Aracne.

Sayles, J. (1998). *Men with Guns & Lone Star*. London: Faber & Faber.

Scandura, G. L. (2004). 'Sex, Lies and TV: Censorship and Subtitling', *Meta* XLIX (1): 125–34.

Shaviro, S. (2010). 'Post-Cinematic Affect: On Grace Jones, Boarding Gate and "Southland Tales"', *Film Philosophies* 14(1): 1–102.

Shepherd, J. (1991). *Music as Social Text*. Cambridge: Polity Press.

Schiffrin, D. (1988). *Discourse Markers*. Cambridge: Cambridge University Press.

Shingler, M. (2007). 'Fasten Your Seatbelts and Prick up Your Ears: the Dramatic Human Voice in Film', *Scope. An Online Journal of Film Studies* 8 <http://www.scope.nottingham.ac.uk/article.php?issue=5&id=128&section=article&q=gaze> (last accessed on 15 February 2013).

Silverman, K. (1988). *The Acoustic Mirror: The Female Voice in Psychoanalysis and Cinema*. Bloomington, IN: Indiana University Press.

Simpson, P. (1993). *Ideology, Language and Point of View*. London and New York: Routledge.

Sinha, A. (2004). 'The Use and Abuse of Subtitles', in Egoyan, A. and Balfour, I. (eds), *Subtitles: on the Foreignness of Film*, pp. 171–90. Cambridge, MA: MIT Press.

Smith, J. (1996). 'Unheard Melodies? A Critique of Psychoanalytic Theories of Film Music', in Bordwell, D. and Carrol, N. (eds), *Post-Theory: Reconstructing Film Studies*, pp. 230–47. Madison: University of Wisconsin Press.

Smith, J. (1999). 'Movie Music as Moving Music: Emotion, Cognition and the Film', in Plantinga, C. and Smith, G. M. (eds), *Passionate Views: Film, Cognition, and Emotion*, pp. 146–67. Baltimore: Johns Hopkins University Press.

Smith, M. (1995). *Engaging Characters. Fiction, Emotion and the Cinema*. Oxford: Clarendon Press.

Smith, S. (2005). *The Musical. Race, Gender and Performance*. London and New York: Wallflower Press.

Smith, S. (2007). 'Voices in Film', in Gibbs, J. and Pye, D. (eds), *Close-Up 02*, pp. 159–238. London & New York: Wallflower Press.

Spadoni, R. (2007). *Uncanny Bodies: The Coming of Sound Film and the Origins of the Horror Genre*. Berkeley: University of California Press.

Spiegl, A. (2013). 'New Voices For The Voiceless: Synthetic Speech Gets An Upgrade' <http://www.npr.org/blogs/health/2013/03/11/173816690/new-voices-for-the-voiceless-synthetic-speech-gets-an-upgrade> (last accessed 26 March 2015).

Stern, L. and Kouvaros, G. (1999). *Falling for You: Essays on Cinema and Performance*. Sydney: Power Publications.

Stuller, J. K. (2013). *Fan Phenomena: Buffy the Vampire Slayer*. Exeter: Intellect.

Susam-Sarajeva, S. (2006). 'Rembetika Songs and Their "Return" to Anatolia', in Polezzi, L. (ed.), *Translation, Travel, Migration*, special issue of *The Translator* 12(2): 253–78.

Susam-Sarajeva, S. (forthcoming). *Translation and Popular Music: Transcultural Intimacy in Turkish-Greek Relations*. Oxford: Peter Lang.

Tagg, P. (1990). 'Music in Mass Media Studies: Reading Sounds, for Example', in Roe, K. and Carlsson, U. (eds), *Popular Music Research*, Nordicom-Sweden 2: 103–15.

Taylor, C. (2003). 'Multimodal Transcription in the Analysis, Translation and Subtitling of Italian Films', *The Translator* 9(2): 191–205.

Taylor, C. (2006). 'The Translation of Regional Variety in the Films of Ken Loach', in Armstrong, N. and Federici, F. M. (eds), *Translating Voices, Translating Regions*, pp. 37–52. London: Aracne.

Thomas, D. (2006). 'Reading Buffy', in Gibbs, J. and Pye, D. (eds), *Close-Up 01*, pp. 167–244. London and New York: Wallflower Press.

Thomson, D. (1967). *Movie Man*. New York: Stein and Day.

Thompson, K. (2003). *Storytelling in Film and Television*. Cambridge, MA: Harvard University Press.

Thompson, R. J. (1997). *Television's Second Golden Age: From Hill Street Blues to ER*. Syracuse, NY: Syracuse University Press.

Tolkien, J. R. R. (1954). *The Lord of the Rings*. London: Allen and Unwin.

Tomaszkiewicz, T. (2001). 'La structure des dialogues filmiques: conséquences pour le sous-titrage', in Ballard, M. (ed.), *Oralité et Traduction*, pp. 281–399. Arras: PU.

Tomaszkiewicz, T. (2009). 'Linguistic and Semiotic Approaches to Audiovisual Translation', in Freddi, M. and Pavesi, M. (eds), *Analysing Audiovisual Dialogue. Linguistic and Translational Insights*, pp. 19–31. Bologna: Clueb.

Turnbull, S. (2004). 'Not Just Another Buffy Paper: Towards an Aesthetic of Television', *Slayage. The International Online Journal of Buffy Studies* 4(1–2) [13–14]

<http://slayageonline.com/essays/slayage13_14/Turnbull.htm> (last accessed on 26 March 2015).

Turnbull, S. (2005). 'Moments of Inspiration. Performing Spike', *European Journal of Cultural Studies* 8(3): 367–73.

Turner, V. (1967). 'Betwixt and Between: The Liminal Period in Rites de Passage', in Turner, V, *The Forest of Symbols: Aspects of Ndembu Ritual*, pp. 93–111. Ithaca, NY: Cornell University Press.

Turner, V. (1981). 'Social Dramas and Stories about Them', in Mitchell, W. I. T. (ed.), *On Narrative*, pp. 137–64. Chicago: University of Chicago Press.

Uspensky, B. (1973). *A Poetics of Composition*, trans. by Zavarin, V. and Wittig, S. Berkeley: University of California Press.

Vandaele, J. (2002). '(Re-)Constructing Humour: Meanings and Means', *The Translator* 8(2): 149–72.

Van Leeuwen, T. (1999). *Speech, Music, Sound*. London: Macmillan.

Vanoye, F. (1985). 'Conversations publiques', in Vanoye, F. (ed.), *La parole au cinéma/ Speech in Film*, special issue of *Iris* 3(1): 99–118.

Wehn, K. (1996). 'Die deutschen Synchronization(en) von "Magnum, P.I." Rahmenbedingungen, serienspezifische Übersetzungsprobleme und Unterschiede zwischen Original- und Synchronfassungen'. Halle-Wittenburg: Halma-Hallische Medienarbeiten 2 <http://www.medienkomm.uni-halle.de/publikationen/halma/hallische_medienarbeiten_2/> (last accessed on 26 March 2015).

Whedon, J. (2004). 'Director's Commentary to "Once More With Feeling"', *Buffy the Vampire Slayer*, Season Six DVD, Twentieth Century Fox Home Entertainment.

Whitman-Linsen, C. (1992). *Through the Dubbing Glass*. Frankfurt a/M.: Peter Lang.

Wilcox, R. (2002). '"Every Night I Save You": Buffy, Spike, Sex and Redemption', *Slayage. The Online Journal of Buffy Studies* 5 (May) <http://slayageonline.com/essays/slayage5/wilcox.htm> (last accessed on 26 March 2015).

Wilcox, R. (2005). *Why Buffy Matters*. London and New York: I. B Tauris.

Williamson, M. (2005). *The Lure of the Vampire. Gender, Fiction and Fandom from Bram Stoker to Buffy*. London and New York: Wallflower Press.

Williamson, M. (2005a). 'Spike, Text and Subtext. Intertextual Portrayals of the Sympathetic Vampire on Cult Television', *European Journal of Cultural Studies* 8(3): 289–311.

Wood, R. (1960/1). 'New Criticism?', *Definition* 3, 9–11.

Woolf, V. (1925/1994). 'The Russian Point of View', in *The Essays of Virginia Woolf*, ed. by McNeille, A., Vol. 4, pp. 181–89. London: Hogarth Press.

Zabalbeascoa, P. (1993). 'Developing Translation Studies to Better Account for Audiovisual Texts and Other New Forms of Text Production', PhD thesis, Universitat de Lleida.

Zabalbeascoa, P. (1994). 'Factors in Dubbing Television Comedy', *Perspectives. Studies in Translatology* 1: 89–100.

Zabalbeascoa, P. (1996a). 'Translating Jokes for Dubbed Television Situation Comedies', in Delabastita, D. (ed.), *The Translator: Studies in Intercultural Communication. Wordplay and Translation*, pp. 252–57. Manchester: St. Jerome.

Zabalbeascoa, P. (1996b). 'La traducción de la comedia televisiva: implicaciones teóricas', in Bravo, J. M. and Nistal, F. (eds), *A Spectrum of Translation Studies*, pp. 173–201. Valladolid: Universidad de Valladolid.

Zabalbeascoa, P. (1997). 'Dubbing and the Non-verbal Dimension', in Poyatos, F. (ed.), *New Perspectives and Challenges in Literature, Interpretation and the Media*, pp. 327–42. Amsterdam: John Benjamins.

Zabalbeascoa, P. (2005). 'Humour and Translation – an Interdiscipline', *Humour* 18(2): 185–207.

Index

NEW TRENDS IN TRANSLATION STUDIES

In today's globalised society, translation and interpreting are gaining visibility and relevance as a means to foster communication and dialogue in increasingly multicultural and multilingual environments. Practised since time immemorial, both activities have become more complex and multifaceted in recent decades, intersecting with many other disciplines. *New Trends in Translation Studies* is an international series with the main objectives of promoting the scholarly study of translation and interpreting and of functioning as a forum for the translation and interpreting research community.

This series publishes research on subjects related to multimedia translation and interpreting, in their various social roles. It is primarily intended to engage with contemporary issues surrounding the new multidimensional environments in which translation is flourishing, such as audiovisual media, the internet and emerging new media and technologies. It sets out to reflect new trends in research and in the profession, to encourage flexible methodologies and to promote interdisciplinary research ranging from the theoretical to the practical and from the applied to the pedagogical.

New Trends in Translation Studies publishes translation- and interpreting-oriented books that present high-quality scholarship in an accessible, reader-friendly manner. The series embraces a wide range of publications – monographs, edited volumes, conference proceedings and translations of works in translation studies which do not exist in English. The editor, Professor Jorge Díaz Cintas, welcomes proposals from all those interested in being involved with the series. The working language of the series is English, although in exceptional circumstances works in other languages can be considered for publication. Proposals dealing with specialised translation, translation tools and technology, audiovisual translation and the field of accessibility to the media are particularly welcomed.